LEISURE ARTS PRESENTS

THE SPIRIT OF CHRISTMAS

CREATIVE HOLIDAY IDEAS
BOOK EIGHT

A time of merriment and good cheer, Christmas is filled with all the things we love most. The tree is trimmed with treasured ornaments and twinkling lights, and gaily wrapped packages entice us to guess their contents. Children eagerly send their last-minute requests to Santa Claus, and the sweet smells of holiday baking fill the house. When all the preparations are complete, family and friends come together to celebrate the birth of Christ and share the joy of the season. To make your Yuletide even more special, this volume is filled with wonderful ideas for handmade decorations and gifts, as well as delicious holiday recipes. May you and your family experience all the wonders of Christmas!

LEISURE ARTS, INC.
Little Rock, Arkansas

THE SPIRIT OF CHRISTMAS

BOOK EIGHT

"... and it was always said of him, that he knew how to keep Christmas well, if any man alive possessed the knowledge. May that be truly said of us, and all of us!"

— From *A Christmas Carol* by Charles Dickens

EDITORIAL STAFF

Editor-in-Chief: Anne Van Wagner Childs
Executive Director: Sandra Graham Case
Executive Editor: Susan Frantz Wiles
Publications Director: Carla Bentley
Creative Art Director: Gloria Bearden
Production Art Director: Melinda Stout

PRODUCTION

DESIGN
Design Director: Patricia Wallenfang Sowers
Senior Designer: Donna Waldrip Pittard
Designers: Diana Heien Suttle, Linda Diehl Tiano, Rebecca Sunwall Werle, and Patricia Ladd Elrod
Design Assistants: Kathy Womack Jones and Karen Story Tyler

FOODS
Foods Editor: Celia Fahr Harkey, R.D.
Assistant Foods Editor: Jane Kenner Prather
Test Kitchen Assistant: Nora Faye Spencer Clift

TECHNICAL
Managing Editor: Kathy Rose Bradley
Senior Editor: Ann Brawner Turner
Technical Writers: Chanda English Adams, Emily Jane Barefoot, Leslie Schick Gorrell, Candice Treat Murphy, Kimberly J. Smith, Linda Luder, and Anita Lewis

EDITORIAL
Associate Editor: Linda L. Trimble
Senior Editorial Writer: Tammi Williamson Bradley
Editorial Writer: Terri Leming Davidson
Copy Editor: Laura Lee Weland

ART
Book/Magazine Art Director: Diane M. Ghegan
Senior Production Artist: Michael A. Spigner
Photography Stylists: Karen Smart Hall and Christina Tiano

ADVERTISING AND DIRECT MAIL
Copywriters: Steven M. Cooper, Marla Shivers, and Tena Kelley Vaughn
Designer: Rhonda H. Hestir
Art Director: Jeff Curtis
Production Artist: Linda Lovette Smart
Typesetters: Cindy Lumpkin and Stephanie Cordero

BUSINESS STAFF

Publisher: Steve Patterson
Controller: Tom Siebenmorgen
Retail Sales Director: Richard Tignor
Retail Marketing Director: Pam Stebbins
Retail Customer Services Director: Margaret Sweetin
Marketing Manager: Russ Barnett
Executive Director of Marketing and Circulation: Guy A. Crossley
Fulfillment Manager: Byron L. Taylor
Print Production Manager: Laura Lockhart
Print Production Coordinator: Nancy Reddick Lister

Library of Congress Catalog Card Number 93-80809
International Standard Book Number 0-942237-36-6

TABLE OF CONTENTS

THE SIGHTS OF CHRISTMAS

Page 6

TABLE OF CONTENTS
(Continued)

THE SHARING OF CHRISTMAS

Page 92

THE TASTES OF CHRISTMAS

Page 112

COZY LITTLE BUFFET 114

A GLORIOUS GATHERING 120

BUSY ELVES' BRUNCH....................128

HEAVENLY CONFECTIONS 134

THE SIGHTS OF CHRISTMAS

For many of us, the holiday season begins when we pull out our collection of decorations to dress up the house. Trimming the tree becomes a family affair, often with cherished heirloom ornaments displayed alongside newer treasures. We also enjoy spreading the festive mood throughout the house with smaller trees and other merry accents. Adding a special charm to the season, handcrafted decorations receive a place of honor in our homes — and in our hearts. As you prepare for the holidays this year, take a little extra time to truly enjoy the sights of Christmas.

SNOWMEN'S FROLIC

Who can resist the fun of building a snowman on a frosty winter day? Created just for kids, this bright collection is perfect for the family room or playroom, and it's sure to delight youngsters — and the young at heart. A smiling snowman clears a path with his trusty shovel, while dozens of his jolly friends romp on the star-studded tree. More of the roly-poly fellows appear in starring roles on whimsical stockings, a fleecy afghan, and a cozy sweatshirt. These cold-weather companions are sure to inspire hopes for a white Christmas! And after an afternoon of playing in the snow, what could be more warming than a basket of freshly baked cookies and some hot cocoa — served in colorful snowman mugs, of course! Instructions for the projects shown here and on the following pages begin on page 14. Come on and join the merriment of the Snowmen's Frolic!

(Opposite) The fun-filled **Snowmen's Frolic Tree** *(page 14)* is decorated with rosy-cheeked **Snowman Face Ornaments** *(page 16)* and fluffy **Snowballs** *(page 15)*. There's a plentiful supply of **Snow Shovel Ornaments** *(page 16)* made from painted cardboard and pencils, and padded felt **Star Ornaments** *(page 16)* brighten the branches of the tree. Purchased garlands, red ball ornaments, and frosty snowball lights round out the trimmings. *(Above)* Children will love discovering their Christmas treats tucked in the tumbling **Snowman Stockings** *(page 18)*.

(Opposite) Your little ones will be warm and snug in these appliquéd sweatshirts! The **Snowman Sweatshirt** *(page 17)* sports a smiling snowman and a sprinkling of stars, and the **"Let It Snow" Sweatshirt** *(page 14)* features a bright checked scarf and a pair of mittens. *(Above)* Perfect for wrapping up in on a chilly day, the appliquéd **Snowman Throw** *(page 17)* is easy to make from cuddly fleece fabric.

SNOWMEN'S FROLIC TREE

(Shown on page 10)

Reminiscent of childhood romps in the snow, this lively tree is full of smiling snowmen and other snowy delights.

Brightening the snowy scene, a string of unique 1 1/2" dia. snowball lights is wrapped around the six-foot-tall tree. Multicolored wooden bead, iridescent bead, and plastic ice crystal garlands also entwine the snow-laden branches.

Snowballs (page 15) are "thrown" onto the tree, along with purchased red satin ball ornaments. Miniature Snow Shovel Ornaments (page 16) crafted from cardboard and pencils, and felt Star Ornaments (page 16) help carry out the festive mood. Finally, happy Snowman Face Ornaments (page 16) made from stuffed fleece peek out from among the branches, spreading good cheer and expressing their wish for a white Christmas.

Drifts of white batting wrap the base of the tree for a snowy skirt, and a dusting of artificial snow is sprinkled over the whole tree, bringing smiles to all the snowmen's faces.

"LET IT SNOW" SWEATSHIRT (Shown on page 12)

You will need a children's white sweatshirt, a 9" square of fabric for scarf, a 7" square of washable felt for mittens, fusible interfacing, paper-backed fusible web, tear-away stabilizer, thread to match fabric and felt, coordinating embroidery floss, tracing paper, and white vinegar.

1. Wash, dry, and press shirt and scarf fabric. Unwrap floss skeins and soak floss and felt for a few minutes in a mixture of 1 cup water and 1 tablespoon vinegar; allow to dry and press felt.

2. Follow manufacturer's instructions to fuse interfacing, then web, to 1 side of felt and to wrong side of fabric.

3. Trace scarf and mitten patterns onto tracing paper; cut out.

4. Place scarf pattern right side down on paper backing side of fabric and mitten pattern right side down on paper backing side of felt; use a pencil to draw around patterns. Cut out shapes along drawn lines. Turn mitten pattern over and repeat to cut 1 mitten in reverse.

5. (Note: Refer to photo for remaining steps.) Remove paper backing from scarf and mittens; arrange on shirt and fuse in place. Using matching thread and a medium width zigzag stitch with a short stitch length, follow **Machine Appliqué**, page 158, to stitch along edges of appliqués.

6. Trace "Let it snow" pattern onto tracing paper. To transfer pattern to shirt, turn pattern over and use a pencil to draw over lines of pattern on back of tracing paper. Place pattern right side up with words along edge of scarf. Use the edge of a spoon or coin to rub over lines of pattern. Use 6 strands of floss and Running Stitch, page 159, to stitch over transferred words. Remove any visible markings.

7. For each snowflake, use 4 strands of floss to work 3 long stitches; work 1 small stitch over centers of long stitches (**Fig. 1**).

Fig. 1

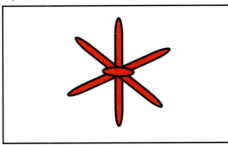

8. For fringe at each end of scarf, thread a needle with two 6" lengths of floss. Working from right side, take needle down through shirt near 1 corner of scarf and bring needle up approx. 1/16" away. Knot ends of floss together close to fabric; trim ends 1 1/2" from knot. Repeat to make fringe across each end of scarf.

9. To launder shirt, turn shirt wrong side out; machine wash and line dry.

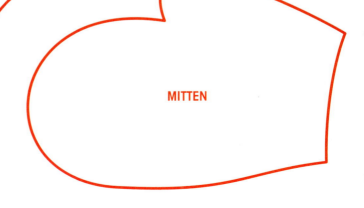

SCARF

MITTEN

14

TABLETOP SNOWMAN (Shown on page 8)

You will need one 4" dia., one 5" dia., and one 6" dia. plastic foam ball; polyester bonded batting; four 5" x 7" pieces of white polyester fleece for arms; one 2" x 10" strip and one 2" x 13" strip of fabric for scarf; a 3" square of orange felt; a 3" x 4" piece of pink felt; polyester fiberfill; black embroidery floss; white thread; two 5/16" dia. black shank buttons for eyes; three 7/8" dia. red buttons for front of snowman; two 1" lengths of 1 3/4" long red loop fringe; drawing compass; tracing paper; utility knife; a candle or block of paraffin (optional); fabric marking pencil; straight pins; and thick craft glue.

ARM

1. (**Note:** To make cutting plastic foam balls easier, run blade of knife over candle or paraffin to coat blade with wax.) Use knife to cut 1/2" from 1 side (bottom) of 4" plastic foam ball; cut 1/2" from opposite sides (top and bottom) of 5" and 6" balls.
2. Draw a 13" dia. circle on tracing paper; cut out. Use pattern to cut 2 circles from batting. Cut a 9" x 17" piece and a 10" x 20" piece from batting.
3. For head, layer batting circles together. Center 4" ball bottom side up on batting circles. Wrap batting circles around ball. Easing and smoothing wrinkles as necessary and trimming away any excess batting, pin edges of batting to bottom of ball.

4. For middle of snowman, position 9" x 17" batting piece with long edges at top and bottom. Center 5" ball on batting with flat sides at top and bottom. Overlapping short edges, wrap batting around ball. Easing and smoothing wrinkles as necessary and trimming away any excess batting, pin long edges of batting to top and bottom of ball.
5. For bottom of snowman, repeat Step 4 to cover 6" ball with 10" x 20" batting piece.
6. (**Note:** Refer to photo for remaining steps. Allow to dry after each glue step.) Glue bottom of 4" ball to top of 5" ball. With batting seams aligned at back, glue top of 6" ball to bottom of 5" ball.
7. For patterns, trace arm and nose patterns onto tracing paper. For cheek pattern, draw a 1 1/2" dia. circle on tracing paper. Cut out patterns.
8. For arms, use pattern and follow **Sewing Shapes**, page 158, to make 2 arms from fleece pieces, leaving short straight edge of each arm open for turning. Lightly stuff arms with fiberfill; sew final closures by hand.
9. To attach arms to snowman, cut a 3" long slit in batting at each side of middle ball. Place square end of 1 arm into each slit and glue in place. Glue each slit closed.

10. For nose, use pattern to cut nose from orange felt. Slightly overlap and glue straight edges of felt together; secure with pins until glue is dry. Stuff nose with fiberfill; glue nose to face.
11. For cheeks, use pattern to cut 2 circles from pink felt. Glue cheeks to face.
12. Use 6 strands of black floss and Running Stitch, page 159, to stitch mouth.
13. Glue black buttons to face for eyes.
14. For each red button on front of snowman, stitch through button with white thread; knot and trim thread at back of button. Glue buttons to snowman.
15. For scarf, press long edges of 2" x 13" fabric strip 1/2" to wrong side. With wrong side of strip facing snowman, wrap strip around neck, overlapping and gluing ends near 1 side of neck.
16. Press each short edge of remaining fabric strip 1/2" to wrong side. With fringe extending 1" beyond pressed edge, center and glue 1 length of fringe along each short edge on wrong side of strip. Press each long edge 1/2" to wrong side; glue in place. Loosely knot strip at center; glue knot over overlapped ends of strip on snowman.

NOSE

STAR BASKET AND SNOWMAN MUGS (Shown on pages 8 and 9)

For basket, you will need an approx. 8" dia. basket, a Charles Craft Royal Blue Royal Classic bread cover (14 ct), yellow embroidery floss, a 19" square of coordinating fabric, thread to match fabric, hot glue gun, glue sticks, and 1 Star Ornament (page 16).
For each mug, you will need a Crafter's Pride Stitch-A-Mug™ with Vinyl-Weave® insert, a 4 1/2" x 11 1/4" piece of blue fabric, a 4" square of white polyester fleece, a 1" x 2" piece of orange felt, a 1 1/2" x 3" piece of pink felt, two 5mm black half-beads, black embroidery floss, loose artificial snow (available at craft stores), thick craft glue, drawing compass, and tracing paper.

BASKET

1. Use 6 strands of yellow floss and Running Stitch, page 159, to stitch 3/4" from edges of bread cover.
2. Press each edge of fabric square 1/4" to wrong side; press 1/4" to wrong side again and machine stitch in place.

3. Line basket with fabric square and bread cover. Referring to photo, glue Star Ornament to basket.

MUG

1. Take mug apart. Center mug insert on wrong side of fabric piece; glue in place. Fold short edges of fabric over insert and glue in place; repeat with long edges. Allow to dry.
2. For face and cheek patterns, draw one 2 1/2" dia. circle and one 3/4" dia. circle on tracing paper. Trace nose pattern onto tracing paper. Cut out patterns.
3. Use patterns to cut face from fleece, nose from orange felt, and cheeks from pink felt.
4. Glue face to center of fabric-covered insert. Glue nose and cheeks to face. Glue half-beads to face for eyes. Allow to dry.
5. Use 6 strands of black floss and Running Stitch, page 159, to stitch mouth.
6. Place insert in mug and sprinkle approx. 2 teaspoons of artificial snow into

mug between insert and mug. Reassemble mug. Mug should be hand washed.

NOSE

SNOWBALLS
(Shown on page 10)

For each snowball, you will need a 2" dia. to 2 3/4" dia. plastic foam ball, a 9" circle of polyester bonded batting, straight pins, and loose artificial snow (available at craft stores).

1. Center foam ball on batting circle. Wrap batting around ball. Easing and smoothing wrinkles as necessary and trimming away any excess batting, pin edges of batting to ball.
2. Roll covered ball in artificial snow.

SNOWMAN FACE ORNAMENTS (Shown on page 10)

For each ornament, you will need two 7" squares of white polyester fleece for face, two 2" x 10" strips of fabric for scarf, a 1" x 2" piece of orange felt, a 2" x 4" piece of pink felt, white thread, black embroidery floss, two 5/16" dia. black shank buttons for eyes, two 1" lengths of 1 3/4" long red loop fringe for scarf, polyester fiberfill, drawing compass, tracing paper, fabric marking pencil, and thick craft glue.

1. For face and cheek patterns, draw a 4 1/2" dia. circle and a 1" dia. circle on tracing paper. Trace nose pattern onto tracing paper. Cut out patterns.

2. Use face pattern and follow **Sewing Shapes**, page 158, to make face from fleece pieces. Stuff face with fiberfill; sew final closure by hand.

3. Use patterns to cut nose from orange felt and cheeks from pink felt.

4. (**Note:** Refer to photo for remaining steps.) Glue nose and cheeks to face. Glue buttons to face for eyes. Allow to dry.

5. Use 6 strands of black floss and Running Stitch, page 159, to stitch mouth.

6. For scarf, press long edges of 1 fabric strip 1/2" to wrong side. With wrong side of strip toward face, wrap and glue strip around bottom of face, overlapping ends 1/2" at back and trimming to fit.

7. Press each short edge of remaining strip 1/2" to wrong side. With fringe extending 1" beyond pressed edge, center and glue 1 length of fringe along each short edge on wrong side of strip. Press each long edge 1/2" to wrong side; glue in place. Loosely knot strip at center; glue knot to strip at bottom of face.

NOSE

SNOW SHOVEL ORNAMENTS (Shown on page 10)

For each ornament, you will need an unsharpened wooden pencil, 2 3/4" of twisted paper wire (available at craft stores), lightweight cardboard, red and silver spray paint, tracing paper, scrap paper, transparent tape, hot glue gun, and glue sticks.

1. Remove eraser from metal tip of pencil. Spray paint pencil red; allow to dry.

2. (**Note:** Refer to photo for remaining steps.) For shovel handle, wrap paper wire around finger to form a circle; twist ends together. Flatten circle to form handle shape. Glue ends of paper wire into metal tip of pencil.

3. For scoop, trace scoop pattern onto tracing paper; cut out. Use pattern to cut scoop from cardboard. For creases in scoop, refer to **Fig. 1** to draw lines on scoop. Place a ruler next to 1 line on scoop and bend scoop slightly along line; unbend. Repeat for remaining lines.

Fig. 1

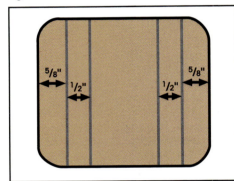

4. Glue bottom 2" of pencil to top center back of scoop. Bend each side of scoop slightly toward back around pencil.

5. Use scrap paper to cover wooden part of pencil between metal tip and scoop; tape in place. Spray paint handle, metal tip of pencil, and scoop silver; allow to dry. Remove paper.

STAR ORNAMENTS
(Shown on page 10)

For each ornament, you will need two 5 1/2" squares of yellow felt, a 5 1/2" square of polyester bonded batting, thread to match felt, removable fabric marking pen, and tracing paper.

1. Trace large star pattern onto tracing paper; cut out.

2. Place batting square between felt squares; pin layers together. Use fabric marking pen to draw around pattern on top felt square.

3. Using a medium width zigzag stitch with a short stitch length, stitch over drawn lines.

4. Cut out star 1/16" outside stitching lines.

SCOOP

LARGE STAR

SNOWMAN SWEATSHIRT (Shown on page 12)

You will need a children's blue sweatshirt; a 9" x 11" piece of white polyester fleece for snowman; a 2½" x 11" strip of fabric for scarf; the following pieces of washable felt: a 4" x 16" piece of yellow, a 1" x 2" piece of orange, and a 2" x 3½" piece of pink; white thread and thread to match yellow felt, scarf fabric, and shirt; black embroidery floss and floss to coordinate with scarf fabric; medium weight fusible interfacing; paper-backed fusible web; tear-away stabilizer; two ¼" dia. black shank buttons for eyes; two ¹¹/₁₆" dia. red buttons for front of snowman; tracing paper; drawing compass; washable fabric glue; seam ripper; a safety pin; and white vinegar.

1. Wash, dry, and press shirt and scarf fabric. Unwrap floss skeins and soak floss and felt for a few minutes in a mixture of 2 cups water and 2 tablespoons vinegar; allow to dry and press felt.
2. Follow manufacturer's instructions to fuse interfacing, then web, to white fleece and yellow felt.
3. For cheek pattern, draw a 1" dia. circle on tracing paper. Trace snowman, small star, and nose patterns onto tracing paper. Cut out patterns.
4. For appliqués, use patterns to cut snowman from white fleece and 4 stars from yellow felt. Cut nose from orange felt and cheeks from pink felt.
5. (**Note:** Refer to photo for Steps 5 - 11. For appliqué, follow **Machine Appliqué**, page 158, using a medium width zigzag stitch with a short stitch length.) Remove paper backing from appliqués. Fuse snowman to shirt. Use white thread to stitch over raw edges of snowman. Fuse 3 stars to shirt front. Use yellow thread to stitch over raw edges of stars.
6. For star on sleeve, begin above cuff and use seam ripper to open bottom 7" of right sleeve seam. Fuse star to sleeve. Use yellow thread to stitch over raw edges of star. Turn shirt wrong side out and sew sleeve back together.
7. Glue nose and cheeks to face; allow to dry. Use 6 strands of black floss and Running Stitch, page 159, to stitch mouth.
8. Use white thread to sew red buttons to front of snowman and black buttons to face for eyes.
9. For scarf, match right sides and fold fabric piece in half lengthwise. Using a ¼" seam allowance and leaving an opening for turning, use matching thread to sew raw edges together; clip corners diagonally, turn right side out, and press. Sew final closure by hand.

10. For fringe on scarf, thread a needle with two 6" lengths of coordinating floss. Take a stitch through both fabric layers close to end of scarf. Knot ends of floss together close to fabric; trim ends 1¼" from knot. Repeat to make fringe across each end of scarf.
11. Loosely knot scarf at center. Use safety pin on wrong side of shirt to attach knot of scarf to snowman.
12. To launder shirt, remove scarf. Turn shirt wrong side out and machine wash; line dry.

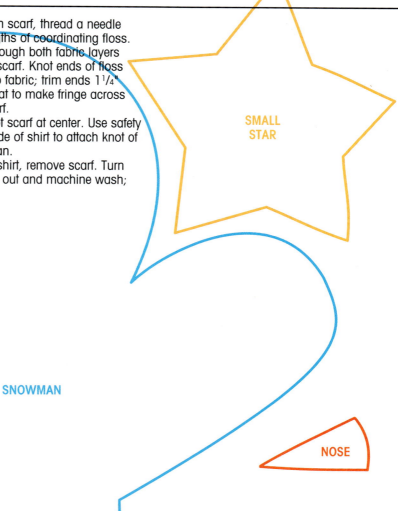

SMALL STAR

SNOWMAN

NOSE

SNOWMAN THROW (Shown on page 13)

You will need 1¾ yds of 60"w polar fleece for throw; a 9" x 11" piece of white polyester fleece for snowman; a 2½" x 11" strip of fabric for scarf; the following pieces of washable felt: a 10" square of yellow, a 1" x 2" piece of orange, and a 2" x 3½" piece of pink; black embroidery floss and floss to coordinate with scarf fabric; white thread and thread to match yellow felt and scarf fabric; two ¼" dia. black shank buttons for eyes; two ¹¹/₁₆" dia. red buttons for front of snowman; medium weight fusible interfacing; paper-backed fusible web; tear-away stabilizer; pressing cloth; tracing paper; chalk pencil; washable fabric glue; drawing compass; yardstick; a safety pin; and white vinegar.

1. Wash and line dry polar fleece. Wash, dry, and press white fleece piece and scarf fabric. Unwrap floss skeins and soak floss and felt for a few minutes in a mixture of 2 cups water and 2 tablespoons vinegar; allow to dry and press felt.

2. Trim selvages from polar fleece. Use chalk pencil and yardstick to draw a line 3½" from each short edge of fabric. Cutting from edge of fleece to drawn line, cut ⅜"w fringe along each short edge.
3. Follow Steps 2 - 4 of Snowman Sweatshirt instructions, this page, to make 1 snowman and 4 small star appliqués and to cut out nose and cheeks; use large star pattern, page 16, to make 2 large star appliqués.
4. (**Note:** For appliqué, follow **Machine Appliqué**, page 158, using a medium width zigzag stitch with a short stitch length.) Remove paper backing from appliqués and arrange on 1 corner of throw. Using pressing cloth, fuse appliqués to throw. Use matching thread to stitch over raw edges of appliqués.
5. To complete snowman, follow Steps 7 - 11 of Snowman Sweatshirt instructions.
6. To launder throw, remove scarf; machine wash and line dry.

SNOWMAN STOCKINGS (Shown on page 11)

For each stocking, you will need a 12" x 18" piece of white polyester fleece for snowman, two 12" x 20" fabric pieces for stocking, a 2" x 7" fabric strip for hanger, white thread and thread to match stocking fabric, a 1" x 2" piece of washable orange felt, a 2" x 4" piece of washable pink felt, two ¼" dia. black shank buttons for eyes, three ¹¹/₁₆" dia. red buttons for front of snowman, black embroidery floss, paper-backed fusible web, tear-away stabilizer, tracing paper, washable fabric glue, white vinegar, removable fabric marking pen, drawing compass, and 1 Star Ornament (page 16).

1. Wash, dry, and press fleece piece and fabric pieces for stocking and hanger. Unwrap floss skein and soak floss and felt for a few minutes in a mixture of 1 cup water and 1 tablespoon vinegar; allow to dry and press felt.

2. Follow manufacturer's instructions to fuse web to 1 side of fleece.

3. Matching dotted lines and aligning arrows, trace top and bottom of body pattern for snowman A, this page, or snowman B, page 19, onto tracing paper. Trace arm pattern for snowman A, this page, or snowman B, page 19, onto tracing paper. Trace nose pattern, page 19, onto tracing paper. For cheek pattern, draw a 1¼" dia. circle on tracing paper. Cut out patterns.

4. (**Note:** Refer to photo for remaining steps.) Place snowman body and arm patterns right side down on paper backing side of fleece; use a pencil to draw around patterns. Cut out shapes along drawn lines.

5. Remove paper backing from arm piece. Referring to ●'s on body pattern, fuse arm to body. Remove paper backing from body. Referring to **Diagram A**, this page, for snowman A or **Diagram B**, page 19, for snowman B, center and fuse snowman to 1 stocking fabric piece (front) with bottom of snowman 2" above 1 short edge (bottom) of fabric piece.

6. Using white thread and a medium width zigzag stitch with a short stitch length, follow **Machine Appliqué**, page 158, to stitch over raw edges of snowman arm and body. For snowman B, stitch detail line under chin.

7. Use patterns to cut nose from orange felt and cheeks from pink felt. Trim 1 cheek to fit along edge of face. Glue nose and cheeks to snowman. Allow to dry.

8. Use 6 strands of black floss and Running Stitch, page 159, to stitch mouth. Using white thread, sew black buttons to face for eyes and red buttons to front of snowman.

9. To draw bottom of stocking shape, refer to **Diagram A**, this page, or **Diagram B**, page 19, and use fabric marking pen to draw a line close to bottom edge of snowman shape; to complete stocking shape, use a ruler to extend lines upward to 2" above top of snowman and to draw a line for top of stocking shape (top of stocking shape should be approx. 7¼" wide). Cutting ½" outside drawn line, cut out stocking front.

10. Place stocking front right side down on right side of remaining stocking fabric piece; use fabric marking pen to draw around stocking front. Cut stocking back from fabric piece.

11. Place stocking front and back right sides together. Leaving top edge open and being careful not to stitch through edges of snowman, use a ½" seam allowance to sew pieces together. Clip curves.

12. Press top edge of stocking ½" to wrong side and glue to secure; allow to dry. Turn stocking right side out and press.

13. For hanger, press each long edge of fabric strip ½" to wrong side. With wrong sides together, press strip in half lengthwise. Glue pressed edges together; allow to dry. Matching ends, fold strip in half to form a loop. Place ends of loop inside stocking at heel-side seamline with approx. 1½" of loop extending above stocking; tack in place.

14. Glue Star Ornament to stocking.

DIAGRAM A

SNOWMAN A BODY TOP

2"

2"

SNOWMAN A BODY BOTTOM

SNOWMAN A ARM

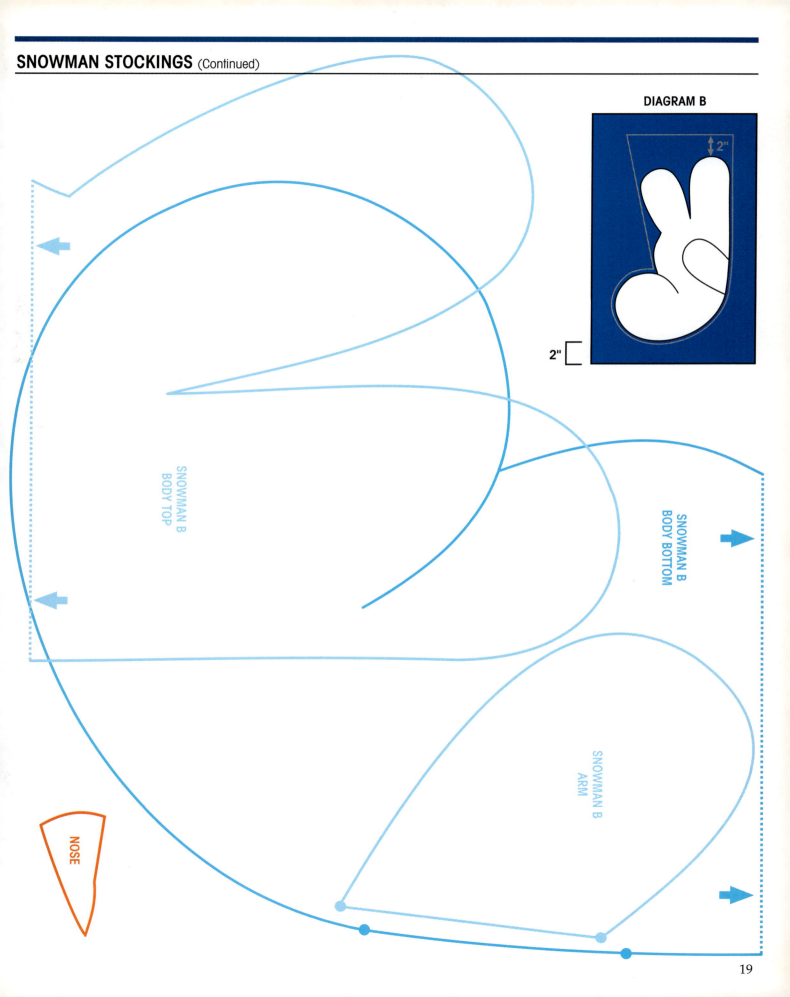

DIAGRAM B

2"

2"

SNOWMAN B
BODY TOP

SNOWMAN B
BODY BOTTOM

SNOWMAN B
ARM

NOSE

ANGELS OF GOLD

As the celestial messengers who heralded the first Holy Night with songs of praise and thanksgiving, angels symbolize the peace and goodwill of the holiday season. Reflecting their purity and majesty, this splendid collection is breathtakingly fashioned in pristine white and opulent gold. Gilded crosses, golden harps, and tiny white lights nestled among the greenery accentuate the harmonious charm of the tree. You'll experience the joy of that very first Christmas with these divine decorations! Instructions for the projects shown on these pages begin on page 26.

Two members of the heavenly host share the glad tidings of the Christ Child's birth in the **"Peace" Scherenschnitte** (*page 30*). (*Opposite*) The **Angels of Gold Tree** (*page 26*) is crowned with a **Centerpiece Angel** (*page 28*) and adorned with a chorus of **Scherenschnitte Angel Ornaments** (*page 30*). Creamy white magnolia blossoms, a rich **Fabric Twist Garland** (*page 29*), golden harps and crosses, shining stars, twinkling lights, and ornamental glass balls enhance the seasonal symphony.

The simple, yet exquisite, **Scalloped Tree Skirt** (*page 29*) is constructed from ivory damask and ivory-and-gold striped fabrics and trimmed with gold braid and gold tassels. (*Opposite*) Greet your holiday guests with these decorative door wreaths and a gracious garland. Gold-brushed leaves, purchased magnolia blossoms, and other elements from the tree add a glittering touch of elegance to the entryway and coordinating gift packages.

You're sure to treasure all the mementos displayed in this **Elegant Covered Photo Album** (*page 26*). Dressed up with golden trim and beaded fleur-de-lis appliqués, it's a lovely keepsake to be enjoyed during the holidays and all through the year.

Imagine the rich surprises you'll find hidden inside this exquisite creation! Gold cording, beads, and a tassel complete the look of the stunning **Beaded Stocking** (*page 26*).

A pair of **Centerpiece Angels** (*page 28*) creates a joyous duet in this heavenly scene. Sprigs of greenery, glass ball ornaments, and miniature gold-burnished instruments accentuate their glorious song.

ANGELS OF GOLD TREE
(Shown on page 21)

Clad in creamy ivory and shimmering gold, the heavenly messengers on this magnificent tree herald the Christmas message of joy and peace to all.

Providing an illuminating backdrop for the angels, the first additions to this dazzling seven-foot-tall tree are strands of tiny white lights, some enhanced by star-shaped gold filigree covers.

A variety of purchased ornaments also glimmers upon the tree. Included among these are shiny ivory and gold glass balls and crystal icicle, teardrop, and finial ornaments. As a gentle reminder of the true meaning of the season, three styles of golden crosses, each approx. 4" long, are hung with bows tied from gold wired ribbon, heightening the radiance of the tree. Miniature wooden harps burnished with gold Rub 'n Buff® play across the branches, and even old glass ball ornaments from Christmases past find a place on the tree when they're refurbished with matte gold spray paint.

Made from a lightly stuffed tube of fabric encircled with purchased cord and bead garlands, each length of luxurious Fabric Twist Garland (page 29) is decorated with gilded leaf ornaments and anchored by lovely silk magnolia blossoms. Winding among the delicate Scherenschnitte Angel Ornaments (page 30), which are cut from ivory parchment paper, the fabric garlands create a golden path to the glorious 14" tall Centerpiece Angel (page 28) at the top of the tree. She's attired in a lavishly decorated robe and has richly appointed wings. The star she holds proclaims her message of "Peace on Earth." Like heavenly clouds, sparkling gold curly ting-ting, purchased at a florist shop, is tucked into the branches beneath her.

Completing the tree's majestic image, the exquisite Scalloped Tree Skirt (page 29) is fashioned from damask and trimmed with silky cording and tassels.

ELEGANT COVERED PHOTO ALBUM (Shown on page 24)

You will need a photo album, fabric to cover album, low-loft polyester bonded batting, 1½"w decorative gold ribbon, 1"w gold trim, two 2½" long beaded fleur-de-lis appliqués (available at fabric stores), lightweight cardboard, hot glue gun, and glue sticks.

1. To cover outside of album, measure length (top to bottom) and width of open album. Cut a piece of batting the determined measurements. Cut a piece of fabric 2" larger on all sides than batting.
2. Glue batting to outside of album.
3. Center open album on wrong side of fabric piece. Fold corners of fabric diagonally over corners of album; glue in place. Fold short edges of fabric over side edges of album; glue in place. Fold long edges of fabric over top and bottom edges of album, trimming fabric to fit ¼" under album hardware; glue in place.
4. For trims, cut 1 length of ribbon and 2 lengths of trim 4" longer than length (top to bottom) of album. Referring to photo, glue trims to front of album, gluing ends to inside of album. Glue appliqués to trims.
5. To cover inside of album, cut two 2"w fabric strips from fabric same length as length (top to bottom) of album. Press ends of each strip ½" to wrong side. Center and glue 1 strip along each side of album hardware with 1 long edge of each strip tucked ½" under album hardware.
6. Cut 2 pieces of cardboard ½" smaller on all sides than front of album. Cut 2 pieces from fabric 1" larger on all sides than 1 cardboard piece.
7. Center 1 cardboard piece on wrong side of 1 fabric piece. Fold corners of fabric diagonally over corners of cardboard piece; glue in place. Fold edges of fabric over edges of cardboard piece; glue in place. Repeat to cover remaining cardboard piece.
8. Center and glue covered cardboard pieces inside front and back of album.

BEADED STOCKING (Shown on page 24)

You will need two 14" x 20" fabric pieces for stocking, two 14" x 20" fabric pieces for stocking lining, two 10" x 17" fabric pieces for cuff and cuff lining, ⅝ yd of ³⁄₁₆" dia. metallic gold twisted cording with flange for cuff trim, 8" of ³⁄₁₆" dia. metallic gold twisted cord for hanger, a 5" long tassel, beads (see beading key, page 27), beading needle, beading thread, sewing thread to match fabrics, lightweight fusible interfacing, tracing paper, graphite transfer paper, removable fabric marking pen, and fabric glue.

1. Matching dotted lines and aligning arrows, trace top and bottom of stocking pattern, page 27, onto tracing paper; cut out.
2. For stocking, use stocking pattern and fabric pieces and follow **Sewing Shapes**, page 158, leaving top edge of stocking open; do not turn right side out. Repeat to make stocking lining from lining fabric pieces; turn lining right side out.
3. Matching wrong sides, insert stocking into lining; pin top edges together.
4. For cuff, follow manufacturer's instructions to fuse interfacing to wrong side of 1 cuff fabric piece. Use cuff pattern, page 27, and follow **Tracing Patterns**, page 158, extending pattern 3½" at sides. Use pattern to cut cuff and cuff lining from fabric pieces.
5. Matching edges, place cuff pattern on right side of interfaced cuff fabric piece. Use transfer paper to lightly transfer beading design onto fabric. Referring to photo and beading key, page 27, sew beads to cuff.
6. (**Note:** Use a ¼" seam allowance for Step 6.) Matching right sides and raw edges, sew cuff and cuff lining pieces together along bottom edge; trim seam allowance at point and clip curves. Unfold cuff and lining; press seam allowance open. Match right sides and short edges (side edges) and fold cuff and lining in half; sew short edges together. Press seam allowance open. Matching wrong sides of cuff and lining, fold cuff in half with right side of lining facing out.
7. For cuff trim, begin at back seam of cuff and glue flange of cording to wrong side of cuff along bottom edge, trimming cording to fit.
8. With stocking toe pointing right and point of cuff at center front, slip cuff over stocking, matching raw edges of cuff and stocking; pin edges together.
9. For hanger, fold cord in half. Matching ends of cord to raw edges of fabrics, insert cord between cuff and stocking at heel-side seamline; pin in place. Use a ½" seam allowance to sew cuff and hanger to stocking. Turn stocking right side out. Fold cuff down over stocking.
10. Tack tassel to point of cuff.

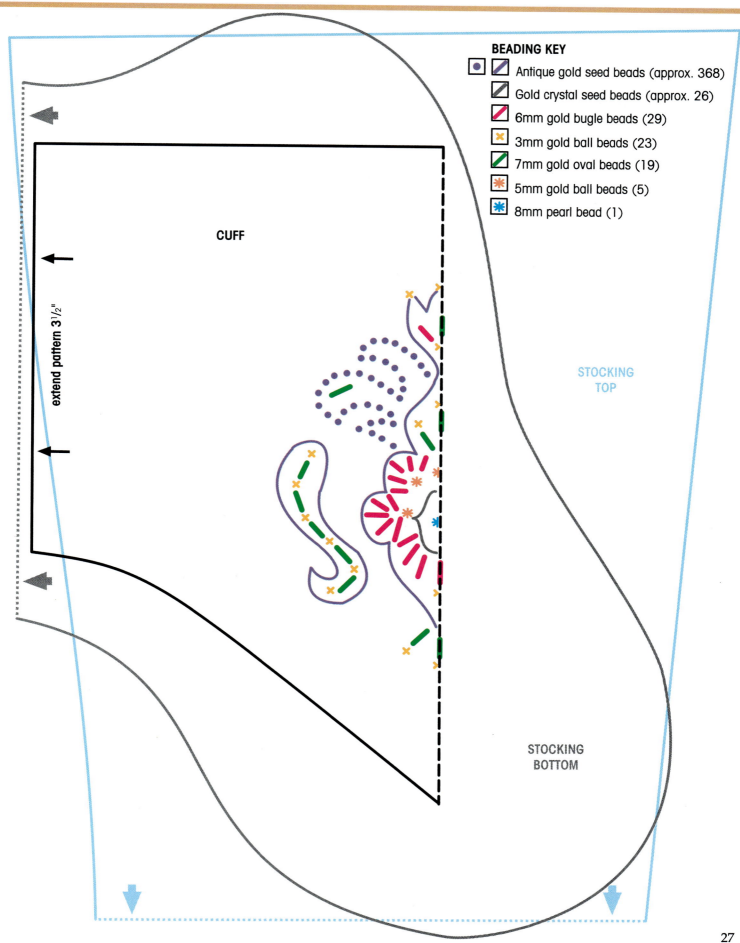

BEADING KEY

- Antique gold seed beads (approx. 368)
- Gold crystal seed beads (approx. 26)
- 6mm gold bugle beads (29)
- 3mm gold ball beads (23)
- 7mm gold oval beads (19)
- 5mm gold ball beads (5)
- 8mm pearl bead (1)

CUFF

extend pattern 3½"

STOCKING TOP

STOCKING BOTTOM

CENTERPIECE ANGELS (Shown on page 25)

For each angel, you will need a 'Just For Keeps'® 3"h doll head and 1¹/₂" long doll arms; a 17" x 29¹/₂" piece of heavy weight fabric for robe; a 13¹/₂"h x 3¹/₂" dia. Steeple People™ papier mâché cone; 4¹/₂" of ¹/₂"w gold picot trim for neckline; 1³/₄ yds of ³/₁₆" dia. gold twisted cord for halo, waist tie, and trim on wings; 1²/₃ yds of ¹/₈" dia. gold twisted cord, 1 yd of ¹/₂"w gold loop fringe, and 1¹/₃ yds of ³/₈"w gold gimp trim for trim on wings; one 1¹/₄ yd length each of 2¹/₂"w and 2³/₈"w wired gold ribbon for shawl; heavy thread; metallic gold spray paint; spray paint to match robe fabric; Sable Brown and Chocolate Deco Art™ Ultra™ Gloss Acrylic Enamel paint and small round paintbrush to paint hair (optional); light brown waterbase stain; foam brush; soft cloth; cosmetic blush (optional); 24" of 20-gauge florist wire for arms; masking tape; large resealable plastic bag; fabric stiffener; stainless steel pins; 16" of string; 31" of 26-gauge paddle wire; two ³/₄"w gold stars (ours were cut from wired star garland); lightweight cardboard; plastic wrap; waxed paper; drawing compass; craft knife; ice pick or nail; tracing paper; matte clear acrylic spray; hot glue gun; glue sticks; and fabric glue.

For musical instrument, you will need a 4" to 5"h wooden musical instrument and gold Rub 'n Buff® metallic finish (optional).

For "Peace on Earth" sign, you will **also** need heavy ivory parchment paper, gold felt-tip pen with fine point, spray adhesive, metallic gold dimensional paint in squeeze bottle with very fine point, and very fine gold glitter.

1. Cover work surface with waxed paper.
2. (**Note:** Follow Step 2 if Centerpiece Angel will be used as a tree topper.) Use craft knife to cut bottom from cone; discard gravel.
3. Use craft knife to cut 1" from top of cone. Spray paint cone to match robe fabric; allow to dry.
4. (**Note:** Use hot glue for all glue steps unless otherwise indicated.) Use craft knife to cut an approx. ¹/₄" dia. hole in side of each shoulder of doll head. Glue head to top of cone. To make openings in cone for wire for arms, insert ice pick through hole in 1 shoulder and make a hole in side of cone; repeat to make a hole in opposite side of cone. Bend 24" wire length in half. Referring to **Fig. 1**, insert bent wire through holes in shoulders and cone. Center wire and wrap wire extending from holes in shoulders with masking tape.

Fig. 1

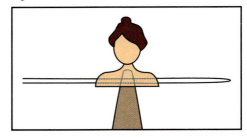

5. (**Note:** For all painting steps, allow to dry after each paint color. Follow Step 5 to paint doll hair, if desired.) Mix 1 part Sable Brown paint with 1 part Chocolate paint. Use paint mixture to paint hair. Use undiluted Chocolate paint to shade hair.
6. Allowing to dry between coats, apply 2 coats of acrylic spray to doll head and arms.
7. To antique doll head and arms, use foam brush to apply stain to doll head and arms; use soft cloth to wipe away excess stain. If desired, repeat process to make some areas darker. Allow to dry.
8. If desired, apply cosmetic blush to cheeks.
9. Repeat Step 6.
10. Cover doll head with plastic wrap. Bend and arrange wire for arms down and around toward front of angel.
11. For neck opening of robe, fold fabric piece in half from top to bottom and again from left to right. Mark center of fabric; unfold fabric. Use compass to draw a 1¹/₂" dia. circle at center of fabric. Cut out circle. Using heavy thread, baste ¹/₈" from edge of opening in fabric.
12. For robe, place fabric piece in plastic bag and pour fabric stiffener over fabric; work stiffener into fabric to saturate. Remove fabric from bag.
13. (**Note:** Refer to photos for remaining steps. Complete Steps 13 - 18 before fabric dries.) With long edges of fabric piece at sides of cone, place neck opening of robe over doll head. Pull ends of basting thread, gathering fabric around neck; knot thread and trim ends.
14. Fold each long edge of fabric ³/₈" to wrong side; pin to secure.
15. To gather waist, wrap string around back of cone (under back of robe) and around front of cone (over front of robe) approx. 2" below neckline; tie string in front. Adjust gathers at front of robe.
16. For sides of robe, begin at bottom of robe and overlap side edges of front of robe ¹/₂" over side edges of back of robe, going approx. 7" up side edges; pin edges together.

17. Placing paddle wire in fold of fabric, fold bottom edge of robe ¹/₂" to wrong side; pin to secure.
18. Arrange robe, leaving approx. ¹/₄" openings around string at each side of waist. Allow robe to dry.
19. Remove plastic wrap from head, pins from robe, and string from waist. Glue arms to ends of wire for arms.
20. Use fabric glue to glue picot trim along neckline of robe, overlapping ends at back.
21. (**Note:** To prevent cord from fraying after cutting, apply fabric glue to ¹/₂" of cord around area to be cut, allow to dry, and then cut.) For halo, cut a 5¹/₄" length of ³/₁₆" dia. cord; hot glue ends of cord together. Glue ends of cord to back of angel's head.
22. For waist tie, cut a 26" length of ³/₁₆" dia. cord. Thread cord around waist through openings in robe; tie into a bow at front. Glue 1 star to each end of tie.
23. For wings, trace wing pattern onto tracing paper; cut out. Use pattern to cut 2 wings from cardboard. Spray paint both sides of each wing gold.
24. Referring to pattern and trim key, this page, cut and glue trims to wings.
25. Glue inner edge of each wing to top center back of robe.
26. For shawl, fold ends of each ribbon length ¹/₂" to wrong side. Place ribbons together. Center ribbons under wings and arrange over shoulders and behind hands.
27. For musical instrument, follow manufacturer's instructions to lightly rub a small amount of Rub 'n Buff® on instrument to highlight if desired. Place instrument in arms.
28. For "Peace on Earth" sign, trace large and small star patterns onto tracing paper; cut out. Use patterns to cut large star from cardboard and small star from heavy paper. Spray paint front and back of large star gold. Use gold pen to write "Peace on Earth" on small star. Use spray adhesive to glue small star to center of large star. Use gold dimensional paint to outline small star and paint dots just inside outline. While paint is still wet, sprinkle with glitter. Allow to dry; shake gently to remove excess glitter. Place sign in arms.

TRIM KEY

🟩	³/₈"w gold gimp trim
🟧	¹/₈" dia. gold twisted cord
🟥	¹/₂"w gold loop fringe
🟦	³/₁₆" dia. gold twisted cord

SCALLOPED TREE SKIRT (Shown on page 23)

You will need a 55" square of medium to heavy weight solid color fabric for skirt, 1/2 yd of 44"w striped fabric for scallops, 1/2 yd of 44"w fabric to line scallops, 3 1/4 yds of 1/4"w decorative braid, 5 1/4 yds of 1/2" dia. twisted cord, 1 1/4 yds of 1/4"w flat gold braid, five 5" long tassels, thread to match fabrics, 1/4"w double-fold bias tape to match tree skirt fabric, 1/2"w paper-backed fusible web tape, tracing paper, fabric marking pencil, string, thumbtack, yardstick, fabric glue, transparent tape, hot glue gun, and glue sticks.

1. Matching right sides, fold tree skirt fabric in half from top to bottom and again from left to right. Use fabric marking pencil to mark center of square. Unfold fabric once.

2. To mark outer guideline, tie 1 end of string to fabric marking pencil. Insert thumbtack through string 26 1/2" from pencil. Referring to **Fig. 1**, insert thumbtack in fabric at center point (A) and mark 1/2 of a circle.

Fig. 1

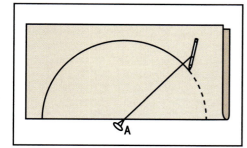

3. Referring to **Fig. 2**, insert thumbtack in fabric at 1 edge of drawn half circle (B) and mark 1/4 of a circle. Repeat, placing thumbtack at opposite edge of half circle (C).

Fig. 2

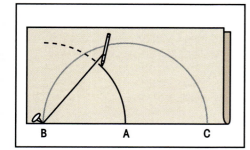

4. To mark inner cutting line, repeat Step 2, inserting thumbtack through string 1 1/4" from pencil.

5. To mark outer cutting line, refer to **Fig. 3** and use yardstick and fabric marking pencil to draw 3 sides of a hexagon.

Fig. 3

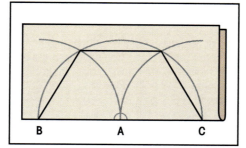

6. Cutting along drawn lines through both fabric layers, cut out inner circle and hexagon. For opening in back of skirt, cut fabric along 1 fold from outer edge to inner circle.

7. To cover raw edge of inner circle, insert edge into fold of bias tape, trimming bias tape to fit; use fabric glue to secure.

8. To hem skirt, follow manufacturer's instructions to fuse web tape to wrong side along outer edges of skirt. Do not remove paper backing. Lightly press edge to wrong side along inner edge of tape. Unfold edge and remove paper backing; refold edge and fuse in place. Repeat to hem opening edges.

9. For scallop pattern, follow **Tracing Patterns**, page 158, for top and bottom of pattern. Matching dotted lines and aligning arrows, tape pattern pieces together.

10. Matching long arrows on pattern to stripes on fabric and leaving at least 1/2" between scallops, draw around scallop pattern 6 times on wrong side of scallop fabric. Pin scallop fabric and lining fabric right sides together. Sew fabric pieces together directly on drawn lines. Leaving a 1/4" seam allowance around each shape, cut out scallops. Clip corners and curves. For opening for turning, carefully cut an approx. 2 1/2" slit in lining side of each scallop near center of pointed end. Turn right side out and press.

11. (**Note:** Refer to photo for remaining steps.) To attach each scallop to skirt, center scallop along 1 straight edge of skirt with curved part of scallop extending beyond edge of skirt; pin in place. Sew scallop to skirt along straight edges.

12. (**Note:** To prevent ends of braid or cord from fraying after cutting, apply fabric glue to 1/2" of braid or cord around area to be cut, allow to dry, and then cut.) Hot glue 1/4"w decorative braid along straight edges of each scallop.

13. Beginning at skirt opening, hot glue cord along edges of skirt; at each hexagon point, extend cord to form a 2" long loop.

Secure loop by wrapping a 4" length of flat braid around base of loop; hot glue to secure.

14. Hot glue 1 tassel to each loop. Wrap a 4" length of flat braid around each tassel; hot glue to secure.

FABRIC TWIST GARLAND
(Shown on page 23)

For each length of garland (we used 7 lengths for our seven-foot-tall tree), you will need a 9"w strip of fabric cut from selvage to selvage (we used 50"w fabric), polyester fiberfill, lengths of 1/8" dia. gold twisted cord and bead garlands cut 10" longer than fabric strip, thread to match fabric, florist wire, wire cutters, 2 to 4 silk magnolia blossoms with leaves, gold Rub 'n Buff® metallic finish (optional), and 2 to 4 purchased 4" long gold leaf ornaments.

1. Matching right sides, fold fabric strip in half lengthwise. Using a 1/4" seam allowance, sew long edges together to form a tube. Turn tube right side out.

2. Gather tube 2" to 3" from 1 end; wrap tightly with wire to secure. Lightly stuff tube with fiberfill. Wrap remaining end of tube with wire to secure.

3. Wrap cord and bead garlands loosely around stuffed tube; wire ends of cord and garlands at ends of tube to secure.

4. (**Note:** Our purchased magnolia blossoms have gold highlighted leaves. For gold highlights on plain silk leaves, follow manufacturer's instructions to apply Rub 'n Buff® metallic finish to leaves.) Wire garland length to tree. Wire 1 magnolia blossom at each end of garland. Wire additional magnolia blossoms and leaf ornaments to garland as desired.

SCALLOP BOTTOM

SCALLOP TOP

SCHERENSCHNITTE ANGEL ORNAMENTS (Shown on page 23)

For each ornament, you will need an 8½" x 11" piece of natural parchment scherenschnitte paper; craft knife with extra blades; cutting mat or thick layer of newspapers; tagboard (manila folder) for backing; spray adhesive; metallic gold spray paint; Design Master™ glossy wood tone spray (available at craft stores and florist shops); metallic gold dimensional paint in squeeze bottle with very fine point; gold glitter; tracing paper; and **either** graphite transfer paper, and removable tape to trace pattern **or** matte clear acrylic spray to seal photocopy of pattern.

1. (**Note:** Pattern shown makes a right-facing ornament. For left-facing ornament, trace gold lines of angel pattern onto tracing paper, turn pattern over, and then follow instructions.) Use gold lines of angel pattern and follow Steps 1 and 2 of "Peace" Scherenschnitte instructions, this page.

2. For ornament backing, trace blue lines of angel pattern onto tracing paper; cut out. Use pattern to cut backing from tagboard.

3. Spray paint both sides of backing gold; allow to dry. Lightly spray edges of backing with wood tone spray; allow to dry.

4. Follow Step 3 of "Peace" Scherenschnitte instructions, positioning angel on painted tagboard.

5. Use dimensional paint to paint lines on angel where glitter is desired; while paint is still wet, sprinkle painted lines with glitter. Allow to dry; shake gently to remove excess glitter.

"PEACE" SCHERENSCHNITTE
(Shown on page 20)

For 11" x 14" scherenschnitte picture, you will need an 11" x 17" piece of natural parchment scherenschnitte paper; craft knife with extra blades; cutting mat or thick layer of newspapers; an 11" x 17" piece of metallic gold mat board; spray adhesive; desired frame with 11" x 14" opening (we used a custom frame); and **either** tracing paper, graphite transfer paper, and removable tape to trace pattern, **or** matte clear acrylic spray to seal photocopy of pattern.

1. (**Note:** Follow Step 1 to transfer pattern, page 31, to scherenschnitte paper **or** photocopy design directly onto center of scherenschnitte paper and spray lightly with acrylic spray to prevent smearing.) Trace pattern onto tracing paper. Center pattern on 1 side (wrong side) of scherenschnitte paper and tape 1 edge in place. Place transfer paper, coated side down, under pattern. Holding papers in place, lightly draw over lines of pattern to transfer pattern to scherenschnitte paper. Remove pattern and transfer paper.

2. (**Note:** Work slowly and change blades often for best results.) Place scherenschnitte paper on cutting mat. Beginning at center of design and working toward outer edges, use craft knife to cut out design.

3. Apply spray adhesive to wrong side of scherenschnitte. Carefully position scherenschnitte on mat board, guiding loose areas into place. Press firmly to secure.

4. Trim scherenschnitte to 11" x 14" with design centered; insert in frame.

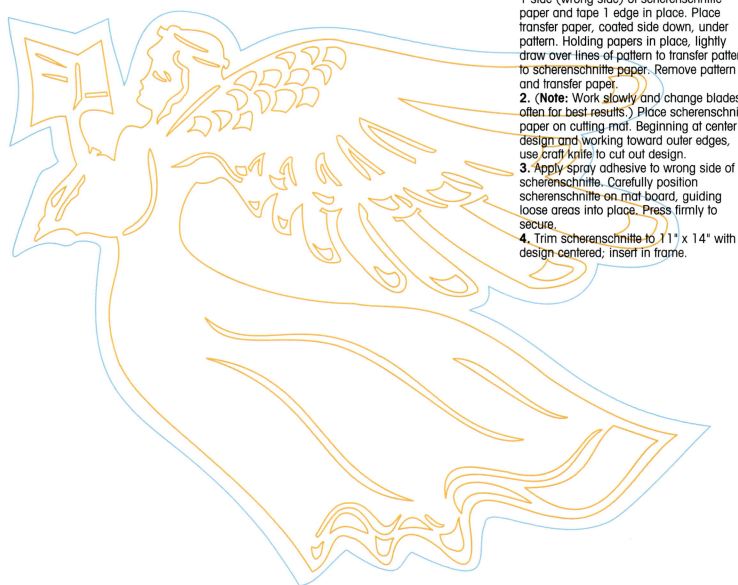

VISIONS OF SANTA

We all have our own vision of Santa Claus, shaped by family traditions and our childhood imaginations. Some of us see him as a rotund, jolly elf; others envision a tall, thin bishop in a richly embroidered robe. But always he is a generous spirit, a bringer of gifts, and a friend to children of all ages. Paying tribute to the many faces of Santa, this country collection features several images of the red-suited visitor. His rosy-cheeked visage adorns the tree with cheer, along with plaid bows and natural trimmings, and a length of red-checked fabric serves as a homey tree skirt. Handmade accents, including stockings and a painted sled, spread the Christmas spirit to every corner. Instructions for the projects shown here and on the following pages begin on page 38. May the magic of Santa Claus bring added enchantment to your celebration!

Sewn from green-striped ticking fabric and bordered with a bright red ruffle, this **Elfish Santa Pillow** *(page 43)* is wonderfully whimsical! Santa's hat is dressed up with textured trim and a shiny jingle bell.

The **Celestial Santa Ornament** *(page 39)* is easy to create by painting a crescent-shaped Santa on a purchased papier mâché ball. Textured paint adds a three-dimensional look to his hat and beard.

Stamped with stars or a checkerboard pattern, inexpensive craft paper is transformed into merry **Stamped Gift Wrap** *(page 39)*. The coordinating **Star and Celestial Santa Gift Tags** *(page 39)* dress up your holiday surprises.

Adorned with a kindly St. Nick, our **Painted Sled** *(page 40)* makes a festive country decoration for any room.

Celebrating the delightful anticipation of Christmas Eve, the **Visions of Santa Tree** *(page 38)* is trimmed with Santas of all shapes and sizes! The **Celestial Santa Ornaments** *(page 39)* are sprinkled with stars, and the **"Icicle" Santa Ornaments** *(page 44)* are shaped from sculpting compound. Painted **Folk-Art Santas** *(page 40)* hold strings of country hearts, and the cone-shaped **Papier Mâché Santas** *(page 38)* carry bags of toys. The **Elfish Santa Ornaments** *(page 42)* sport caps with shiny jingle bells. Two purchased garlands — one of wooden beads and one of silk holly and grapevine — add to the country charm of the tree. Plaid wired ribbon bows, pinecones, and purchased wooden snowflakes complete the trimmings.

Using your imagination and ornaments from the tree, you can create charming little scenes like this one. Here, a **Papier Mâché Santa** (*page 38*) is arranged with greenery, pinecones, a candle, and a pair of woolly sheep.

These old-fashioned stockings are all ready to be filled with treats from Santa's pack! The patchwork **Checkerboard Stocking** (*page 45*) is tied with embroidery floss, and the **Homespun Stocking** (*page 45*) is sewn from cozy plaid fabric. Both stockings feature coffee-dyed muslin cuffs embroidered with a loved one's name.

VISIONS OF SANTA TREE (Shown on page 33)

Trimmed with images of Santa, this magical tree recreates many of our childhood visions of that charming old character — a kind-faced bringer of gifts, an impish elf, an ancient man with a long white beard. These gentlemen will warm the hearts of all who see them.

Forming a natural backdrop for the many Santas, two purchased garlands are wound through the branches of this 7½-foot-tall tree. The first is made of intertwined lengths of ¼" diameter rough brown rope, artificial holly, and dried grapevine which are wired together. The second is a ½" diameter natural wooden bead garland.

Among the branches of the tree are five unique Santa ornaments. Created from purchased papier mâché balls, our Celestial Santa Ornaments (page 39) feature a crescent moon Santa with a snowy beard. Each Folk-Art Santa (page 40) is made from muslin, stuffed, and then painted. The "Icicle" Santa Ornaments (page 44) are sculpted from Mâché Clay (an air-drying clay) and then painted. A special painting technique gives each Papier Mâché Santa (this page) an aged appearance, and the Elfish Santa Ornaments (page 42) are made by layering painted canvas shapes on a stuffed and painted muslin base.

To further the natural look, pinecones are wired to the tree, and purchased 3¼" diameter pressed wood snowflake ornaments surround the Santas. Wired to the tips of several branches, bows tied from 2¼" wide red and green plaid wired ribbon provide bright color in contrast with the more rustic elements. For an informal tree topper, a multi-loop bow fashioned from the same ribbon is wired to the top of the tree. A cheery length of fabric wraps the base of the tree in warm red and white checks.

Wouldn't Santa be surprised and delighted to find a few of these familiar faces on your tree this holiday season?

PAPIER MÂCHÉ SANTAS (Shown on page 37)

For each Santa, you will need a 9"h plastic foam cone; instant papier mâché (we used Celluclay® Instant Papier Mâché); white, ivory, light yellow, dark yellow, peach, dark red, brown, dark brown, green, and blue acrylic paint; small round and flat paintbrushes; gesso; foam brushes; soft cloth; toothpicks; waxed paper; matte clear acrylic spray; craft glue; and 8" of florist wire, hot glue gun, and glue sticks for attaching Santa to tree (optional).

1. Cover work area with waxed paper. Follow manufacturer's instructions to mix papier mâché.
2. (**Note:** Refer to **Diagram** and photo when shaping Santa; use measurements given as general guidelines. When applying features, blend edges of shapes into wet papier mâché on cone.) Use fingertips to spread a thin layer of craft glue, then a smooth ⅛" thick layer of papier mâché onto sides and top of cone. For tip of hat, build up top of cone ½" with papier mâché.
3. For face, use a toothpick to lightly outline a 1½" dia. circle in wet papier mâché 2¼" from top of Santa.
4. For fur trim on hat, form a 5¼" long, ⅜" dia. roll of papier mâché. Overlapping top edge of face, apply roll to Santa, joining ends at back.
5. Form a ¼" thick beard shape from papier mâché; apply to Santa around bottom of face. Apply a ¼" thick layer of papier mâché along sides of face and to back of head for hair.
6. Use small pieces of papier mâché to form nose and mustache; apply to face.
7. For sleeves and mittens, form two 3" long, ¾" dia. rolls of papier mâché.

Apply 1 roll to each side of Santa. For fur trim on sleeves, form two 1" long, ⅜" dia. rolls of papier mâché. Apply 1 roll to each arm ½" from bottom of arm. Use a toothpick to separate thumb from hand on each mitten.
8. For fur trim at bottom of coat, form a 10¾" long, ⅜" dia. roll of papier mâché; apply to Santa along bottom edge, joining ends at back.
9. Form a ¼" thick bag shape from papier mâché; apply to coat, connecting top of bag to mitten.
10. Use a toothpick to add texture to mustache, beard, hair, and fur trims.
11. (**Note:** Drying may take 2 days or longer; drying time may be shortened by placing Santa in front of a fan.) Allow Santa to dry completely.
12. Use fingers to spread a thin layer of craft glue, then a smooth ⅛" thick layer of papier mâché onto bottom of Santa. Lay Santa on side and allow papier mâché to dry completely.
13. Use foam brush to apply 1 coat of gesso to Santa. Allow to dry.
14. (**Note:** Refer to photo to paint Santa. To give Santa an antique look, an undercoat of paint is applied to hat and coat before basecoat is applied; when painting basecoats, allow edges of undercoat to show through. Use flat paintbrushes to paint undercoat and basecoats; use round paintbrushes to paint outlines and details. Allow to dry after each paint color.) For undercoat, paint hat and coat light yellow. For basecoats, paint mustache, beard, hair, and fur trims ivory; paint face peach; paint coat and hat dark red; paint mittens green; and paint bag dark yellow.
15. Mix 1 part brown paint with 1 part

water. Use mixture to outline fur trims, bottom of beard, bag, and mittens. Use undiluted dark brown paint to outline arms.
16. Use dark red paint to paint mouth and blue paint to paint eyes. Use a toothpick to paint 2 small white spots in each eye for highlights. Paint white eyebrows on Santa. Mix 1 part dark red paint with 1 part water; use mixture to paint cheeks. Paint dark brown stars on bag. Highlight mustache, beard, hair, and fur trims with white.
17. Allowing to dry after each coat, apply 2 coats of acrylic spray to Santa.
18. To antique Santa, mix 1 part brown paint with 1 part water. Working on 1 small area at a time, use foam brush to apply mixture to mustache, beard, hair, fur trim, and bag; use soft cloth to wipe away excess paint. Allow to dry. If desired, repeat process to make some areas darker.
19. Repeat Step 17.
20. If attaching Santa to tree, hot glue center of wire to bottom of Santa.

DIAGRAM

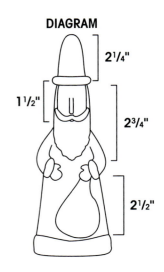

CELESTIAL SANTA ORNAMENTS (Shown on page 34)

For each ornament, you will need a 4" dia. papier mâché ball; peach, dark pink, dark red, metallic gold, and black acrylic paint; Duncan Snow Accents™; small round and flat paintbrushes; brown waterbase stain; plastic or coated paper plate; paper towels; brown permanent felt-tip pen with fine point; a ½" dia. unfinished wooden bead; 6" of jute twine; tagboard (manila folder); drawing compass; craft knife; hot glue gun; and glue sticks.

1. For template to draw crescent shape, use compass to draw a 3¼" dia. circle on tagboard. Use craft knife to cut out circle; discard circle.
2. (**Note:** Use a glass or cup with an opening slightly smaller than ball to hold ornament while working.) Use template and a pencil to lightly draw circle on ball.
3. Referring to photo and **Fig. 1**, draw a crescent shape, approx. 1" wide at widest point, in circle. Draw a straight line on crescent for bottom edge of hat. Sketch outline of face on crescent.

Fig. 1

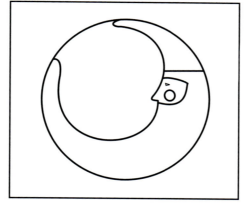

4. (**Note:** Refer to photo to paint Santa. Use round paintbrushes to paint hat, face, and details on face. Allow to dry after each paint color.) Paint hat dark red. Leaving a small triangular area unpainted for eye, paint face peach. Paint dark pink cheek on face. Mix 1 part dark pink paint and 1 part peach paint; use mixture to highlight cheek. Using tip of paintbrush handle or a

toothpick, paint a small black dot in unpainted triangle for eye.
5. Use round paintbrush and a stamping motion to apply an approx. ¼" dia. dot of Snow Accents™ at tip of hat for pom-pom. For hat trim, hair, mustache, and beard, use flat paintbrush and a stamping motion to apply Snow Accents™ to ornament, filling in unpainted areas of crescent shape; allow to dry.
6. Use pencil to sketch stars on ornament as desired. Use round paintbrush to paint stars gold. Using tip of a paintbrush handle and gold paint, paint rows of dots around each star. Use brown pen to outline stars.
7. To antique areas painted with Snow Accents™, pour stain onto plate. Dip crumpled paper towel in stain; do not saturate. Blot on a clean paper towel to remove excess stain. Using a light stamping motion, apply stain to areas painted with Snow Accents™. Allow to dry.
8. Erase any visible pencil lines.
9. For hanger, glue ends of twine into hole of bead. Glue bead to top of ornament.

STAMPED GIFT WRAP (Shown on page 34)

You will need brown craft paper, 1/16" thick crafting foam, utility scissors, small flat paintbrush, hot glue gun, and glue sticks. **For star gift wrap,** you will **also** need a 4" x 5" wood piece cut from 1 x 6 lumber for stamp, metallic gold acrylic paint, brown permanent felt-tip pen with fine point, and tracing paper. **For checkerboard gift wrap,** you will **also** need a 3" x 4" wood piece cut from 1 x 6 lumber for stamp and red acrylic paint.

STAR GIFT WRAP
1. For stamp, trace star patterns onto tracing paper; cut out. Use a pencil to draw around stars on crafting foam. Use scissors to cut stars from foam. Glue stars to wood piece.
2. Use paintbrush to apply gold paint evenly to stars on stamp. Use stamp to stamp stars on craft paper. Reapplying paint as necessary, repeat as desired.
3. Use tip of paintbrush handle and gold paint to paint rows of dots around stars. Allow to dry.
4. Use brown pen to outline each star.

CHECKERBOARD GIFT WRAP
1. For stamp, use a ruler and pencil to draw six 1" squares on craft foam. Use scissors to cut squares from foam. Refer to **Fig. 1** to glue squares to wood piece.

Fig. 1

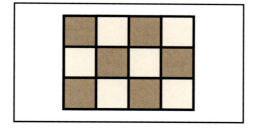

2. Use paintbrush to apply red paint evenly to squares on stamp. Reapplying paint as necessary, begin at bottom left corner of craft paper and use stamp to stamp a row of checks onto paper, working from left to right. Working from right to left and lining up squares, reverse stamp and stamp a second row of checks onto paper just above first row. Reversing stamp for each row, repeat as desired.

STAR AND CELESTIAL SANTA GIFT TAGS (Shown on page 34)

For each tag, you will need a 4" x 8" piece of cream-colored heavy paper, rubber cement, brown permanent felt-tip pen with fine point, and hole punch (optional). **For star tag,** you will **also** need a 3½" square of Star Gift Wrap (this page). **For celestial Santa tag,** you will **also** need a 3½" square of brown craft paper; peach, dark pink, dark red, and black acrylic paint; Duncan Snow Accents™; small round and flat paintbrushes; brown waterbase stain; plastic or coated paper plate; paper towels; and drawing compass.

STAR TAG
1. Matching short edges, fold heavy paper in half.

2. Glue gift wrap square to front of tag. Use pen to draw dashed lines around edge of gift wrap square to resemble stitching.
3. If desired, punch hole in tag.

CELESTIAL SANTA TAG
1. Use compass to lightly draw a 3" dia. circle at center of craft paper square.
2. Drawing a crescent shape approx. ¾" wide at widest point, follow Steps 3 - 5, 7, and 8 of Celestial Santa Ornaments instructions, this page, to sketch and paint Santa.
3. Follow Star Tag instructions to complete tag.

FOLK-ART SANTAS (Shown on page 36)

For each Santa, you will need two 8" x 12" muslin pieces; polyester fiberfill; ecru thread; medium weight cardboard or mat board; white, dark yellow, peach, dark peach, pink, dark red, dark green, light blue green, brown, light grey, and black acrylic paint; liner, small round, and small flat paintbrushes; gesso; foam brushes; brown waterbase stain; soft cloth; black permanent felt-tip pen with fine point; drawing compass; freezer paper; tracing paper; graphite transfer paper; stylus or ball-point pen that does not write; spring-type clothespins; fine sandpaper; tack cloth; plastic or coated paper plates; paper towels; toothpicks; removable tape; craft glue; matte clear acrylic spray; and 8" of florist wire, hot glue gun, and glue sticks for attaching Santa to tree (optional).

1. For sewing pattern, place freezer paper shiny side down over Santa pattern, page 41, and trace outline of pattern, including seam allowance at bottom; cut out.
2. Pin muslin pieces together. Center pattern shiny side down on muslin pieces. Use a warm dry iron to press pattern onto muslin (pattern will adhere to muslin).
3. Using a short machine stitch and leaving bottom edge open, sew muslin pieces together close to side and top edges of pattern. Use a pencil to draw a straight line along bottom edge of pattern. Peel pattern from muslin. (Pattern may be used more than once.) Cut out Santa $1/8$" outside stitching line and along drawn line. At $1/4$" intervals, clip curved edges to $1/16$" from stitched line. Turn Santa right side out.
4. For base of Santa, use compass to draw two $2^5/8$" dia. circles on cardboard; cut out.
5. (**Note:** Use craft glue for Step 5.) Stuff Santa with fiberfill to $1/2$" from opening. Insert 1 cardboard circle $1/2$" inside bottom of Santa. At $1/2$" intervals, clip fabric extending beyond cardboard to $1/16$" from cardboard. Glue clipped edges to bottom of cardboard; allow to dry. Glue remaining cardboard circle to bottom of Santa. Use clothespins to hold cardboard circle on Santa until glue is dry.
6. Lightly sanding and wiping with tack cloth between coats, apply 3 coats of gesso to Santa, allowing to dry between coats.
7. For painting pattern, trace Santa pattern, page 41, onto tracing paper, omitting seam allowance at bottom; cut out. Draw around pattern on uncoated side of transfer paper; cut out transfer paper.

8. (**Note:** Red lines on pattern indicate basecoat areas. Blue areas indicate highlighting or shading. Grey lines indicate details.) To transfer pattern to Santa, place transfer paper and pattern on front of Santa with coated side of transfer paper against Santa and edges of pattern and transfer paper lined up with seams of Santa. Tape pattern and transfer paper in place. Use stylus to draw over red lines of pattern. Repeat to transfer bottom coat trim to back of Santa.
9. (**Note:** Refer to photo for remaining steps. Read Painting Techniques, page 41, before painting. Allow to dry after each paint color.) Apply basecoats as follows:
   - Hat and coat – dark red
   - Face – peach
   - Hat trim, heart on tip of hat, cuffs, hair, mustache, beard, and bottom coat trim – white
   - Mittens, boots, and bottom of Santa – black
   - Hanging hearts – dark yellow
10. Apply shading and highlighting as follows:
   - Face – shade with dark peach along top and sides of face and top of nose
   - Cheeks – shade with pink along tops of cheeks
   - Hat trim, cuffs, hair, mustache, and beard – shade with light grey
   - Mittens and boots – highlight with white
   - Coat and hat – shade with black
11. (**Note:** It is best to freehand details as much as possible.) Repeat Step 8 to transfer grey lines on pattern onto Santa.
12. Paint details as follows:
   - Designs on hat trim and heart on tip of hat – dark green with dark red spot strokes
   - Border on heart on tip of hat – dark red
   - Borders on cuffs and bottom coat trim – dark red lines with dark green spot strokes
   - Top hanging heart – dark green leaves, dark red berries and line, and light blue green ribbon
   - Middle hanging heart – dark red star and spot strokes
   - Bottom hanging heart – brown tree trunk, dark green branches with white highlights, and dark red dashed lines
   - Beads joining hearts – dark yellow spot strokes
   - Eyes – black spot strokes
   - Eyebrows – white
   - Mouth – black
   - Lip – dark red

13. Use black pen to draw eyelids and eyelashes; use pen to outline nose on face and leaves, ribbon, and star on hearts.
14. Allowing to dry after each coat, apply 2 coats of acrylic spray to Santa.
15. Working on 1 small area at a time, use foam brush to apply stain to Santa; wipe with soft cloth to remove excess stain. Allow to dry.
16. Repeat Step 14.
17. If attaching Santa to tree, hot glue center of wire to bottom of Santa.

PAINTED SLED
(Shown on page 35)

You will need 1 unfinished decorative wooden sled with a 9" x 16" or larger area for painting; white, dark yellow, peach, dark peach, pink, dark red, green, dark green, light blue green, brown, light grey, and black acrylic paint; liner, small round, and small flat paintbrushes; brown waterbase stain; foam brushes; soft cloth; black permanent felt-tip pen with fine point; tracing paper; graphite transfer paper; stylus or ball-point pen that does not write; fine sandpaper; tack cloth; plastic or coated paper plates; paper towels; toothpicks; matte clear acrylic spray; florist wire; wire cutters; artificial pine branches; stems of artificial red berries; dried grapevine; pinecones; $2^1/4$"w wired ribbon; hot glue gun; and glue sticks.

1. Sand sled and wipe lightly with tack cloth to remove dust.
2. Excluding runners, use foam brush to paint sled green.
3. Omitting seam allowance at bottom of Santa pattern, trace Santa and holly patterns, page 41, onto tracing paper.
4. (**Note:** Refer to photo for remaining steps. Red lines on patterns indicate basecoat areas. Blue areas indicate highlighting or shading. Grey lines indicate details.) Use transfer paper and stylus to transfer red lines on patterns to sled.
5. Follow Step 9 of Folk-Art Santas instructions, this page, to paint basecoats on Santa.
6. For basecoats on holly, paint leaves dark green and berries dark red.
7. Follow Step 10 of Folk-Art Santas instructions to shade and highlight Santa.
8. For holly, shade leaves with black and highlight with white; shade berries with black and highlight with pink.

PAINTED SLED
(Continued)

9. (**Note:** It is best to freehand details as much as possible.) Use transfer paper to transfer grey lines on patterns onto Santa and holly.

10. Follow Steps 12 and 13 of Folk-Art Santas instructions to complete details on Santa.

11. For details on holly, paint tendrils and veins on leaves brown. For white accents, use white to paint spot strokes.

12. To antique sled, follow Steps 14 - 16 of Folk-Art Santas instructions.

13. For trim at top of sled, wire pine branches, berry stems, and lengths of grapevine together. Glue arrangement to 1 runner of sled. Repeat for trim at side of sled. Form a multi-loop bow from ribbon; wrap bow with wire at center to secure. Glue bow to sled. Trim ribbon ends and arrange streamers; glue in place. Glue pinecones around bow.

PAINTING TECHNIQUES

Basecoat – Allowing to dry after each coat, use flat brush to apply 2 to 3 coats of paint.

Float – Dip a flat brush in water. Stroke brush on paper towel, allowing towel to soak up some of the water. Load paint on 1 side of brush. Gently stroke brush on paper plate until stroke leaves a definite line on 1 side and fades to nothing on the other side. Place loaded side of brush next to detail line. Stroke evenly to highlight or shade. Clean brush before reloading. Reload brush for each stroke.

Highlight – Float with a light color of paint.

Load – Dip brush in paint.

Shade – Float with a dark color of paint.

Spot Stroke – Dip tip of paintbrush handle lightly into paint. Lightly dot project surface, reloading each time for spots of equal size. For smaller dots, use a toothpick.

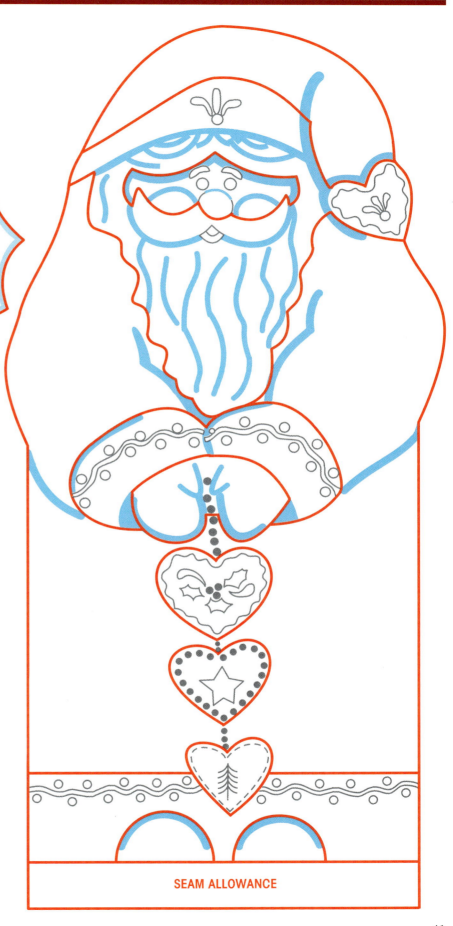

SEAM ALLOWANCE

ELFISH SANTA ORNAMENTS (Shown on page 36)

For each ornament, you will need a 13" square of unbleached muslin; white thread; polyester fiberfill; an 8" x 12" piece of pre-primed artist's canvas (available at art supply stores); white, ivory, light peach, pink, dark red, brown, dark brown, light grey, and black fabric paint; Duncan Snow Accents™; liner, small round, and medium flat fabric paintbrushes; brown waterbase stain; soft cloth; a 15mm jingle bell; 12" of jute twine; tracing paper; removable tape; cardboard covered with waxed paper; hot glue gun; and glue sticks.

1. Trace ornament face pattern, this page, onto tracing paper; cut out. Use pattern to cut 2 pieces from muslin for ornament front and back.

2. (**Note:** Red lines on patterns indicate basecoat areas. Blue areas indicate highlighting or shading. Grey lines indicate details.) For face, place 1 muslin piece (ornament front) over pattern; use a pencil to lightly trace red lines onto muslin.

3. Pin ornament front fabric piece right side up on covered cardboard. Follow Steps 4, 6, and 7 of Elfish Santa Pillow instructions, page 43, to paint face on muslin, painting eyelids white.

4. Place painted muslin piece wrong side up on ornament back muslin piece. Leaving an opening at bottom for turning, use a 1/4" seam allowance to sew pieces together. Turn right side out and stuff bottom of ornament with fiberfill to approx. 1" above forehead. Sew final closure by hand.

5. (**Note:** Refer to photo for remaining steps.) Paint front and back of top portion of ornament (hat) dark red.

6. Trace eyebrow, mustache, and beard patterns, this page, onto tracing paper; cut out. Use a pencil to draw around patterns on canvas for indicated numbers of shapes; cut out shapes.

7. Use flat paintbrush to paint eyebrows, mustache, and beard pieces ivory; allow to dry. Use liner paintbrush to paint light grey

and white lines on eyebrows, mustache, and beard.

8. For hat trim, cut a 2³/₄" x 8¹/₂" strip from muslin. Press each long edge ³/₄" to wrong side.

9. Use flat brush to apply 1 coat of Snow Accents™ to right side of hat trim; allow to dry. Paint hat trim ivory.

10. To antique eyebrows, mustache, beard pieces, and hat trim, mix 1 part stain with 1 part water. Use flat paintbrush to apply mixture to shapes; blot with soft cloth to remove excess stain. Allow to dry.

11. Matching top edges of beard piece A and beard piece B to top of face, glue all 3 beard pieces, mustache, and eyebrows to ornament.

12. Wrap hat trim around ornament, overlapping ends at back; glue to secure.

13. Cut jute in half. Thread 1 length of jute through jingle bell and tie into a bow. Glue to top of hat. For hanger, knot ends of remaining length of jute together. Glue knot to top back of hat.

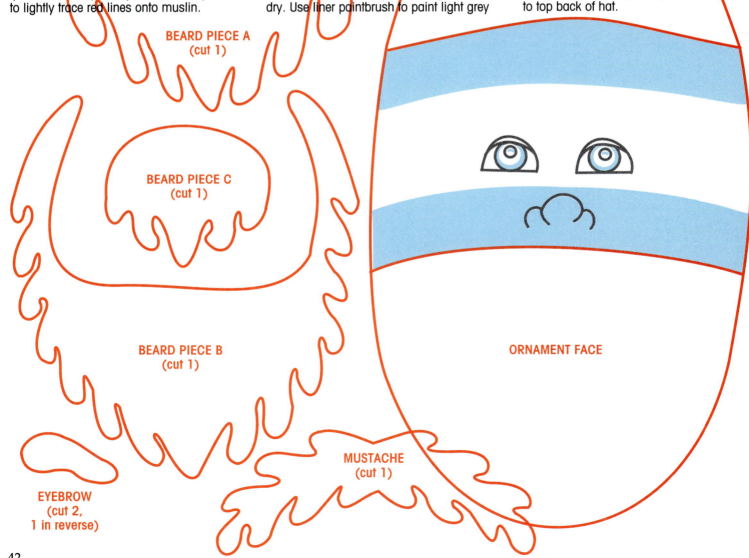

BEARD PIECE A
(cut 1)

BEARD PIECE C
(cut 1)

BEARD PIECE B
(cut 1)

ORNAMENT FACE

EYEBROW
(cut 2,
1 in reverse)

MUSTACHE
(cut 1)

ELFISH SANTA PILLOW (Shown on page 32)

For an approx. 18" x 20" pillow, you will need two 13½" x 16" fabric pieces for pillow front and back; one 3¼" x 1⅔ yd bias fabric strip (pieced as necessary) and 1⅔ yds of ⅝" dia. cord for welting; one 6½" x 4 yd fabric strip for ruffle (pieced as necessary); thread to match fabrics; polyester fiberfill; white, ivory, light peach, pink, dark red, brown, dark brown, light grey, and black fabric paint; Duncan Snow Accents™; liner, small round, and medium flat fabric paintbrushes; brown waterbase stain; soft cloth; 8" of jute twine; a 15mm jingle bell; tracing paper; hot-iron transfer pencil; removable tape; cardboard covered with waxed paper; and washable fabric glue.

1. Wash, dry, and press fabric pieces according to paint manufacturers' recommendations.
2. (**Note:** Follow Steps 2 - 11 to paint Santa. Refer to photo for all painting steps. Red lines on pattern indicate basecoat areas. Blue areas indicate highlighting or shading. Grey lines indicate details.) Trace pillow face pattern, this page, onto tracing paper. Following manufacturer's instructions, use hot-iron transfer pencil to transfer red lines on pattern to center on right side of one 13½" x 16" fabric piece (pillow front).
3. Pin pillow front fabric piece right side up on covered cardboard. Using flat paintbrush, paint hat dark red; before paint dries, shade with dark brown. Allow to dry.
4. Using a flat paintbrush, paint face light peach. Before paint dries, dip a clean flat paintbrush into water, load a small amount of dark brown paint onto brush, and shade top ⅓ of face. Repeat to shade bottom ⅓ of face with pink. Allow to dry.
5. Use flat paintbrush to paint mustache, hair, and beard ivory. Allow to dry.
6. To transfer details of pattern, use a pencil to draw over grey lines on back of traced pattern. Place pattern pencil side down (right side up) on painted Santa; tape to secure. Use the edge of a spoon or coin to rub over detail lines. Remove pattern.
7. (**Note:** When painting details, allow to dry between colors and use round paintbrushes unless otherwise indicated.) Paint irises of eyes brown; before paint dries, shade irises with dark brown. Paint pupils of eyes black, remainder of eyes white, and nose and eyelids light peach. Use liner paintbrush to paint highlights in eyes white and to outline eyes and nose with brown.

8. Use round paintbrush to paint eyebrows ivory. Use liner paintbrush to outline eyebrows, mustache, hair, and beard with light grey. Referring to photo, use liner paintbrush to paint light grey and white lines on eyebrows, mustache, hair, and beard.
9. Follow paint manufacturer's instructions to heat-set design.
10. Using flat paintbrush and a stamping motion, paint trim on hat with Snow Accents™; allow to dry. Paint trim ivory; allow to dry.
11. To antique hat trim, mix 1 part stain with 1 part water. Use flat paintbrush to apply mixture to hat trim; blot with soft cloth to remove excess stain. Allow to dry.
12. For welting, press 1 end of bias strip ½" to wrong side. Center cord on wrong side of bias strip. Matching long edges, fold strip over cord. Using zipper foot, baste along length of strip close to cord; trim seam allowance to ½". Beginning at center bottom and matching raw edges, pin welting to right side of pillow front fabric

piece, clipping seam allowance at corners. Trim cord to fit where ends meet and overlap fabric over ends of cord; baste in place.
13. For ruffle, match right sides and short edges and fold ruffle fabric strip in half. Using a ½" seam allowance, sew short edges together; press seam open. With wrong sides together, match raw edges and press ruffle in half. To gather ruffle, baste ⅜" and ¼" from raw edge. Pull basting threads, gathering ruffle to fit edge of pillow front fabric piece. Matching raw edges, pin ruffle to right side of pillow front fabric piece over welting; baste in place.
14. Matching right sides, place pillow front and back together. Sewing as close as possible to welting and leaving an opening for turning, use zipper foot to sew edges together. Clip corners, turn right side out, and press. Stuff pillow with fiberfill. Sew final closure by hand.
15. Thread twine through jingle bell and tie into a bow; trim ends. Glue bow to tip of hat.

PILLOW FACE

"ICICLE" SANTA ORNAMENTS (Shown on page 36)

For each ornament, you will need 18" of 20-gauge florist wire; natural Mâché Clay no-bake sculpting compound; peach, dark pink, dark red, and black acrylic paint; small paintbrushes; foam brush; brown waterbase stain; aluminum foil; waxed paper; rolling pin; tracing paper; utility scissors; soft cloth; ball-point pen; and matte clear acrylic spray.

1. For hanger, bend wire in half, forming a loop.

2. Leaving top 1/2" of wire exposed, wrap and crush a 12" square of foil firmly between and around ends of loop, forming a 9" long icicle shape (**Fig. 1**). Wrap additional pieces of foil around icicle as needed to fill out shape. Foil icicle should be well shaped and firm before clay is added.

Fig. 1

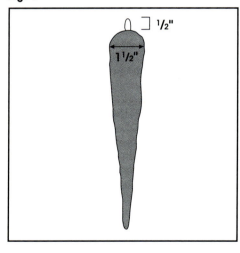

3. Working on waxed paper, use rolling pin to roll out clay to approx. 1/8" thickness.

4. Working with wet hands, apply clay over foil icicle shape, smoothing clay with fingers.

5. Trace eyebrow, mustache, and beard patterns onto tracing paper; cut out.

6. Repeat Step 3. Use pen to draw around patterns on clay for indicated numbers of pieces. Use scissors to cut out pieces. Cut a 1/2" x 5 1/4" strip of clay for hat trim.

7. (**Note:** Refer to photo for remaining steps.) With top of beard 1/2" from top of icicle shape, press beard onto ornament (**Fig. 2**).

Fig. 2

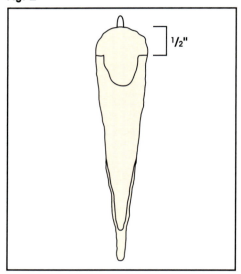

8. Overlapping top edges of beard slightly, press hat trim around ornament, joining and smoothing ends at back. Leaving a small opening above beard for mouth, press mustache onto ornament. Press eyebrows onto ornament.

9. For pom-pom at top of hat, form a 1/2" dia. ball of clay; push ball down over hanging loop onto top of hat and flatten slightly, leaving approx. 1/8" of loop exposed.

10. Use a straight pin to prick hat trim to resemble fur and to score lines into mustache and beard to resemble hair. Allow ornament to dry overnight on waxed paper.

11. (**Note:** Allow to dry after each paint color.) Paint hat, mouth, and back and bottom of ornament dark red. Paint face peach. Paint cheeks dark pink. Using tip of a paintbrush handle or a toothpick, paint a small black dot for each eye.

12. Allowing to dry after each coat, apply 2 coats of acrylic spray to ornament.

13. To antique ornament, mix 1 part stain with 1 part water. Use foam brush to apply mixture to ornament; use soft cloth to wipe away excess stain. Allow to dry.

14. Repeat Step 12.

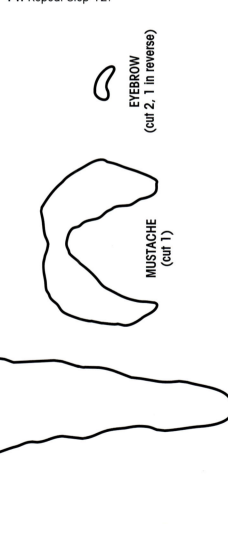

EYEBROW
(cut 2, 1 in reverse)

MUSTACHE
(cut 1)

BEARD
(cut 1)

HOMESPUN STOCKING

(Shown on page 37)

You will need two 12" x 20" print fabric pieces for stocking, two 12" x 20" muslin pieces for lining, one 10" x 13⅛" muslin piece for cuff, one 2" x 8" muslin strip for hanger, thread to match fabrics, embroidery floss for stitching on cuff, instant coffee (optional), removable fabric marking pen, and tracing paper.

1. To coffee-dye fabric, dissolve 2 tablespoons coffee in 2 cups hot water; allow to cool. Soak fabric pieces in coffee several minutes; remove from coffee, allow to dry, and press.

2. Matching dotted lines and aligning arrows, trace top and bottom of stocking pattern, this page, onto tracing paper; cut out.

3. Leaving top edge of stocking open, use pattern and follow **Sewing Shapes**, page 158, to make stocking from stocking fabric pieces; press. Repeat to make lining from lining fabric pieces; do not turn lining right side out.

4. (**Note:** Use a ½" seam allowance for remaining steps.) For cuff, match short edges of muslin piece and sew short edges together to form a tube. Press seam open; turn right side out. Fold bottom raw edge to inside of tube to meet top raw edge; press.

5. Position cuff with fold at bottom and seam at center back. Referring to photo, use fabric marking pen to write name in approx. 2½" high letters on cuff approx. 1" above fold. Refer to photo and use 6 strands of floss and Running Stitch, page 159, to stitch name on cuff. Use 6 strands of floss and Overcast Stitch, page 159, to stitch along bottom edge of cuff. Remove pen lines.

6. Matching raw edges, place cuff over stocking; pin in place. Sew raw edges of stocking and cuff together; press seam allowance to inside of stocking.

7. Press top edge of lining ½" to wrong side. With wrong sides together, insert lining into stocking.

8. For hanger, press muslin strip in half lengthwise; unfold. Press long edges to center; refold strip and sew close to pressed edges. Matching ends, fold strip in half to form a loop. Place ends of loop between lining and stocking at heel-side seamline with 3" of loop extending above stocking; pin in place.

9. Slipstitch lining to stocking, securely sewing hanger in place.

CHECKERBOARD STOCKING (Shown on page 37)

You will need one 15" x 17" piece each of muslin and a contrasting fabric for stocking front, one 23" x 14" muslin piece for stocking front backing, one 12" x 20" fabric piece for stocking back, two 12" x 20" muslin pieces for lining, one 23" x 14" piece of low-loft polyester bonded batting, one 10" x 13⅛" muslin piece for cuff, one 2" x 8" muslin strip for hanger, ecru thread, embroidery floss for ties on stocking front, embroidery floss for stitching on cuff, instant coffee (optional), removable fabric marking pen, and tracing paper.

1. If desired, follow Step 1 of Homespun Stocking instructions, this page, to coffee-dye fabric pieces.

2. (**Note:** Use a ¼" seam allowance unless otherwise indicated.) For stocking front, cut each 15" x 17" fabric piece into seven 2" x 17" strips. Matching right sides and raw edges, sew long edges of strips together, alternating colors of strips (**Fig. 1**). Press seam allowances toward darker fabric.

Fig. 1

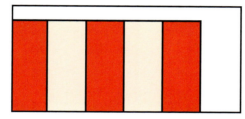

3. Cut pieced panel into eight 2" strips (**Fig. 2**).

Fig. 2

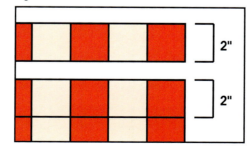

4. Alternating direction of strips and matching right sides and raw edges, sew long edges of strips together, being careful to align seams (**Fig. 3**). Press seam allowances to 1 side.

Fig. 3

5. Matching edges, place batting on stocking front backing muslin piece. Center pieced rectangle right side up on batting. Pin all layers together.

6. To tie layers together, thread a needle with 5" of embroidery floss. Working from right side, take needle down through all 3 layers at 1 corner of 1 square; bring needle up approx. ¹⁄₁₆" away. Tie ends of floss into a square knot next to fabric; trim ends ½" from knot. Repeat for remaining corners of squares on stocking front.

7. Follow Steps 2 - 4 of Homespun Stocking instructions, this page, to make stocking, lining, and cuff from tied stocking front and stocking back, lining, and cuff fabric pieces.

8. Using Cross Stitch, page 158, along bottom edge of cuff, follow Step 5 of Homespun Stocking instructions to embroider stocking.

9. Follow Steps 6 - 9 of Homespun Stocking instructions to complete stocking.

STOCKING BOTTOM

STOCKING TOP

ENCHANTING ELEGANCE

*R*eflecting nature's icy beauty, our Enchanting Elegance collection captures the serenity of an evening stroll through the snowy woods. There, as the last tiny bird sings its twilight song, the flickering of starlight falls through awaiting evergreen branches. This delicate ensemble will brighten your holiday with wintry charm. Instructions for the projects shown here begin on page 48.

Created from one basic pattern and stiffened in six different shapes, exquisite **Crocheted Snowflake Ornaments** (*page 48*) gently drift down the evergreen boughs of our **Enchanting Elegance Tree** (*page 48*). A magical sight, the tree is wrapped in shiny cords, ribbons, and bows. Shimmering miniature lights cast a warming glow on strands of iridescent and silver beads, and sprigs of silk ivy add rich color to the branches. Elegant glass ornaments, white silk poinsettias, and tiny snowbirds enhance the tranquil scene. (*Opposite*) The **Wintry Wreath** (*page 48*) mirrors the beauty of the tree.

ENCHANTING ELEGANCE TREE
(Shown on page 47)

If you're dreaming of a white Christmas, you'll love this elegant tree.

Creating a luxurious garland, strands of iridescent and silver beads, together with 1/2" diameter twisted silver cord, are gracefully draped among the boughs of the tree. Frosty white, silver, and iridescent glass ball ornaments reflect the tiny clear lights, and three styles of silver-drenched glass icicle and pinecone ornaments also highlight the captivating scene.

Six uniquely patterned Crocheted Snowflake Ornaments (this page) drift through the branches of the majestic tree. All made from one basic pattern, the snowflakes are simply shaped differently during the stiffening process.

For a touch of holiday tradition, white silk poinsettias, white artificial holly, and cuttings of green silk ivy are wired to the tree. Bows tied from silver wired ribbon lend a festive air with their long, curling streamers, and a generous length of shiny silver lamé fabric skirts the base of the tree.

A small flock of European blown glass snowbirds alights among the finery, enjoying their wintry surroundings.

WINTRY WREATH
(Shown on page 46)

This frost-covered 22" diameter mixed evergreen wreath brings to mind a forest blanketed with a fresh fall of snow. Wrapped with garlands of iridescent and silver beads and 1/2" diameter twisted silver cord, the artificial wreath also hosts shiny and frosted silver glass ball ornaments in an assortment of sizes. These elements contrast with the delicacy of the beautiful white Crocheted Snowflake Ornaments (this page) sprinkled over the wreath. A multi-loop bow crafted from shimmering silver wired ribbon provides an elegant finishing touch.

CROCHETED SNOWFLAKE ORNAMENTS (Shown on page 46)

SUPPLIES
Bedspread Weight Cotton Thread (size 10): approx. 8 yds for **each** snowflake
Steel crochet hook, size 5 (1.90mm) **or** size needed for gauge
Finishing supplies: fabric stiffener, resealable plastic bag, tracing paper, blocking board or ironing board, plastic wrap, stainless steel pins, terry towel, and paper towels
1/16" dia. silver cord for hangers (optional)

ABBREVIATIONS
ch(s)   chain(s)
Rnd   Round
st   stitch

★ — work instructions following ★ as many **more** times as indicated in addition to the first time.
( ) — work enclosed instructions **as many** times as indicated by the number immediately following **or** contains explanatory remarks.

GAUGE: 38 chs = 4" (DO NOT HESITATE TO CHANGE HOOK SIZE TO OBTAIN CORRECT GAUGE.)

SNOWFLAKE
Ch 6; join with slip st to form a ring.
Rnd 1: ★ Ch 20, slip st in ring, ch 26, slip st in 20th ch from hook, (ch 20, slip st in same ch) twice, ch 6, slip st in ring; repeat from ★ 5 times **more**; finish off.

FINISHING
1. (Note: Follow all steps for each snowflake.) Using a mild detergent and warm water, wash crocheted snowflake; rinse thoroughly. Roll snowflake in terry towel, gently pressing out excess moisture. Lay snowflake flat and allow to dry completely.
2. Pour fabric stiffener into plastic bag; place snowflake in stiffener. Seal bag, pressing out air. Work stiffener into snowflake; allow snowflake to soak for several hours.
3. Trace desired snowflake pattern onto tracing paper. Leaving at least 1" around design, cut out pattern. Place pattern on blocking board and cover with plastic wrap.
4. Remove snowflake from stiffener; squeeze snowflake gently and blot with paper towels to remove excess stiffener. Place snowflake right side up over pattern. Arrange snowflake to fit pattern, using pins to pin snowflake in place. Allow to dry.
5. If hanger is desired, thread a 6" length of silver cord through chain space of ornament; knot ends together.

A FESTIVAL
OF TREES

*F*un *and easy to trim
with handmade ornaments,
tabletop trees are a popular
trend in holiday decorating.
In this festival of small trees
you'll discover wonderful
ideas for spreading the spirit
of the season all through
the house — from a dainty
tea party theme to the
home-baked appeal of our
gingerbread tree. Whether
displayed on the coffee table
or the kitchen counter, these
miniature creations let
you design a tailor-made
celebration that reflects your
individuality. Instructions
for the projects shown here
begin on page 56.*

A radiant sight, the **Starry
Night Tree** (*page 58*) is hung
with shimmering hand-
painted stars and celestial
ball ornaments. Gold bows,
swirls of blue and gold
ribbons, and a star-sprinkled
tree skirt complete the
brilliant display.

Dainty teacups, lacy ornaments, and tiny handkerchief stockings lend an air of romance to this **Holiday Tea Party Tree** (*page 59*). Strings of pearls, a delicate heart tree topper, and a gathered skirt add to the Victorian look.

The homey **Gingerbread Tree** (*page 57*) is a fragrant reminder of Christmases past when children waited eagerly to sample goodies fresh from the oven. Trimmed with spicy cookie ornaments, cinnamon sticks, and dried fruit slices, this simple spoon tree will beckon guests to gather 'round. Be sure to bake extra cookies to share as special holiday treats!

(*Opposite*) Country fun abounds with the "down-on-the-farm" appeal of our **Chicken Scratch Christmas Tree** (*page 56*). Homespun Santa chickens are the stars in this plucky scene, and baby chicks watch the excitement from their own little baskets. Bright gingham bows and red bead garlands add splashes of holiday color. What a delightful accent for a country kitchen!

Blooming with Christmas creativity, the **Homegrown Holiday Tree** (*page 60*) is tended by delightful gardening fairies. Under their watchful care, golden star "flowers" thrive in little terra-cotta pots. *(Opposite)* Nestled among the branches of our **Woodland Frost Tree** (*page 61*) are miniature bird nests, pinecones, twigs, and other woodland elements. Tiny birds and frost-covered birdhouses provide colorful accents for this fresh, sylvan arrangement.

CHICKEN SCRATCH CHRISTMAS TREE (Shown on page 52)

You'd have to get up pretty early on Christmas morning to beat these farm-fresh chickens and their lively offspring! Encircled by garlands of red wooden beads and rope secured with mini clothespins, this whimsical 28" high tree is home to a whole flock of Chicken Star Ornaments and feather-topped Chick-in-a-Basket Ornaments. One chicken rules the roost with a cheerful "Happy Holidays" banner. For a hen-pecking good time, we've also included Birdseed Ball Ornaments and bright red and white gingham bows. Supported by floral foam in a galvanized steel bucket, the tree is displayed on a matching place mat with a few more eggs ready to hatch close by.

BIRDSEED BALL ORNAMENTS

You will need a 1½" dia. plastic foam ball for each ornament, craft sticks, foam brush, craft glue, birdseed, cotton string, and a large piece of plastic foam for drying ornaments.

1. (Note: Follow Steps 1 and 2 for each ornament.) Insert a craft stick into 1 foam ball to use as a handle. Use foam brush to apply a thin coat of craft glue to ball. Roll ball in birdseed to cover. Insert craft stick into large foam piece and allow ball to dry.
2. For hanger, cut a 5" length of string; knot ends together. Remove craft stick from ball and fill hole with glue; press knot of string into hole. Allow to dry.

CHICK-IN-A-BASKET ORNAMENTS

You will need a 2¼" long plastic egg and a small basket for each ornament; yellow craft feathers; orange, yellow, and black acrylic paint pens; wood excelsior; hot glue gun; and glue sticks.

1. (Note: Refer to photo and follow all steps for each ornament.) Glue feathers to top (small end) of egg.
2. Use black paint pen to paint eyes. Use orange and yellow paint pens to paint beak. Allow to dry.
3. Fill basket with excelsior and place egg in basket.

CHICKEN STAR ORNAMENTS

For each ornament, you will need two 8" squares of yellow fabric; an 8" square of polyester bonded batting; red thread; white, orange, and red ¹/₁₆" thick crafting foam; tracing paper; removable fabric marking pen; black permanent felt-tip pen with fine point; pinking shears; hot glue gun; and glue sticks.

1. Trace all patterns onto tracing paper; cut out.
2. For chicken, use fabric marking pen to draw around star pattern on right side of 1 fabric square (backing).
3. Place batting on wrong side of remaining fabric square; place backing right side up on batting and pin layers together. Use red thread to stitch along drawn lines. Leaving a ¹/₄" seam allowance, use pinking shears to cut out star.
4. (Note: Refer to photo for remaining steps.) For wings, fold right star point toward front and stitch close to fold (**Fig. 1**); repeat for left star point.

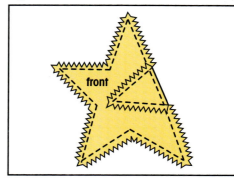

Fig. 1

5. Use hat, hat trim, beak, and foot patterns to cut shapes from indicated colors of crafting foam. Glue shapes to chicken.
6. Use black pen to draw eyes on chicken.
7. For tree topper, use banner pattern to cut banner from white crafting foam. Use black pen to draw dashed lines along edges of banner to resemble stitching and to write "Happy Holidays" on banner. Glue banner to chicken.

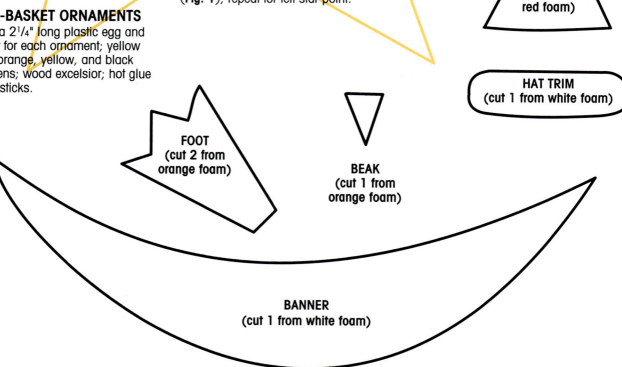

HAT
(cut 1 from red foam)

HAT TRIM
(cut 1 from white foam)

FOOT
(cut 2 from orange foam)

BEAK
(cut 1 from orange foam)

BANNER
(cut 1 from white foam)

GINGERBREAD TREE (Shown on page 53)

Memories of the sweet and spicy aromas of Christmases past were the inspiration for this homey three-foot-tall tree. A perfect touch in the kitchen, the tree has clever wooden spoon branches and is made pretty and fragrant with decorations of greenery, dried fruit, and whole spices. The easy-to-make Spicy Cookie Ornaments are cut in traditional shapes, decorated with candied fruit and blanched almonds, and hung with colorful ribbon ties. With the piquant smells of cinnamon, nutmeg, and other favorite spices coming from your oven, Christmas could not be far away!

WOODEN SPOON TREE

You will need a 1" dia. x 36" long wooden dowel, a dowel end to fit dowel, six 12" long wooden spoons with ³/₈" dia. handles, electric drill, ³/₈" dia. drill bit, hand saw, a 5¹/₂" dia. terra-cotta flowerpot, basket to hold pot, plaster of paris, fabric to cover pot, artificial miniature pine garland with pinecones, preserved cedar, silk leaves, purchased dried orange and apple slices, cinnamon sticks, whole nutmeg, masking tape, hot glue gun, and glue sticks.

1. Referring to **Fig. 1**, use a pencil and ruler to mark placement of branches on dowel. Drilling through center of dowel, drill a ³/₈" dia. hole through dowel at each mark.

Fig. 1

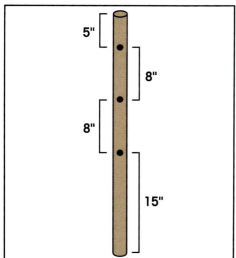

2. (Note: Refer to photo for remaining steps.) For short branches, cut 2 spoons to 7¹/₄" long and 2 to 10" long. Glue spoon handles into holes in dowel. Glue dowel end to top of tree.
3. Use masking tape to seal hole in bottom of flowerpot. Follow manufacturer's instructions to mix enough plaster of paris

to fill pot ³/₄ full. Center bottom of tree in pot. Pour plaster of paris into pot. Secure tree in an upright position until plaster begins to set. Allow plaster to harden. Place pot in basket and cover with fabric.
4. Wrap and glue garland around dowel. Glue cedar, silk leaves, fruit slices, cinnamon sticks, and nutmeg to garland.

SPICY COOKIE ORNAMENTS

You will need all-purpose flour, plastic wrap, rolling pin, tracing paper, paring knife, drinking straw, baking sheets, wire rack, ¹/₈"w satin ribbon for hangers, and the following ingredients:

DOUGH

1 tablespoon ground cinnamon
1 tablespoon ground ginger
2 teaspoons ground allspice
1 teaspoon ground cloves
1 teaspoon ground nutmeg
1 package refrigerated sugar cookie dough
Whole almonds
Red candied cherry halves
Green candied citron pieces

1. Knead spices into cookie dough; wrap dough in plastic wrap and refrigerate for at least 1 hour.
2. To blanch almonds, place almonds in boiling water for 1 minute. Transfer to ice water for 2 - 3 minutes; drain. Peel skins from almonds.
3. Trace patterns onto tracing paper; cut out.
4. Preheat oven to 350 degrees. On a lightly floured surface, use a floured rolling pin to roll out dough to ¹/₈-inch thickness. Place patterns on dough and use knife to cut out cookies. Transfer cookies to ungreased baking sheets. Use straw to make a hole for hanger at top of each cookie. Decorate cookies with blanched almonds, cherry halves, and citron pieces.
5. Bake cookies 13 to 15 minutes or until lightly browned. Transfer to wire rack to cool completely.
6. For hangers, thread 12" lengths of ribbon through holes in cookies.

STARRY NIGHT TREE (Shown on page 50)

Resembling the starry night sky, this tree twinkles and shines with celestial bodies on deep blue fields. Shimmering wired ribbons in gold and midnight blue join gold and blue bead garlands and gold star garland on this three-foot-tall tree. Bows tied from gold ribbon provide more flourishes of shimmering light. With their rich colors, the painted Star Ornaments and Celestial Ball Ornaments enhance the beauty of purchased gold glass star ornaments. Even the base of the tree is wrapped in the splendor of the night sky with the machine-appliquéd Starry Tree Skirt.

STAR ORNAMENTS

For each ornament, you will need poster board, metallic gold acrylic paint, gold glitter acrylic paint, metallic gold and bronze dimensional paint in squeeze bottles with very fine points, small flat paintbrush, 3" of ⅛" dia. gold twisted cord, tracing paper, graphite transfer paper, hot glue gun, and glue sticks.

1. Trace star pattern onto tracing paper. Use transfer paper to transfer outline of star pattern onto poster board; cut out star.
2. (**Note:** Allow to dry after each coat of paint.) Paint both sides of star with metallic gold acrylic paint; repeat with gold glitter acrylic paint.
3. Use transfer paper to transfer details of pattern onto 1 side (front) of star.
4. Referring to pattern, use gold and bronze dimensional paint to paint details on star.
5. For hanger, fold cord in half to form a loop; glue ends to top center back of star.

CELESTIAL BALL ORNAMENTS

For each ornament, you will need a 2¼" dia. blue glass ball ornament, chalk pencil, gold glitter dimensional paint in squeeze bottle, drawing compass, and tagboard (manila folder).

1. For moon template, use compass to draw a 1¾" dia. circle on tagboard; cut out and discard circle.
2. (**Note:** Use a glass or cup with an opening smaller than ornament to hold ornament while working.) Place template on ornament. For outer edge of moon, use chalk pencil to draw around ⅔ of template; refer to photo to draw inner edge of moon. Use chalk pencil to draw various sizes of stars over remainder of ornament.
3. Use gold glitter paint to paint moon and stars; allow to dry.

STARRY TREE SKIRT

You will need a 24" fabric square for tree skirt top, a 24" fabric square for tree skirt lining, a 24" square of antique gold fabric and a 13" x 24" piece of shiny gold fabric for star appliqué, thread to match skirt top fabric, metallic gold appliqué thread, paper-backed fusible web, tear-away stabilizer, acetate for templates, permanent felt-tip pen with fine point, spring-type clothespins, 2¼ yds of ¼" dia. twisted gold cording with flange, a 24" square of tracing paper (pieced as necessary), fabric glue, string, thumbtack, pinking shears, and fabric marking pencil.

1. Follow manufacturer's instructions to fuse web to wrong sides of gold fabrics.
2. For whole point template, use permanent pen to trace gold outline of star point pattern onto acetate. For half point template, trace blue half of star point pattern onto acetate. Cut out templates. Mark right side of half point template.
3. For star pattern, fold tracing paper square in half from top to bottom and again from left to right. Matching folds, fold tracing paper in half diagonally. Referring to **Fig. 1,** place whole point template on

folded tracing paper; draw around long edges of template. Cut along drawn lines and unfold tracing paper. Use star pattern to cut star from antique gold fabric.

Fig. 1

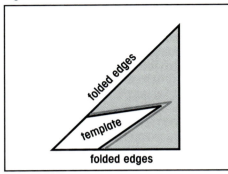

4. With template right side down, draw around half point template 8 times on paper backing side of shiny gold fabric; cut out half points.
5. Remove paper backing from half points and place 1 half point on each point on right side of fabric star; fuse in place. Remove paper backing from star and center star on right side of tree skirt top fabric square; fuse in place.
6. Using gold appliqué thread in top of sewing machine and thread to match skirt fabric in bobbin, follow **Machine Appliqué**, page 158, to stitch over raw edges of star and half points.
7. To mark sewing line on wrong side of skirt top, tie 1 end of string to fabric marking pencil. Insert thumbtack through string 11¼" from pencil. Insert thumbtack through center of star and draw circle.
8. Matching right sides and raw edges, place skirt top on skirt lining fabric; pin in place. Using thread to match fabric and

STAR
POINT

leaving an opening for turning, use a straight stitch to sew top and lining together along drawn circle. Leaving a 1/4" seam allowance, use pinking shears to cut out skirt. Turn skirt right side out and press. Sew final closure by hand.

9. To draw opening at center on right side of skirt, repeat Step 7, inserting thumbtack through string 3/4" from pencil. Draw a straight line from circle to edge of skirt between 2 points of star.

10. Follow **Machine Appliqué**, page 158, to stitch along each side of drawn line and just outside drawn circle (**Fig. 2**). Carefully cut between stitched lines and cut out center circle.

Fig. 2

11. (**Note:** To prevent ends of cording from fraying after cutting, apply fabric glue to 1/2" of cording around area to be cut, allow to dry, and then cut.) Beginning at opening in skirt, glue flange of cording along outer edge on wrong side of skirt, trimming cording to fit; secure cording with clothespins until glue is dry.

HOLIDAY TEA PARTY TREE (Shown on page 51)

Pearl garland, white lace, and soft pink gimp set a feminine mood for this delicate tree. Real antique teacups tied to the tree with satiny pink bows inspire thoughts of warm and pleasant conversation, and iridescent glass ball ornaments reflect the soft afternoon light like pearls. Dainty Ball Ornaments are made by covering a few of the glass ball ornaments with doilies and embellishing them with ribbons and flowers. A doily is also used to trim the sweet Handkerchief Heart Tree Topper, which was fashioned from an antique handkerchief. The miniature Handkerchief Stockings are made from pretty handkerchiefs as well (we found ours at antique stores and flea markets). For the perfect tree skirt, a ribbon is threaded through one long edge of a 42" long lace-trimmed table runner which is then gathered and tied around the base of the tree. A length of soft green fabric is arranged underneath to peek from the edge of the lacy skirt.

DAINTY BALL ORNAMENTS

For each ornament, you will need a 1 1/2" dia. glass ball ornament, a 6" dia. lace doily, a small rubber band, three 14" lengths of 1/16"w to 1/4"w satin ribbon, small silk flowers, hot glue gun, and glue sticks.

1. Center ornament on doily. Bring edges of doily together and gather at top of ornament; wrap rubber band around gathers and top of ornament several times to secure.

2. Tie ribbons into a bow around top of ornament, covering rubber band.

3. Glue flowers to bow.

HANDKERCHIEF STOCKINGS

For each stocking, you will need a handkerchief, lightweight fusible interfacing, thread to match handkerchief, 6" of lace trim (optional), 3 1/2" of 1/8"w satin ribbon, fabric marking pencil, tracing paper, fabric glue, and tissue paper (optional).

1. Trace stocking pattern onto tracing paper; cut out.

2. Follow manufacturer's instructions to fuse interfacing to wrong side of handkerchief.

3. Matching top edge of pattern to 1 edge of handkerchief, place pattern on interfaced side of handkerchief; use fabric marking pencil to draw around pattern. Turn pattern over and repeat. Cut out stocking pieces.

4. Matching right sides and raw edges and using a 1/4" seam allowance, sew stocking pieces together, leaving top edge open. Clip curves, turn stocking right side out, and press.

5. If desired, glue lace trim along top edge of stocking. Allow to dry.

6. For hanger, fold ribbon in half, forming a loop; glue ends inside top of stocking at heel-side seamline. Allow to dry.

7. If desired, lightly stuff stocking with tissue paper.

HANDKERCHIEF HEART TREE TOPPER

You will need a handkerchief, high-loft polyester bonded batting, lightweight fusible interfacing, 6 1/2" dia. lace doily, 12" of 1/2"w lace trim, five 20" lengths of 1/16"w to 1/4"w satin ribbon, fabric marking pencil, poster board, tracing paper, small silk flowers, craft glue, hot glue gun, and glue sticks.

1. Trace heart pattern onto tracing paper; cut out. Use pattern to cut 1 heart from poster board and 3 hearts from batting. Trim 1/2" from edge of 1 batting heart.

2. Follow manufacturer's instructions to fuse interfacing to wrong side of handkerchief. Use fabric marking pencil to draw around heart pattern on interfaced side of handkerchief; cut out heart 1/2" outside drawn line.

3. Place handkerchief heart right side down. Beginning with small batting heart, center batting hearts, then poster board heart, on wrong side of handkerchief heart.

4. (**Note:** Use craft glue for all gluing unless otherwise indicated.) At approx. 1/2" intervals, clip edges of handkerchief heart to 1/8" from edges of poster board heart. Alternating sides and pulling fabric taut, glue edges of handkerchief heart to back of poster board heart.

5. With 1/4" of lace extending beyond edges of heart, glue lace trim along edge on back of heart. With 1 1/2" of doily extending beyond edges of heart, glue doily to back of heart, gathering doily at center of heart as needed. Allow to dry.

6. Tie 4 ribbon lengths together into a bow; trim ends. Hot glue bow to top of heart. Hot glue flowers to bow.

7. For hanger, fold remaining ribbon length in half. Hot glue fold of ribbon to center back of heart.

With its playful Garden Fairy Ornaments, this three-foot-tall tree is perfect for the green thumb — or anyone who wants to spread good wishes! Sprigs of tiny white silk flowers and bright red berries form an airy backdrop for the smiling little fairies. With their glittery wands and Watering Can Ornaments sprinkling goodwill over all, the gossamer-winged creatures grow Sprouting Star Ornaments in miniature clay pots. The tree is supported by floral foam in its own larger pot, which is trimmed, like the smaller pots, with berry red ribbon.

SPROUTING STAR ORNAMENTS

For each ornament, you will need a 1$\frac{7}{8}$"w gold glitter star floral pick, a 1$\frac{3}{4}$"h clay flowerpot, floral foam to fit in pot, Spanish moss, small silk leaves, metallic gold acrylic paint, small flat paintbrush, 6$\frac{1}{2}$" of $\frac{1}{4}$"w satin ribbon, 6" of florist wire, hot glue gun, and glue sticks.

1. Glue floral foam into pot; glue moss over foam. Glue ribbon around rim of pot.
2. Paint gold highlights on leaves; allow to dry. Trim stem of star floral pick 2" below star. (If making Garden Fairy Ornament, set remainder of stem aside.) Glue leaves to stem 1" below star. Insert stem into foam in pot.
3. To attach ornament to tree, glue center of wire to bottom of pot.

WATERING CAN ORNAMENTS

For each ornament, you will need a 4"h galvanized steel watering can, mild liquid dish soap (not lemon scented), white vinegar, black acrylic paint, small flat paintbrush, soft cloth, matte clear acrylic spray, iridescent glitter, three 6" lengths of wired star garland, 6" of florist wire, hot glue gun, and glue sticks.

1. Wash watering can in hot soapy water; rinse well. Rinse can in a solution of 1 part vinegar and 1 part water. Dry can completely.
2. To antique can, mix 1 part water to 1 part black paint. Brush paint mixture on can; use soft cloth to wipe away excess. Allow to dry. Spray can with acrylic spray; while acrylic spray is still wet, sprinkle can with glitter. Allow to dry; shake off excess glitter.
3. Wrap each length of garland loosely around finger to curl. Glue 1 end of each garland length into 1 hole of spout.
4. To attach ornament to tree, glue center of wire to bottom of can.

GARDEN FAIRY ORNAMENTS

For each ornament, you will need a plain canvas garden glove; a 3" square of muslin; 15" of 4"w organdy ribbon for wings; polyester fiberfill; white, peach, dark peach, and black fabric paint; small flat and round paintbrushes; toothpicks; heavy thread to match peach paint; black permanent felt-tip pen with fine point; a 3$\frac{1}{2}$"w silk geranium leaf; curly doll hair; 15" of wired star garland; **either** a 4" length cut from stem of gold glitter star floral pick (from Sprouting Star Ornament) **or** a 4" length cut from a $\frac{1}{8}$" dia. wooden skewer painted with gold glitter paint; florist wire; wire cutters; tracing paper; removable tape; hot glue gun; and glue sticks.

1. (**Note:** Refer to photo for all steps. The body pattern on this page makes a left-flying fairy; for a right-flying fairy, turn pattern over to transfer to glove.) For body, trace body pattern onto tracing paper. Place pattern right side up on thumb and 3 fingers of glove with tips of feet and hands approx. $\frac{1}{4}$" from glove fingertips; modify pattern to fit glove if necessary. To transfer pattern to glove, turn pattern over and use a pencil to draw over lines of pattern on back of tracing paper. Place pattern on glove; tape to secure. Use the edge of a spoon or coin to rub over pattern.
2. (**Note:** Allow to dry after each paint color. Refer to patterns when adding details.) Use flat paintbrush to paint body and cuff of glove peach (**Fig. 1**). Use black pen to outline body and to draw details.

3. For face, use flat paintbrush to paint 1 side of muslin square peach. Trace black lines of face pattern onto tracing paper. To transfer pattern to muslin, turn pattern over and use a pencil to draw over lines of pattern on back of tracing paper. Place pattern right side up on muslin; tape to secure. Use the edge of a spoon or coin to rub over pattern.
4. (**Note:** Use round paintbrush for Step 4 unless otherwise indicated.) Paint irises of eyes black and remainder of eyes white. Mix 1 part dark peach paint with 1 part water; use paint mixture to paint cheeks. Use a toothpick to paint white dots for highlights in eyes and 3 dark peach dots for lips. Use black pen to draw over transferred lines. Cutting just inside outer transferred line, cut out face.

Fig. 1

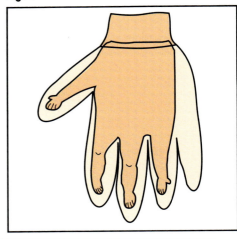

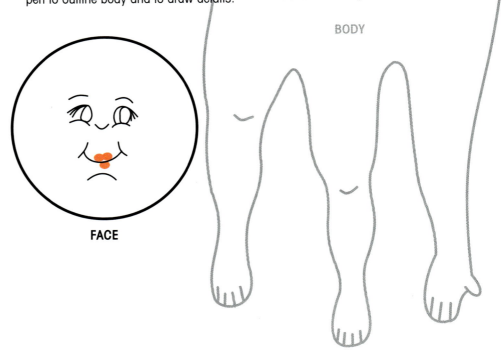

BODY

FACE

HOMEGROWN HOLIDAY TREE (Continued)

5. To form body, refer to **Fig. 2** and fold unpainted finger of glove to back of cuff; wrap wire around base of cuff and finger to secure. Tuck excess glove fabric at center of glove toward back.

Fig. 2

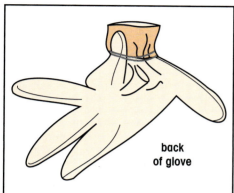

back of glove

6. Baste along top edge of cuff, catching fingertip in basting. Stuff cuff with fiberfill. Pull basting threads, gathering top edge of cuff. Knot thread and trim ends. Whipstitch face to cuff (**Fig. 3**).

Fig. 3

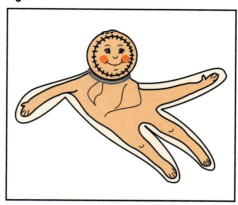

7. Glue hair to head, covering edges of face. Glue leaf to body. For crown, wind garland into an approx. 2" dia. coil; glue to top of head. For wand, glue stem of gold floral pick to hand.

8. For wings, overlap ends of ribbon to form a loop; flatten loop with ends at center. Wrap loop with thread at center to secure; knot thread and trim ends. Glue center of wings to back of angel at shoulder level.

9. For hanger, cut a 6" length of wire. Glue center of wire to back of angel.

WOODLAND FROST TREE (Shown on page 55)

Suggesting a love of nature and a gentle, peaceful Christmas, this woodsy tree is filled with a busy colony of birds.

To enhance the evergreen boughs of this unique three-foot-tall artificial pine tree, preserved oak leaves, birch twigs, and dried mini oak are tucked among the branches and hot glued to the trunk. Small bleached pinecones are hot glued to the tips of some of the tree's branches.

To invite our feathered friends to nest in this woodland setting, a variety of colorful Birdhouse Ornaments has been placed in the tree, along with purchased nests.

One- to two-inch-tall wooden, mushroom, and felt birds of many shapes and colors inhabit nearly every branch of the tree. Each nest holds two or three tiny eggs. For their speckled appearance, we painted the wooden eggs with light grey acrylic paint, then sprayed them lightly with Design Master® glossy wood tone spray (available at craft stores and florist shops).

Sheet moss, oak leaves, and pinecones conceal the base of the tree, and for a frosty look, we sprayed small areas of the tree with water and sprinkled them lightly with mica flakes, a natural glitter-like substance.

BIRDHOUSES AND BIRDHOUSE ORNAMENTS

For each birdhouse or birdhouse ornament, you will need fine sandpaper, tack cloth, paintbrushes, pinecones or birch twigs for roof, mica flakes, utility scissors, spray bottle filled with water, hot glue gun, and glue sticks.

For each birdhouse, you will **also** need 1 unfinished wooden birdhouse (ours are 7 1/4" and 9 1/4" tall); **either** red, light green, and dark green **or** dark yellow, light blue grey, blue, and dark blue acrylic paint; and a soft cloth.

For each birdhouse ornament, you will **also** need 1 unfinished miniature wooden birdhouse (ours are 2 1/4" to 3 1/4" tall) and desired colors of acrylic paint (we used dark yellow, red, light green, and light blue grey).

BIRDHOUSE

1. Sand birdhouse and wipe lightly with tack cloth to remove dust.

2. (**Note:** Refer to photo for remaining steps. Follow Step 2 for red house or Step 3 for blue house. Allow to dry after each paint color.) For red house, paint roof, perch, and base light green. Paint streaks of dark green over light green paint; use soft cloth to wipe away excess paint. Paint remainder of house red.

3. For blue house, paint roof, perch, and base dark yellow. Paint streaks of blue over dark yellow paint; use soft cloth to wipe away excess paint. Paint remainder of house blue. Paint streaks of dark blue and light blue grey over blue paint; use soft cloth to wipe away excess paint.

4. To give birdhouse a weathered look, lightly sand birdhouse so that unpainted areas show through in places. Wipe lightly with tack cloth to remove dust.

5. (**Note:** Follow Step 5 for twig roof or Step 6 for pinecone-shingled roof.) For twig roof, measure depth of roof from front to back. Cut enough twigs the determined measurement to cover roof. Glue twigs to roof.

6. For pinecone-shingled roof, cut scales from pinecones. Glue scales to roof.

7. For "frost" on roof, lightly spray roof with water; lightly sprinkle mica flakes on roof.

BIRDHOUSE ORNAMENT

1. Follow Step 1 of Birdhouse instructions.

2. Paint miniature birdhouse as desired; allow to dry.

3. Follow Steps 4 - 7 of Birdhouse instructions.

NOSTALGIC TOYLAND

Relive the magical memories of childhood with this toy-filled Christmas collection. Decked with favorite old playthings retrieved from the attic (or found at the flea market), the Nostalgic Toyland tree echoes with the carefree laughter of youth. Dainty doll dresses, stuffed animals, books, airplanes, and music-makers are nestled throughout the branches. These sentimental pieces inspire us to remember a more innocent time and become young once again. Resembling giant alphabet blocks — a traditional children's favorite — our handcrafted box ornaments make charming accents, especially when used to display classic rag dolls or cuddly teddy bears. The block designs also appear on the simple welted tree skirt. Adding smiles to this holiday trip down memory lane are papier mâché Santa ornaments with fluffy, snow-white beards. Playful garlands created from dominoes and checkers are simple to make, and a whimsical Tinker Toy® star tops off the fun-filled tree. With instructions beginning on page 68, this nostalgic collection reminds us that Christmas is for children — of all ages.

(Opposite) Displayed alongside prized childhood treasures, fabric-covered **Block Box Ornaments** (*page 68*) look right at home on the **Nostalgic Toyland Tree** (*page 68*). **Ol' Tyme Santa Ornaments** (*page 71*) keep a watchful eye on who's being naughty or nice. Their fur-trimmed hats are actually made from old neckties! Garlands of dominoes and checkers recall the simple pleasures of childhood games, and even the youngest child can help craft the colorful paper chain — it's made from scraps of wrapping paper! Lots of old-fashioned playthings, smiling grandfather clock ornaments, and strands of silvery tinsel complete this memory-filled collection.

(Left) "Lighting" the way for a fun-filled celebration, a playful Tinker Toy® star is placed atop the tree.

(Below) Children's alphabet blocks inspired the clever **Toy Block Tree Skirt** (*page 70*). The block designs were fused onto the skirt, then secured with a machine appliqué stitch.

(*Opposite*) Crafted from homespun fabrics, this **Nine-Patch Doll Quilt** (*page 69*) completes a nostalgic arrangement of love-worn bears and baby dolls. Coordinating fabrics were used to make the **Block Box Ornaments** (*page 68*), delightful places to hide holiday surprises!

(*Left*) The charming **Chimney-Top Stocking** (*page 69*) features painted bricks and an "icicle" cuff. Surrounded by an assortment of miniature toys, an **Ol' Tyme Santa Ornament** (*page 71*) seems to be descending the chimney with a bag of goodies.

(*Below*) It's fun to deliver gifts or showcase your favorite old playthings in this **Covered Toy Box** (*page 68*). The handy fabric-covered container is sure to be treasured for years to come.

NOSTALGIC TOYLAND TREE (Shown on pages 63 and 64)

Take a trip back in time with this seven-foot-tall tree overflowing with remembrances of childhood days.

Strings of large, colorful lights — the kind that were hung on the Christmas tree in years past — set the mood, along with wooden bead garlands and paper chains. Just like the ones we made in grade school, these fun-to-make paper chains are crafted from wrapping paper scraps. We made another garland by drilling holes through dominoes and checkers and stringing them together on white string.

Favorite stuffed animals and dolls, some worn by love and some tea-dyed to appear old, sit among the branches or pop playfully out of the Block Box Ornaments (this page), which are simply gift boxes made to resemble toy blocks with fused-on fabrics. Interspersed throughout the tree are other forgotten treasures — bingo cards, small American flags, doll clothes, and wonderful metal toys such as a telephone, a top, and some bright red airplanes. We discovered some of these items at flea markets and antique stores, and others we uncovered among our own personal stashes of cherished playthings. The papier mâché Ol' Tyme Santa Ornaments (page 71), with hats crafted from men's neckties and genuine fur, add more old-fashioned charm. Purchased clock ornaments, silver tinsel, and well read children's books add to the nostalgic theme.

A clever Tinker Toy® star tops off this delightful array. The Toy Block Tree Skirt (page 70), appliquéd with more familiar toy blocks, covers the base of the tree.

BLOCK BOX ORNAMENTS
(Shown on page 64)

For each ornament, you will need a 4" square unassembled cardboard gift box, a 14" x 18" fabric piece to cover outside of box, a 14" x 18" fabric piece to cover inside of box (optional), fabric scraps to cover sides of box and for letters and design on box, paper-backed fusible web, 2¹/₂"h lettering stencils, disappearing ink fabric marking pen, tracing paper, craft knife, and craft glue (optional).

1. If box does not lie flat as 1 layer, disassemble box until it is 1 layer.
2. Follow manufacturer's instructions to fuse web to wrong sides of 14" x 18" fabric piece(s) and fabric scraps.
3. (**Note:** Protect ironing board cover with a piece of scrap fabric.) To cover outside of box, center box right side down on paper backing side of 14" x 18" fabric piece; use fabric marking pen to draw around box. Cut out fabric just outside drawn lines. Remove paper backing. Lay box right side up on ironing board. Center fabric piece web side down over box. Beginning at center, fuse fabric piece to box. Trim fabric even with edges of box. If box has slits, use craft knife to cut through slits in box. If desired, repeat to cover inside of box.
4. To cover each outside box side, cut a 4" square from fabric scrap. Remove paper backing; fuse fabric square to side of box.
5. For letters on box, use stencils and fabric marking pen to draw letters on right side of fabric scraps; cut out letters. Remove paper backing and fuse letters to sides of box.
6. For design on box lid, trace tree, heart, or star pattern onto tracing paper; cut out. Use pattern to cut shape from fabric scrap. Remove paper backing and fuse to lid.
7. Assemble box, regluing seams if necessary. If desired, glue box closed.

COVERED TOY BOX (Shown on page 67)

You will need an assembled cardboard storage box with lid, fabrics to cover box and lid, print fabrics and black fabric for letters and stars, paper-backed fusible web, 4"h lettering stencils, disappearing ink fabric marking pen, 4 decorative brass corners with screws, hammer, nail, tracing paper, hot glue gun, and glue sticks.

1. To cover box lid, measure length and width of lid, including ends and sides; add 3" to each measurement. Cut a fabric piece the determined measurements. Follow manufacturer's instructions to fuse web to wrong side of fabric piece.
2. Center lid top side down on paper backing side of fabric piece. Use a pencil to draw around lid; remove lid. Draw lines 1" outside original drawn lines, extending lines to edges of fabric. Cut away squares at corners of fabric piece and make a diagonal clip at each corner from outer drawn lines to ¹/₁₆" from inner drawn lines (**Fig. 1**). Remove paper backing.

Fig. 1

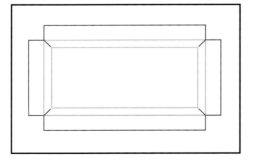

3. Center fabric piece right side up on top of lid. Fuse fabric to top of lid only. Turn lid over.
4. To cover each side of lid, fuse fabric to side of lid; fuse ends of fabric to ends of lid. Fold remaining edge of fabric to inside of lid; fuse in place.

5. To cover each end of lid, fold short edges of fabric at end of lid 1" to wrong side (**Fig. 2**); fuse in place. Fold fabric up and fuse to end of lid. Fold edge of fabric to inside of lid; fuse in place. Glue to secure if necessary.

Fig. 2

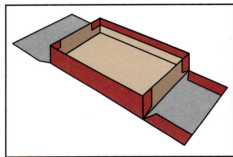

6. Repeat Steps 1 - 5 to cover box.
7. Follow manufacturer's instructions to fuse web to wrong sides of fabrics for letters and stars.
8. For letters, use stencils and fabric marking pen to draw letters on right sides of print fabrics to spell "TOYS." Cut out letters. For stars, trace star pattern onto tracing paper; cut out. Use pattern to cut stars from print fabrics.
9. Remove paper backing from letters and stars; fuse approx. ¹/₂" apart onto black fabric. Leaving approx. ¹/₈" of black fabric around each letter or star, cut out letters and stars. Remove paper backing from letters and stars. Arrange letters and stars on lid; fuse in place.
10. For each decorative corner on lid, place 1 decorative corner over 1 lid corner; use a pencil to mark placement of holes for screws and remove corner. Use hammer and nail to make holes through lid at marks. Replace corner on lid, place screws through holes, and use glue to secure screws on inside of lid.

NINE-PATCH DOLL QUILT (Shown on page 66)

For an approx. 20" x 24½" doll quilt, you will need ⅛ yd each of 3 light and 3 medium 44"w fabrics for blocks, ⅓ yd of very light 44"w fabric for sashing, ⅛ yd of dark 44"w fabric for connecting squares, ¼ yd of 44"w fabric for binding, one 24" x 28½" piece each of fabric for backing and low-loft polyester bonded batting, sewing thread, rotary cutter, cutting mat, ruler, and embroidery floss for ties.

Note: Wash, dry, and press fabrics. For sewing steps, match right sides and raw edges and use a ¼" seam allowance unless otherwise indicated. Press seam allowances toward darker fabric if possible.

1. For blocks, cut two 1½" x 22" strips and one 1½" x 12" strip from each medium fabric and one 1½" x 22" strip and two 1½" x 12" strips from each light fabric.

2. Using 1 light and 1 medium fabric and stitching along long edges, sew 1 light 22" strip between 2 medium 22" strips and 1 medium 12" strip between 2 light 12" strips. Cut across pieced strips to make 1½"w strips (**Fig. 1**). Repeat with remaining light and medium strips.

Fig. 1

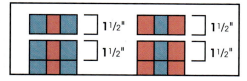

3. To complete a nine-patch block, sew 3 strips together (**Fig. 2**). Repeat for a total of 20 blocks. (You will have extra strips.)

Fig. 2

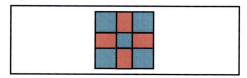

4. For sashing, cut forty-nine 2" x 3½" pieces. For connecting squares, cut thirty 2" squares.

5. (**Note:** Refer to **Diagram** to assemble quilt.) For each sashing row, sew 5 connecting squares and 4 sashing pieces together. For each nine-patch row, sew 5 sashing pieces and 4 nine-patch blocks together. Sew rows together.

6. Place backing fabric wrong side up. Matching edges, place batting on backing. Center quilt top right side up on batting. Smoothing wrinkles, pin layers together.

7. To tie quilt, thread a needle with 5" of floss. Working from right side, take needle down through all 3 layers at center of 1 connecting square; bring needle up approx. ¹⁄₁₆" away. Tie floss into a square knot next to fabric; trim ends ½" from knot. Repeat for remaining squares.

8. Trim batting and backing even with edges of quilt top.

9. For binding, cut a 1½" x 2¾ yd fabric strip (pieced as necessary). Press 1 end of strip ½" to wrong side. Matching wrong sides, press strip in half lengthwise; unfold. Press long raw edges to center; refold binding.

10. Unfold 1 long edge of binding. Beginning with pressed end of binding and matching right side of binding to quilt front, pin unfolded edge of binding along 1 edge of quilt. Mitering binding at corners, continue pinning binding around quilt until ends of binding overlap ½"; trim excess binding. Using pressing line closest to raw edge as a guide, sew binding to quilt. Fold binding over raw edges to back of quilt; hand stitch in place.

DIAGRAM

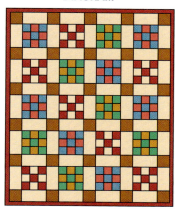

CHIMNEY-TOP STOCKING (Shown on page 67)

You will need four 12" x 18" pieces and a 2" x 8" strip of bleached muslin for stocking, lining, and hanger; a 6" x 15" piece of low-loft cotton batting for cuff; white thread; ½"w paper-backed fusible web tape; red and dark red fabric paint; ½"w flat paintbrush; tracing paper; and disappearing ink fabric marking pen.
For stocking insert, you will need a 6½" x 10" piece of lightweight cardboard, 1 Ol' Tyme Santa Ornament (page 71), large pin back, assorted small toys and ornaments, hot glue gun, and glue sticks.

1. (**Note:** Refer to photo for all steps.) For stocking front, lay one 12" x 18" muslin piece on a protected surface with short edges at top and bottom. Use fabric marking pen and a ruler to draw lines across width of muslin at ¾" intervals. Using drawn lines as guidelines and using red and dark red paints alternately, use paintbrush to paint approx. 1¼" long bricks approx. ¼" apart on muslin piece. Allow to dry. Repeat to paint a second muslin piece for stocking back. Follow manufacturer's instructions to heat-set paint if necessary.

2. Matching dotted lines and aligning arrows, trace top and bottom of stocking pattern, page 27, onto tracing paper; cut out.

3. For stocking, align rows of bricks and pin painted muslin pieces right sides together. Aligning straight edge at top of pattern with 1 row of bricks, draw around stocking pattern on muslin pieces; cut out.

4. Using a ¼" seam allowance and leaving top edge open, sew stocking pieces together. Clip curves and turn right side out; use a pressing cloth to press stocking. Use stocking pattern to make stocking lining from remaining muslin pieces; do not turn right side out.

5. With wrong sides together, insert lining into stocking. Use a ½" seam allowance to sew top edges together.

6. For cuff, make 2" to 3" cuts into 1 long edge of batting piece to resemble icicles. Follow manufacturer's instructions to fuse web tape along remaining long edge on 1 side (wrong side) of cuff; do not remove paper backing. Lightly press edge ½" to wrong side; unfold edge and remove paper backing. With wrong side of cuff facing stocking, place cuff around stocking with short edges of cuff overlapping at heel-side seamline; fold long straight edge of cuff into stocking. Fuse edge of cuff to lining. Hand stitch short edges of cuff together.

7. For hanger, press muslin strip in half lengthwise; unfold. Press long edges to center; refold strip and sew close to pressed edges. Matching ends, fold strip in half to form a loop. Place ends in stocking at heel-side seamline with 2" of loop extending above stocking; tack in place.

8. For insert, trim cardboard piece to fit snugly in top of stocking with ¾" of cardboard exposed at top; place cardboard in stocking. Glue pin back to back of Ol' Tyme Santa Ornament; pin ornament to center of exposed cardboard. Arrange and glue toys and ornaments to cardboard.

TOY BLOCK TREE SKIRT (Shown on page 65)

You will need two 56" squares of fabric (pieced as necessary) for tree skirt top and lining, fabrics for appliqués, a 2¹⁄₂" x 4³⁄₄ yd bias strip (pieced as necessary) and 4³⁄₄ yds of ³⁄₈" dia. cord for welting, thread to match skirt top fabric, thread for appliqués (we used fine clear nylon thread), paper-backed fusible web, tear-away stabilizer, tracing paper, fabric marking pencil, thumbtack, and string.

1. Fold lining fabric square in half from top to bottom and again from left to right.
2. To mark outer cutting line, tie 1 end of string to fabric marking pencil. Insert thumbtack through string 27" from pencil. Insert thumbtack in fabric as shown in **Fig. 1** and mark ¹⁄₄ of a circle.

Fig. 1

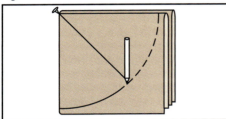

3. To mark inner cutting line, repeat Step 2, inserting thumbtack through string 2" from pencil.
4. Cutting through all layers of fabric, cut out lining along marked lines. For opening at back of lining, cut through 1 layer of fabric along 1 fold from outer to inner edge.
5. Use lining as a pattern to cut skirt top from remaining fabric square.
6. Follow **Tracing Patterns**, page 158, to make patterns for large, medium, and small block shapes, page 71, and large, medium, and small block sides, this page.
7. For 3 sets of block appliqués, place fusible web paper side up over traced patterns and remaining patterns, this page and page 71; leaving at least 1" between shapes, trace each pattern 3 times onto web. For remaining block side appliqués, turn traced block side patterns over and trace each pattern 3 times again onto web. Cut out shapes approx. ¹⁄₂" outside drawn lines.
8. Follow manufacturer's instructions to fuse web shapes to wrong sides of appliqué fabrics. Cut shapes from fabrics along drawn lines. Do not remove paper backing.
9. (**Note:** Refer to photo for Step 9.) To assemble each large block appliqué, remove paper backing from 2 large block sides. Matching outer edges, place block sides on 1 large block shape; fuse in place. Remove

paper backing from one "A," one "E," and 1 tree shape. Arrange pieces on block shape and fuse in place. Repeat to assemble remaining large block appliqués. Using corresponding letters and shapes, repeat to assemble each medium and small block appliqué.
10. Omitting tear-away stabilizer, follow **Machine Appliqué**, page 158, to stitch over all raw edges within each block appliqué.
11. Remove paper backing from block appliqués. Referring to photo, arrange appliqués on tree skirt top and fuse in place. Follow **Machine Appliqué**, page 158, to stitch over remaining raw edges of appliqués.
12. For welting, center cord lengthwise on wrong side of bias strip. Matching long edges, fold strip over cord. Using zipper foot, machine baste along length of strip close to cord.

13. Matching raw edges, baste welting along outer edge on right side of tree skirt top; trim welting to fit. At each end of welting, open fabric and trim 1" from cord.
14. Place skirt top and lining right sides together. Using a zipper foot and stitching as close as possible to welting, sew outer curved edges together. Leaving an opening for turning along 1 opening edge, use a ¹⁄₂" seam allowance to sew opening edges and inner curved edges together. Clip seam allowances, turn right side out, and press. Sew final closure by hand.

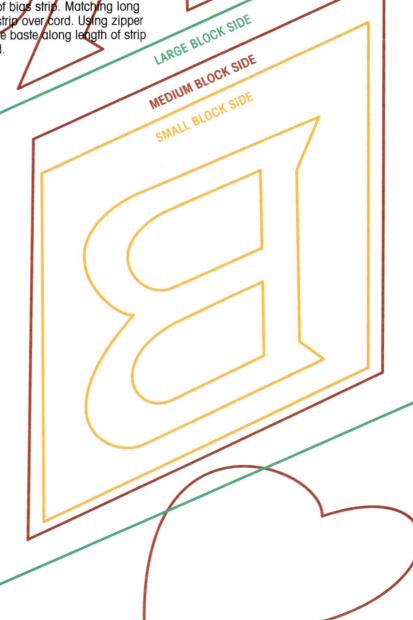

LARGE BLOCK SIDE

MEDIUM BLOCK SIDE

SMALL BLOCK SIDE

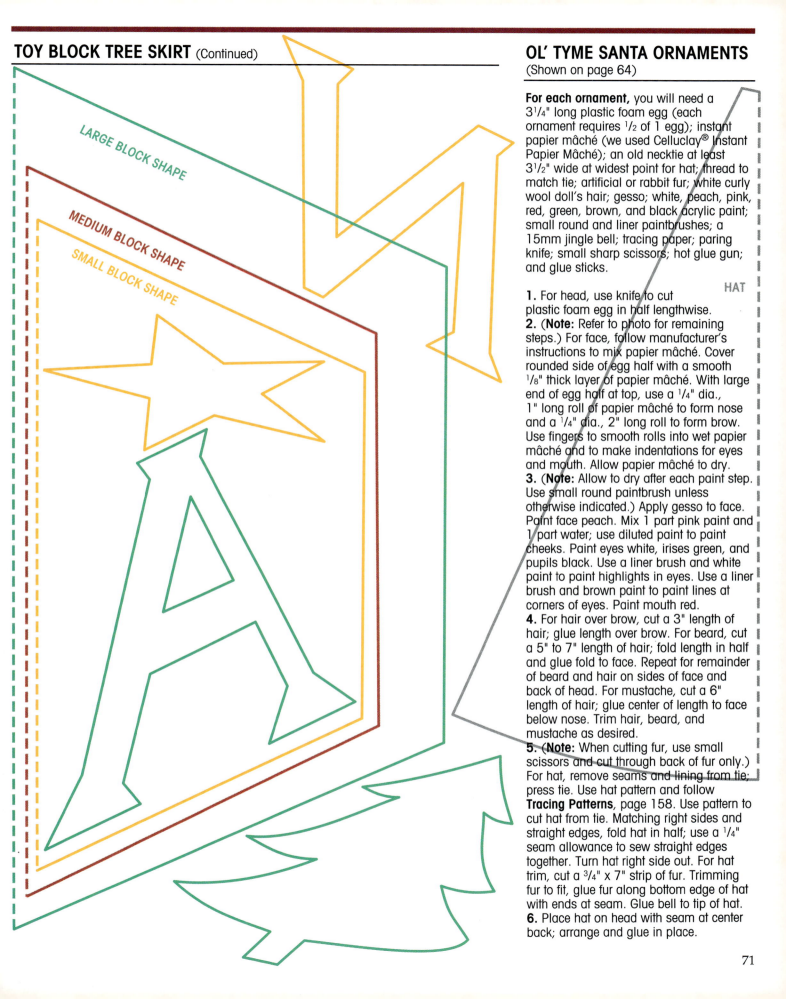

TOY BLOCK TREE SKIRT (Continued)

LARGE BLOCK SHAPE

MEDIUM BLOCK SHAPE

SMALL BLOCK SHAPE

OL' TYME SANTA ORNAMENTS

(Shown on page 64)

For each ornament, you will need a 3$^1/4$" long plastic foam egg (each ornament requires $^1/2$ of 1 egg); instant papier mâché (we used Celluclay® Instant Papier Mâché); an old necktie at least 3$^1/2$" wide at widest point for hat; thread to match tie; artificial or rabbit fur; white curly wool doll's hair; gesso; white, peach, pink, red, green, brown, and black acrylic paint; small round and liner paintbrushes; a 15mm jingle bell; tracing paper; paring knife; small sharp scissors; hot glue gun; and glue sticks.

HAT

1. For head, use knife to cut plastic foam egg in half lengthwise.
2. (**Note:** Refer to photo for remaining steps.) For face, follow manufacturer's instructions to mix papier mâché. Cover rounded side of egg half with a smooth $^1/8$" thick layer of papier mâché. With large end of egg half at top, use a $^1/4$" dia., 1" long roll of papier mâché to form nose and a $^1/4$" dia., 2" long roll to form brow. Use fingers to smooth rolls into wet papier mâché and to make indentations for eyes and mouth. Allow papier mâché to dry.
3. (**Note:** Allow to dry after each paint step. Use small round paintbrush unless otherwise indicated.) Apply gesso to face. Paint face peach. Mix 1 part pink paint and 1 part water; use diluted paint to paint cheeks. Paint eyes white, irises green, and pupils black. Use a liner brush and white paint to paint highlights in eyes. Use a liner brush and brown paint to paint lines at corners of eyes. Paint mouth red.
4. For hair over brow, cut a 3" length of hair; glue length over brow. For beard, cut a 5" to 7" length of hair; fold length in half and glue fold to face. Repeat for remainder of beard and hair on sides of face and back of head. For mustache, cut a 6" length of hair; glue center of length to face below nose. Trim hair, beard, and mustache as desired.
5. (**Note:** When cutting fur, use small scissors and cut through back of fur only.) For hat, remove seams and lining from tie; press tie. Use hat pattern and follow **Tracing Patterns**, page 158. Use pattern to cut hat from tie. Matching right sides and straight edges, fold hat in half; use a $^1/4$" seam allowance to sew straight edges together. Turn hat right side out. For hat trim, cut a $^3/4$" x 7" strip of fur. Trimming fur to fit, glue fur along bottom edge of hat with ends at seam. Glue bell to tip of hat.
6. Place hat on head with seam at center back; arrange and glue in place.

BOUNTIFUL GLORY

*S**ince Renaissance times, people have adorned their homes with gilded fruit to reflect
the glory of Christmas. The vibrance of our bountiful collection continues this jubilant tradition
as we celebrate the birth of the Christ Child. Bearing a fruitful motif, an array of topiaries,
table accents, and gift wrap abounds with elegance. Even the branches of our opulent tree are laden
with gold-brushed fruit, handcrafted medallions, and an assortment of glimmering purchased
ornaments. You can easily create your own exquisite celebration with inexpensive items
from your local craft shop. Instructions for the projects begin on page 76.*

The glory of the Newborn King is captured in cross stitch in this touching depiction of the **Madonna and Child** *(page 77)*.
Jeweled **Medallion Ornaments** *(page 76)* bring a regal touch to the display. *(Opposite)* Garlands of **Gilded Fruit and
Artichokes** *(page 79)* are draped around the **Bountiful Glory Tree** *(page 76)*, along with gold beads, twisted cord, and
metallic ribbon. Standing in an ornate urn, the tree is finished with purchased ball ornaments and pheasant feathers.

(*Opposite*) Your home will take on a stately air when you display **Elegant Topiaries** (*page 76*) in classic containers. A decorator table becomes a rich holiday feature when veiled in the flowing fabric poufs of our **Elegant Table Skirt** (*page 79*). The **Fruitful Table Topper** (*page 79*), painted with fruit stamps and golden accents, completes the setting.

(*Left*) Luxurious **Gilded Fruit and Artichokes** (*page 79*) become a magnificent Christmas centerpiece when arranged in an ornate bowl. To achieve the gilded look, selected pieces are brushed with metallic paint or highlighted with gold leaf.

(*Below*) Gifts become special treasures when wrapped in our **Fruitful Gift Wrap** (*page 78*). Coordinating stamped tags, opulent ribbons, and gilded grape leaves enhance the memorable presentation.

BOUNTIFUL GLORY TREE
(Shown on page 73)

The glory of nature abounds on this classic 6½-foot-tall tree with its rich tones of gilded fruit, shimmering ribbons and garlands, and sparkling ornaments.

For a unique display, the tree is placed in an elegant 28" tall painted plaster urn. To create the luxurious garlands that are draped around the tree, Gilded Fruit and Artichokes (page 79), including pears, grapes, apples, and artichokes, are wired to leafy purchased garlands of small green apples, cherries, raspberries, and pomegranates. Metallic gold and bronze acrylic paint and composite gold leaf are used to highlight the fruit.

Additional garlands of gold beads, rich ³⁄₈" dia. twisted burgundy and gold cord, 3"w burgundy ribbon with gold edging, and 5"w variegated wired ribbon enhance the subtle shadings of the fruit. A length of the twisted cord is tied into a double-loop bow to crown the tree. Deep red glass ball ornaments in a generous 4" dia. size add elegance, while individual pheasant feathers tucked among the branches add natural color and softness to the tree.

Contributing bits of sparkle and brilliance are the bejeweled Medallion Ornaments (this page), which are simple to craft from poster board, fabric, paint, and acrylic jewels.

MEDALLION ORNAMENTS (Shown on page 72)

For each ornament, you will need a 5" square of metallic gold fabric; a 5" square of white poster board; paper-backed fusible web; metallic gold dimensional paint in squeeze bottle with a very fine tip; the following acrylic jewels: four 10mm red, four 7 x 15mm gold, and four 6mm blue; a 15mm half pearl; gold glitter; jewel glue; 7" of ¹⁄₁₆" dia. gold twisted cord for hanger; Sulky® fabric transfer pen; utility scissors; and tracing paper.

1. Follow manufacturer's instructions to fuse web to wrong side of fabric. Remove paper backing and fuse fabric to poster board.

2. Trace pattern onto tracing paper. Following manufacturer's instructions, use transfer pen to transfer pattern to fabric side of covered poster board.
3. Cut out medallion.
4. (**Note:** Refer to photo and pattern for Steps 4 - 6.) Spread glue on medallion where indicated by shaded area on pattern. While glue is still wet, sprinkle glitter over glue. Allow to dry; shake off excess glitter.
5. Glue jewels and half pearl to medallion where indicated by X's on pattern.
6. Use paint to paint over transferred lines and dots on medallion; allow to dry.
7. For hanger, knot ends of cord together; glue knot to back of medallion.

ELEGANT TOPIARIES (Shown on page 74)

For each topiary, you will need a decorative pot (pot for each cone topiary should have an opening same diameter as bottom of cone), sheet moss, hot glue gun, and glue sticks.
For round topiary, you will **also** need floral foam to fit in pot, desired size plastic foam ball, twigs for trunk (we used willow twigs), utility scissors, gilded artificial grapes and leaves (see Gilded Fruit and Artichokes, page 79), and gold twisted cord.
For each cone topiary, you will **also** need desired size plastic foam cone and items for decorating topiary (we used gold mesh ribbon, gold wired ribbon, and a Medallion Ornament, this page).
For pear topiary, you will **also** need floral foam to fit in pot, a gilded artificial pear (see Gilded Fruit and Artichokes, page 79), twigs for trunk (we used willow twigs), utility scissors, gold twisted cord, and craft knife.
For artichoke topiary, you will **also** need floral foam to fit in pot and a gilded

artificial artichoke with stem (see Gilded Fruit and Artichokes, page 79).

ROUND TOPIARY
1. Glue floral foam in pot to within ¹⁄₂" of rim. Glue sheet moss over foam, covering foam completely.
2. For trunk, cut twigs 4" longer than desired finished height of trunk. Glue twigs together. Insert 1 end of twig bundle 2" into plastic foam ball; glue to secure. Insert remaining end of twig bundle 2" into floral foam in pot; glue to secure.
3. Glue sheet moss over ball, covering ball completely.
4. Glue grapes and leaves to ball and to moss in pot as desired. Tie cord into a bow around trunk of tree; knot and fray each end of cord.

CONE TOPIARY
1. Glue base of plastic foam cone into top of pot.

2. Glue sheet moss over cone, covering cone completely.
3. Decorate topiary as desired.

PEAR TOPIARY
1. Follow Step 1 of Round Topiary instructions to prepare pot.
2. For trunk, cut twigs to 4" longer than desired finished height of trunk. Glue twigs together. Measure diameter of twig bundle; use craft knife to cut an "X" in bottom of pear approx. same size as diameter of twig bundle. Insert 1 end of twig bundle 2" into fruit; glue to secure. Insert remaining end of twig bundle 2" into floral foam in pot; glue to secure.
3. Knot cord around trunk. Fray ends of cord.

ARTICHOKE TOPIARY
1. Follow Step 1 of Round Topiary instructions to prepare pot.
2. Insert stem of artichoke in center of moss; glue to secure.

MADONNA AND CHILD (Shown on page 72)

You will need a 12" x 14" piece of Cream Lugana (25 ct), embroidery floss (see color key), embroidery hoop (optional), and desired frame (we used a custom frame).

Follow Working Over Two Fabric Threads, page 159, to work design. Except as noted in color key, use 2 strands of floss for Cross Stitch, 1 for Backstitch, and 1 strand of floss and 1 strand of Kreinik Balger® Blending Filament for Half Cross Stitch. Frame as desired.

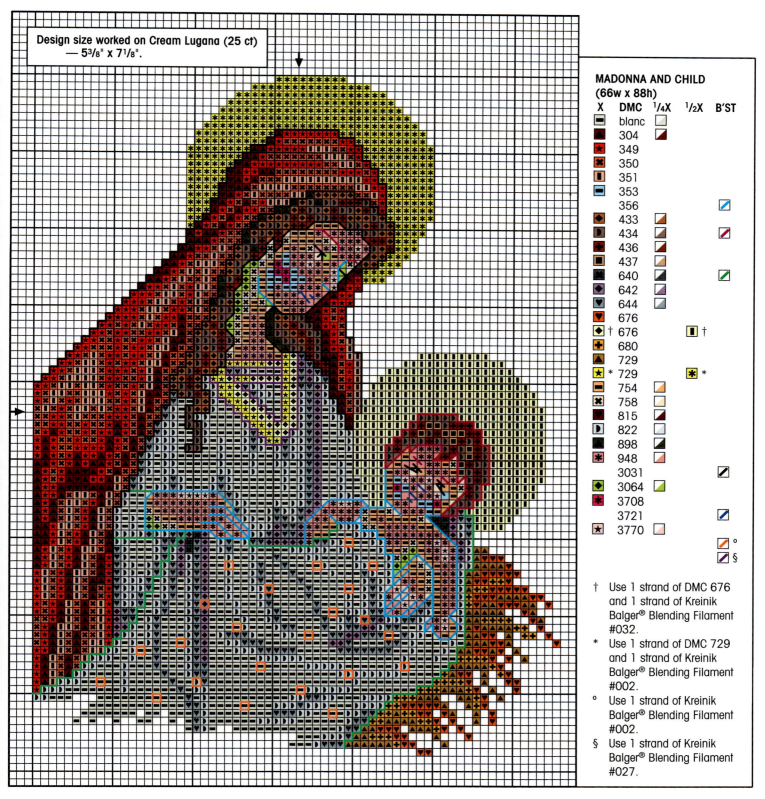

Design size worked on Cream Lugana (25 ct) — 5³⁄₈" x 7¹⁄₈".

MADONNA AND CHILD
(66w x 88h)

X	DMC	¼X	½X	B'ST
	blanc			
	304			
	349			
	350			
	351			
	353			
	356			
	433			
	434			
	436			
	437			
	640			
	642			
	644			
	676			
†	676			†
	680			
	729			
*	729			*
	754			
	758			
	815			
	822			
	898			
	948			
	3031			
	3064			
	3708			
	3721			
	3770			
				°
				§

† Use 1 strand of DMC 676 and 1 strand of Kreinik Balger® Blending Filament #032.

* Use 1 strand of DMC 729 and 1 strand of Kreinik Balger® Blending Filament #002.

° Use 1 strand of Kreinik Balger® Blending Filament #002.

§ Use 1 strand of Kreinik Balger® Blending Filament #027.

FRUITFUL GIFT WRAP AND TAGS (Shown on page 75)

You will need ivory parchment paper or lightweight watercolor paper for gift wrap; a 3³/₄" x 6¹/₂" piece of ivory parchment paper or watercolor paper for each gift tag; ¹/₁₆" thick crafting foam; blocks of wood for stamps (at least ¹/₂" thick and large enough to accommodate stamp designs); the following colors of Accent® Crown Jewels™ acrylic paint: Imperial Antique Gold, Crown Red Velvet, Duchess Rose, Queen's Emerald, and Fabergé Purple; Duncan Precious Metals Polished Copper acrylic paint; Duncan Decorator Acrylics Opaque Evergreen acrylic paint; Deco Art™ Americana™ Country Red acrylic paint; small flat and liner paintbrushes; permanent felt-tip pen with fine point; tracing paper; hot glue gun; and glue sticks.

GIFT WRAP

1. For stamps, trace fruit and leaf patterns, this page and page 79, onto tracing paper; cut out.
2. Use permanent pen to draw around patterns on crafting foam. Cut out shapes.

3. Referring to patterns for arrangement of shapes on wood blocks, group grapes together on 1 block and pear leaves together on another block. Place remaining fruits and leaves on separate blocks. Pressing shapes firmly onto blocks before glue hardens, glue shapes to blocks.
4. (**Note:** Refer to photo for remaining steps. Refer to color key, this page, for Step 4. Practice stamping designs on scrap paper.) Use flat paintbrush to apply base color evenly to stamp. If highlight color is used, use flat brush to apply highlight color along 1 side of shape on stamp, blending colors together slightly. Press stamp onto paper; carefully lift stamp. Repeat to paint fruit on paper as desired. Allow to dry.
5. (**Note:** Use liner paintbrush for Step 5.) Use Imperial Antique Gold to paint highlights along 1 side of each grape and to paint veins on leaves and tendrils around grape clusters. Use Crown Red Velvet to shade 1 side of each plum if desired; use Imperial Antique Gold to paint highlights along opposite side of each plum. Use Imperial Antique Gold or Polished Copper to paint stems on pears.

GIFT TAG

1. Use flat paintbrush and Imperial Antique Gold paint to paint a ¹/₄"w border along each edge on 1 side of paper; allow to dry.
2. With painted side out, match short edges and fold paper in half.
3. Follow Steps 1 - 3 of Gift Wrap instructions to make desired stamps.
4. Follow Steps 4 and 5 of Gift Wrap instructions to paint design on front of tag.

COLOR KEY
PEAR
  Base color – Imperial Antique Gold
  Highlight color – Polished Copper
PLUM
  Base color – 1 part Duchess Rose mixed with 1 part Country Red
GRAPES
  Base color – 1 part Crown Red Velvet mixed with 1 part Fabergé Purple
LEAVES
  Base color – 1 part Queen's Emerald mixed with 1 part Evergreen

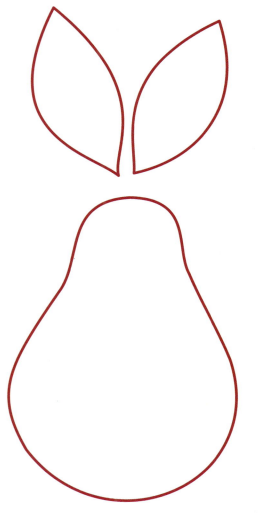

FRUITFUL GIFT WRAP AND TAGS (Continued)

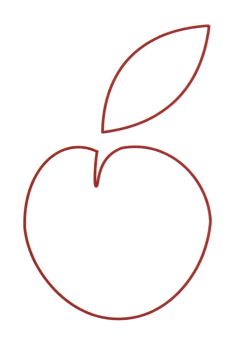

GILDED FRUIT AND ARTICHOKES (Shown on page 75)

You will need artificial fruit, artichokes, and leaves (we used swags made of pears, grapes, and leaves; individual stems of plastic artichokes and apples; and latex grape leaves).
For overall highlights, you will need metallic gold acrylic paint, metallic bronze acrylic paint (optional), and a small fan paintbrush.
For gold leaf, you will need composite gold leaf (not 24K gold leaf) and gold leaf adhesive size (available at craft stores), a 2" square of cellulose sponge, plastic or coated paper plate, and a stiff-bristled toothbrush.

Note: Both techniques may be used on the same piece of fruit or leaf.

APPLYING OVERALL HIGHLIGHTS
1. (**Note:** Follow Step 1 for highlighting with gold only or Step 2 for highlighting with gold and bronze. Refer to photo for either step.) Use paintbrush to lightly brush streaks of gold paint on fruit or leaf; allow to dry.

2. Use paintbrush to lightly brush streaks of gold paint on fruit or leaf; before paint dries, repeat to brush streaks of bronze paint on fruit or leaf. Allow to dry.

APPLYING GOLD LEAF
1. (**Note:** When applying gold leaf, work with dry hands in a draft-free area. If necessary, apply talcum powder to hands to absorb any moisture. Refer to photo for Steps 1 and 2.) Pour a small amount of adhesive size onto plate. Lightly dip sponge piece in plate, picking up a small amount of adhesive size. Use sponge to stamp a thin layer of adhesive size onto portion of fruit or leaf where highlighting is desired; allow to dry just until clear and tacky. If first coat of adhesive size loses its tack, apply a second coat.
2. Carefully apply pieces of gold leaf to adhesive size. For worn appearance, use toothbrush to brush excess gold leaf from fruit or leaf.

ELEGANT TABLE SKIRT WITH FRUITFUL TABLE TOPPER (Shown on page 74)

For table skirt, you will need fabric for skirt and 1"w paper-backed fusible web tape.
For table topper, you will need fabric for topper; 1/2" dia. multi-colored twisted cording with flange; 3/16" dia. metallic gold twisted cord; four 2 1/2" long tassels; 5"w variegated wired ribbon; safety pins; 1"w paper-backed fusible web tape; 1/16" thick crafting foam; blocks of wood for stamps (at least 1/2" thick and large enough to accommodate stamp designs); the following colors of Accent® Crown Jewels™ acrylic paint: Imperial Antique Gold, Crown Red Velvet, Duchess Rose, Queen's Emerald, and Fabergé Purple; Duncan Precious Metals Polished Copper acrylic paint; Duncan Decorator Acrylics Opaque Evergreen acrylic paint; Deco Art™ Americana™ Country Red acrylic paint; textile medium; small flat and liner paintbrushes; permanent felt-tip pen with fine point; tracing paper; fabric glue; hot glue gun; and glue sticks.

TABLE SKIRT
1. Add together the diameter of table and twice the height of table; add 40". Cut a square of fabric the determined size. (Follow web tape manufacturer's instructions to piece fabric pieces together if necessary.)

2. To hem skirt, follow manufacturer's instructions to fuse web tape along edges on wrong side of fabric; do not remove paper backing. Lightly press edges to wrong side along inner edge of tape. Unfold edges and remove paper backing. Refold edges and fuse in place.
3. Center skirt on table. Tuck hemmed edge of fabric under at floor and arrange folds for "pouf" effect.

TABLE TOPPER
1. Add together the diameter of table plus twice the desired drop length of table topper; add 2". Cut a square of fabric the determined size.
2. Follow Step 2 of Table Skirt instructions to hem edges of table topper.
3. For painted design along edges of table topper, follow Steps 1 - 3 of Gift Wrap instructions, Fruitful Gift Wrap and Tags, page 78, to make stamps. Following paint manufacturers' instructions to mix textile medium with paints, follow Steps 4 and 5 of Gift Wrap instructions to paint design. Use liner paintbrush and green paint mixture to paint green vines between fruit.
4. Follow manufacturers' instructions to heat-set design.

5. (**Note:** To prevent ends of cording or cord from fraying after cutting, apply fabric glue to 1/2" of cording or cord around area to be cut, allow to dry, and then cut.) Hot glue flange of 1/2" dia. cording along edge on wrong side of table topper. Hot glue 3/16" dia. cord to right side of table topper along inner edge of 1/2" dia. cording. Hot glue 1 tassel to each corner of table topper.
6. Place table topper on table. Measure around edge of tabletop. Cut a length of ribbon 40" longer than the determined measurement. Loosely knot ribbon as desired. Drape ribbon along edge of tabletop, using safety pins to secure.

NOAH AND FRIENDS

*D*uring the holidays, our hearts and minds are drawn to the Bible and the wonderful Christmas miracle that we celebrate. Along with the story of the Nativity, we delight in turning to other favorite passages, like the account of Noah and the Great Flood. This timeless story has captured imaginations for generations, and Noah's Ark toys were especially well-liked back when Bible-related playthings were the only ones children could play with on Sundays. With the enduring popularity of the theme, you'll discover a host of creative ways to display these projects — at Christmastime and throughout the year (for example, the patchwork tree skirt is really a cozy bed quilt!). Instructions for the projects shown on these pages begin on page 84.

With the aid of his trusty staff, **Noah** (*page 86*) watches over the **Animals Two By Two** (*page 87*). His flowing robe and shawl are easily fashioned from twisted paper. Realistic markings and furry manes add to the appeal of the button-jointed animals. (*Opposite*) A menagerie of elephants, lions, giraffes, camels, and zebras parade around the **Noah and Friends Tree** (*page 84*). Resembling raindrops, tiny white lights fall gently through the branches. Their warming glow is matched by raffia-tied candle lights and tin-punched star ornaments. Painted with simple phrases, the touching **Story Heart Ornaments** (*page 84*) eloquently recount this favorite Bible story.

Bordered by animal pairs, the **Noah's Ark Wall Hanging** (*page 90*) dramatically recalls the fateful forty-days-and-forty-nights adventure. Buttons, fabric yo-yos, and appliquéd waves embellish this starry night scene.

A multitude of coordinating fabrics was used to create the rustic **Noah's Patchwork Stocking** (*page 84*). Whether filled with greenery and used as a decorative accent or stuffed with delightful surprises, its charming simplicity will be appreciated season after season. Edged with deep sea-blue paint, the **Story Heart Ornaments** (*page 84*) have a fabric backing for added dimension.

After serving as a unique Christmas tree skirt, the **Noah's Star Quilt** (*page 84*) doubles as a warming coverlet for a twin bed through the rest of the winter.

NOAH AND FRIENDS TREE
(Shown on page 81)

One of our most beloved Bible stories, the story of Noah is one of faith and promise. Invite Noah and his friends into your home this Christmas to share in the great promise that this season brings.

Small clear lights, along with purchased 9" tall candle lights decorated with raffia bows, light the way for the crew on Noah's tree. Strands of wooden bead garland loosely hang from the branch tips of our seven-foot-tall tree, giving the feeling of the rolling waves that Noah and the animals must have encountered. Purchased punched metal star ornaments add to the warm glow that surrounds this tree.

Among these lights of hope parade the Animals Two By Two (page 87). Made from muslin, these charming hand-painted animals have button-jointed legs, furry manes, and yarn tails. Hanging among the animals, the Story Heart Ornaments (this page) tell the captivating story of Noah.

Wrapped around the base of the tree is the cozy Noah's Star Quilt (this page), which is also ample enough to cover a twin bed on a cold winter evening.

STORY HEART ORNAMENTS
(Shown on page 83)

For each ornament, you will need an approx. $3^3/8$"w heart-shaped wooden cutout, a 5" square of blue print fabric, medium weight fusible interfacing, blue acrylic paint to match fabric, a stencil brush, paper towels, raffia, a large wooden bead, a large button, black permanent felt-tip pen with medium point, hot glue gun, and glue sticks.

1. Dip brush in paint; remove excess on paper towel until brush is almost dry. Using a stamping motion, paint approx. 1" along edges of heart; allow to dry.
2. Referring to photo, use pen to write desired phrase on heart; we wrote "the Lord spoke to Noah," "forty days and nights," "rain fell on the earth," "two of every kind," "every kind of bird," and "a promise kept."
3. Follow manufacturer's instructions to fuse interfacing to wrong side of fabric square. Glue heart to center on right side of fabric square. Cutting approx. $3/8$" from wooden heart, cut out fabric heart.
4. For hanger, cut two $8^1/2$" lengths of raffia. Knot raffia lengths together at 1 end; glue knot to back of heart. Knot raffia at top of heart. Thread bead and button onto raffia. Knot raffia at remaining end.

NOAH'S PATCHWORK STOCKING
(Shown on page 83)

You will need two 12" x 20" fabric pieces for stocking, two 12" x 20" fabric pieces for stocking lining, fabric scraps for cuff, a 6" x $13^1/4$" fabric piece for cuff lining, a 2" x 8" fabric strip for hanger, thread to match fabrics, fabric marking pencil, and tracing paper.

1. Matching dotted lines and aligning arrows, trace top and bottom of stocking pattern, page 45, onto tracing paper; cut out.
2. Leaving top edge open, use stocking pattern and follow **Sewing Shapes,** page 158, to make stocking from stocking fabric pieces. Repeat for stocking lining; do not turn lining right side out.
3. (**Note:** For Steps 3 and 4, match right sides and raw edges and use a $1/4$" seam allowance; press seam allowances to 1 side.) For top section of cuff, cut seventeen $1^1/4$" x $3^1/2$" strips from fabrics; sew strips together along long edges to form a $3^1/2$" x $13^1/4$" pieced strip. For middle section of cuff, cut six $2^5/8$" x $1^3/4$" strips from fabrics; sew strips together along short edges to form a $1^3/4$" x $13^1/4$" pieced strip.
4. Sew top and middle sections together along 1 long edge. Sew 1 long edge of cuff lining fabric piece to remaining long edge of middle section.
5. Matching right sides and short edges, fold cuff in half. Using a $1/2$" seam allowance, sew short edges together to form a tube. Press seam open; turn cuff right side out. Fold raw edge of cuff lining to inside of tube to meet raw edge of cuff (cuff lining will extend $3/4$" below cuff seamline); press.
6. Matching raw edges, place cuff over stocking with seamline at center back. Using a $1/2$" seam allowance, sew cuff to stocking. Press seam allowance $1/2$" to inside of stocking.
7. For lining, press top edge of lining $1/2$" to wrong side. Insert lining into stocking.
8. For hanger, press long edges of fabric strip $1/2$" to wrong side. With wrong sides together, press strip in half lengthwise; sew close to pressed edges. Matching ends, fold hanger in half to form a loop. Place ends of loop between stocking and lining at heel-side seamline with approx. $2^1/2$" of loop extending above stocking; pin in place.
9. Slipstitch lining to stocking and, at the same time, securely sew hanger in place.

NOAH'S STAR QUILT
(Shown on page 83)

For an approx. $65^1/2$" x $89^1/2$" quilt, you will need the following 44/45"w fabrics for star (square-in-square) blocks: $5/8$ yd of medium fabric for center squares, $7/8$ yd of light fabric for inner triangles, and one $2/3$ yd piece each of 2 dark fabrics for outer triangles; one 42" x 52" piece each of very light and light fabric for quarter-square blocks; $5/8$ yd of 44/45"w medium fabric for inner border; $7/8$ yd of 44/45"w dark fabric for outer border; $5/8$ yd of 44/45"w medium fabric for binding; one 81" x 96" piece each of backing fabric (pieced as necessary) and polyester bonded batting; sewing and quilting thread to coordinate with fabrics; rotary cutter, mat, and ruler; fabric marking pencil; and silver marking pencil.

Note: Before beginning project, wash, dry, and press all fabrics. We recommend using a rotary cutter for all cutting. For sewing steps, match right sides and raw edges and use a $1/4$" seam allowance unless otherwise indicated. Press seam allowances toward darker fabric when possible.

1. (**Note:** Follow Steps 1 - 3 to make 35 star blocks.) For center squares, cut thirty-five $4^1/2$" squares. For inner triangles, cut seventy $3^3/4$" squares; cut each square in half diagonally to make 140 triangles. For outer triangles, cut thirty-five $4^7/8$" squares from each fabric; cut each square in half diagonally to make a total of 140 triangles (70 from each fabric).
2. Sew 2 inner triangles to opposite edges of 1 center square (**Fig. 1**). Sew 2 inner triangles to remaining edges of square (**Fig. 2**). Repeat to sew remaining inner triangles to remaining center squares, forming 35 pieced squares.

Fig. 1   **Fig. 2**

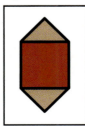   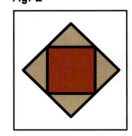

3. Sew 2 outer triangles from 1 dark fabric to opposite edges of 1 pieced square (**Fig. 3**, page 85). Sew 2 outer triangles from second dark fabric to remaining edges of square (**Fig. 4**, page 85). Repeat for remaining pieced squares.

Fig. 3

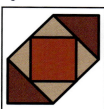

Fig. 4

Fig. 7

4. (Note: Follow Steps 4 - 6 to make 35 quarter-square blocks.) Matching right sides and raw edges, place very light and light 42" x 52" fabric pieces together; pin at edges to secure. Referring to grey lines in **Fig. 5**, use fabric marking pencil and ruler to draw a grid of eighteen 9¼" squares on wrong side of top fabric piece. Referring to blue lines in **Fig. 5**, draw diagonal lines across grid, forming an "X" in each square. Referring to **Fig. 6**, sew fabric pieces together, stitching ¼" on each side of diagonal lines that go from upper left to lower right.

Fig. 5

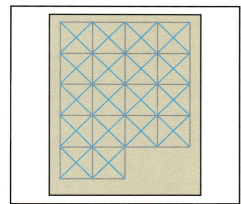

Fig. 6

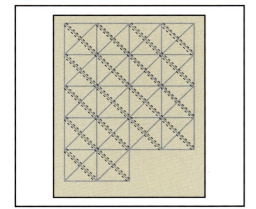

5. Cut along all drawn lines to make 72 diagonal half blocks.
6. Sew 2 corresponding half blocks together for each block (**Fig. 7**).

7. (Note: Diagram, this page, shows top half of quilt only.) Referring to **Diagram,** arrange blocks into 10 rows of 7 blocks each, alternating star blocks with quarter-square blocks. Sew blocks into rows; sew rows together.
8. For inner border, cut two 2¼" x 60" fabric strips for top and bottom and two 2¼" x 88" strips for sides of quilt top.
9. Center and sew one 60" strip to top of quilt top and remaining 60" strip to bottom of quilt top. Trim strips even with sides of quilt top. Repeat to sew remaining inner border strips to sides of quilt top.
10. For outer border, cut two 3¼" x 64" fabric strips for top and bottom and two 3¼" x 94" strips for sides of quilt top. Repeat Step 9 to sew strips to quilt top.
11. Referring to **Diagram,** use silver pencil and ruler to mark quilting lines on quilt top.
12. Place backing fabric wrong side up. Place batting on backing fabric. Center quilt top right side up on batting. Pin layers

together. Basting from center outward, baste layers together to each corner and to each side. With basting lines 3" to 4" apart, baste from top to bottom and from side to side. Baste ½" from each edge of quilt top.
13. Working from center of quilt outward, follow **Quilting,** page 159, to quilt "in the ditch" (close to seamlines) around inner square of each star block and along all marked quilting lines.
14. Trim batting and backing even with edges of quilt top.
15. For binding, cut a 2" x 9 yd fabric strip (pieced as necessary). Press 1 end of binding ½" to wrong side. Matching wrong sides, press strip in half lengthwise; unfold. Press long raw edges to center; refold binding.
16. To bind edges of quilt, unfold 1 long edge of binding. Beginning with pressed end of binding at least 3" away from a corner and matching right side of binding to quilt front, pin unfolded edge of binding along 1 edge of quilt. Using pressing line closest to raw edge as a guide, sew binding to quilt. Mitering binding at corners, continue pinning and sewing binding around quilt until ends of binding overlap ½"; trim excess binding. Fold binding over raw edges to back of quilt; hand stitch in place. Remove basting threads from quilt.

DIAGRAM

NOAH (Shown on page 80)

You will need an empty 3-liter plastic soft drink bottle, a 3" long plastic foam egg, papier mâché (we used Celluclay® instant papier mâché), 34" of approx. 60"w tan twisted paper, 1¼ yd of approx. 7¾"w blue-green twisted paper (untwisted), two 8" lengths of approx. 7¾"w black twisted paper (untwisted) and two 2" x 8" strips of polyester bonded batting for hands, 24" of 8-gauge wire for arms, florist wire, light grey wool doll's hair, thread to match hair, a 3¼" x 29" torn fabric strip for head wrap, peach and pink acrylic paint, paintbrushes, Design Master® glossy wood tone spray (available at craft stores and florist shops), raffia, 40" of ¼"w jute braid trim, 1⅓ yds of jute twine, two 5mm black half-beads for eyes, a large wooden bead and a large button for belt trim, a crooked twig for staff, 1 small sprig each of preserved boxwood and preserved cedar, black embroidery floss, a rubber band, masking tape, wire cutters, pliers, approx. 2 cups gravel (we used aquarium gravel), craft glue, hot glue gun, and glue sticks.

1. Remove lid from bottle and discard. Pour gravel into bottle.
2. For head, place small end of egg in opening of bottle. Push egg down onto bottle until total height of bottle and egg measures approx. 15½".
3. Follow manufacturer's instructions to mix a small amount of papier mâché. Apply a smooth ⅛" thick layer of papier mâché over egg and 2" of bottle below egg to form neck (**Fig. 1**). Allow to dry.

Fig. 1

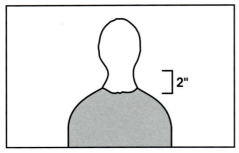

4. Paint papier mâché peach; allow to dry.
5. For robe, cut an 18" length of tan twisted paper and untwist. Use craft glue to glue short edges of paper piece together to form a tube; allow to dry.

6. Place robe over bottle. Gather top edge of robe tightly around neck; wrap rubber band tightly around top of robe and neck to secure robe in place. Fold bottom edge of robe 3" to wrong side. Refer to photo to arrange robe.
7. For arms, use pliers to bend each end of 8-gauge wire length ¼" to 1 side. Wrap wire with masking tape.
8. (**Note:** Follow Step 8 for each hand.) Beginning with 1 end of batting strip, wrap one 2" x 8" batting strip around 1 end of 8-gauge wire length; use masking tape to secure. Beginning with 1 long edge of 1 black paper piece and placing end of batting-covered wire at center, wrap paper piece around end of wire over batting; use masking tape to secure. Twist paper slightly at end of wire and batting; knot a length of floss tightly around paper at twist (**Fig. 2**). Referring to **Fig. 3**, turn free end of paper wrong side out over batting. Referring to **Fig. 4**, secure free end of paper with masking tape to form wrist. Put a drop of craft glue into opening at end of hand and press opening closed; allow to dry.

Fig. 2

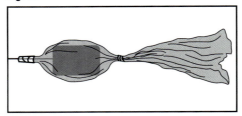

Fig. 3

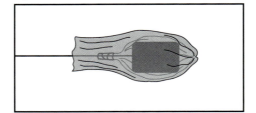

Fig. 4

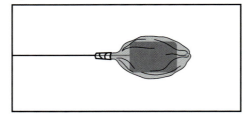

9. For sleeves, untwist remainder of tan paper. Cut a 16" x 30" piece from paper. Use craft glue to glue long edges of paper piece together to form a tube; allow to dry.
10. Center arms in sleeve tube. Gather center of sleeve tube around center of arms; wrap with florist wire to secure. Hot glue center of arms to center back of robe at neck. Roll up bottom of each sleeve approx. 2½". Referring to photo, arrange arms and sleeves.
11. Tie jute braid trim into a knot around robe at waist. Cut three 40" lengths of raffia. Tie raffia lengths together into a bow around robe at waist. Thread bead onto 1 end of raffia lengths; knot raffia lengths below bead. Thread button onto remaining end of raffia lengths approx. 4" from end; knot raffia lengths below button and again approx. 1" from end.
12. For beard, cut one approx. ½" dia., 8" length of hair and fold length in half; hot glue fold to face. Repeat for remainder of beard and to cover sides and back of head with hair. For center part at top of head, glue folds of hair lengths along each side of a line from center of forehead to center back of head. For mustache, cut an approx. ¾" dia., 6" length of hair. Knot a length of thread tightly around center of hair length; trim ends of thread. Hot glue center of hair length to face above beard. Trim beard, hair, and mustache as desired.
13. Hot glue half-beads to face for eyes.
14. Mix 1 part pink paint with 1 part water; use diluted paint to paint cheeks on face.
15. For head wrap, match wrong sides and fold fabric strip in half lengthwise. Referring to photo, wrap fabric strip around head twice and hot glue at side of head to secure. Cut a 12" length and a 1 yd length of jute twine and two 1 yd lengths of raffia. Knot short length of twine around ends of fabric at side of head. Wrap raffia lengths and remaining twine length together around head wrap and knot at side of wrap. Tuck boxwood and cedar sprigs into knots at side of wrap; hot glue in place.
16. For shawl, lightly spray blue-green paper piece with wood tone spray; allow to dry. Drape shawl around shoulders and roll up approx. 4" at each end of shawl. Place staff at side behind 1 arm.

For each animal, you will need two 14" squares of muslin, one 14" square of low-loft polyester bonded batting, four ³/₄" dia. black buttons, polyester fiberfill, ecru sewing thread, black embroidery floss, black wool yarn, 22" of jute twine for hanger (optional), small flat paintbrush, waxed paper, tracing paper, hot glue gun, and glue sticks.

For camel, you will **also** need light rust, rust, and dark brown acrylic paint; small sponge piece; small round paintbrush; and 4" of rust wool yarn for tail.

For lion, you will **also** need dark yellow acrylic paint, a 4" x 6" piece of light tan artificial fur, Design Master® glossy wood tone spray (optional; available at craft stores and florist shops), 4" of light brown wool yarn for tail, and small sharp scissors.

For zebra, you will **also** need light beige and black acrylic paint, small round paintbrush, stencil brush, acetate for stencil, permanent felt-tip pen with fine point, craft knife, cutting mat or thick layer of newspapers, removable tape (optional), paper towels, 3¹/₂" of 1" long black fringe for mane, and two 4" lengths of black wool yarn for tail.

For giraffe, you will **also** need very dark yellow and dark brown acrylic paint, small round paintbrush, stencil brush, acetate for stencil, permanent felt-tip pen with fine point, craft knife, cutting mat or thick layer of newspapers, removable tape (optional), paper towels, 4¹/₂" of 1" long brown fringe for mane, and 4" of brown wool yarn for tail.

For elephant, you will **also** need light grey, grey, and dark grey acrylic paint; small sponge piece; small round paintbrush; and 4" of grey wool yarn for tail.

CAMEL

1. For camel, trace body, front leg, and back leg of camel pattern, this page, separately onto tracing paper.
2. With batting between muslin pieces, layer and pin muslin and batting pieces together.
3. Leaving at least 1" between shapes, use a pencil to draw around body pattern once and each leg pattern twice on top muslin piece. Using a short straight stitch and stitching directly on drawn lines, sew layers together.
4. (**Note:** Refer to photo for remaining steps. For painting steps, cover work area with waxed paper; allow to dry after each paint color.) Use flat paintbrush to apply

rust paint to both sides of each shape, extending paint approx. ¹/₄" outside sewn lines.
5. Cutting approx. ¹/₈" outside sewn lines, cut out each shape.
6. Apply a second coat of rust paint to both sides of each shape, including edges.
7. Referring to pattern for arrangement of legs, place body between front legs and back legs. Use a pencil to lightly mark inside top of each leg.
8. Place legs with marked side down. Use dampened sponge piece to lightly stamp both sides of body and unmarked side of each leg with light rust paint. Use round paintbrush to paint a dark brown hoof on unmarked side of each leg.
9. To stuff each leg, cut an approx. 1" long opening on marked side at center of widest part of leg; stuff leg with a small amount of fiberfill.
10. (**Note:** Refer to pattern to assemble camel. Attach legs to camel with marked sides facing body.) To attach front legs to body, thread a needle with floss; knot ends together. Bring needle up through 1 leg at pink ●, through body at pink ●, and through remaining leg at pink ●. Pull floss until legs are tight against body. Thread needle through 1 button and take needle back through legs and body. Thread needle through a second button and bring needle back through legs and body. Repeat to make several more stitches through buttons, legs, and body. Knot floss between body and 1 leg and trim ends. Repeat to attach back legs to body at pink ◆'s.
11. Using 1 strand of black yarn, work a French Knot, page 159, on each side of camel's head for eyes.
12. For tail, knot 1 end of rust yarn length; trim short end of yarn close to knot. Glue knot to camel and fray yarn. Trim tail as desired.
13. If hanger is desired, knot center of twine. Glue knot to top center back of camel.

LION

1. For lion, use lion pattern, page 88, and follow Steps 1 - 6 of Camel instructions, painting shapes dark yellow.
2. Follow Step 7 of Camel instructions to mark inside top of each leg.
3. Follow Steps 9 - 11 of Camel instructions to stuff and attach legs and to make eyes.
4. Using light brown yarn, follow Step 12 of Camel instructions to make tail. Knot end of tail.

5. For mane, trace mane pattern (shown in gold), page 88, onto tracing paper; cut out. Draw around pattern on back of fur; turn pattern over and draw around pattern again. Using small scissors and cutting through back of fur only, cut out manes. If desired, lightly spray fur with wood tone spray; allow to dry. Referring to pattern, glue 1 mane to each side of lion.
6. If hanger is desired, knot center of twine. Glue knot to top center back of lion.

ZEBRA

1. For zebra, use zebra pattern, page 88, and follow Steps 1 - 6 of Camel instructions, painting shapes light beige.
2. Follow Step 7 of Camel instructions to mark inside top of each leg.
3. Using zebra stripe pattern (shown in green), page 88, follow **Stenciling**, page 158, to stencil black stripes on each side of body and on unmarked sides of legs. Use round paintbrush to extend stripes to edges of each shape and to paint a black hoof on unmarked side of each leg.
4. Follow Steps 9 - 11 of Camel instructions to stuff and attach legs and to make eyes.
5. Using both lengths of black yarn, follow Step 12 of Camel instructions to make tail.
6. For mane, refer to pattern and glue finished edge of fringe along 1 side of neck between pink ✳'s.
7. If hanger is desired, knot center of twine. Glue knot to top center back of zebra.

GIRAFFE

1. For giraffe, use giraffe pattern, page 89, and follow Steps 1 - 6 of Camel instructions, painting shapes very dark yellow.
2. Follow Step 7 of Camel instructions to mark inside top of each leg.
3. Using giraffe spot pattern (shown in green), page 89, follow **Stenciling**, page 158, to stencil dark brown spots on each side of body and on unmarked sides of legs. Use round paintbrush to paint a dark brown hoof on unmarked side of each leg.
4. Follow Steps 9 - 11 of Camel instructions to stuff and attach legs and to make eyes.
5. Using brown yarn, follow Step 12 of Camel instructions to make tail.
6. For mane, refer to pattern and glue finished edge of fringe along 1 side of neck between pink ✳'s.
7. If hanger is desired, knot center of twine. Glue knot to top center back of giraffe.

Continued on page 88

ANIMALS TWO BY TWO (Continued)

ELEPHANT

1. For elephant, use elephant pattern, page 90, and follow Steps 1 - 6 of Camel instructions, page 87, making 1 body, 2 front legs, 2 back legs, and 2 ears and painting shapes light grey.

2. Follow Step 7 of Camel instructions to mark inside top of each leg and each ear.

3. Follow Step 8 of Camel instructions to paint elephant, including ears, using grey paint for sponge painting and dark grey paint to paint feet.

4. Follow Steps 9 - 11 of Camel instructions to stuff and attach legs and to make eyes. Referring to pattern, glue ears to elephant.

5. Using grey yarn, follow Step 12 of Camel instructions to make tail. Knot end of tail.

6. If hanger is desired, knot center of twine. Glue knot to top center back of elephant.

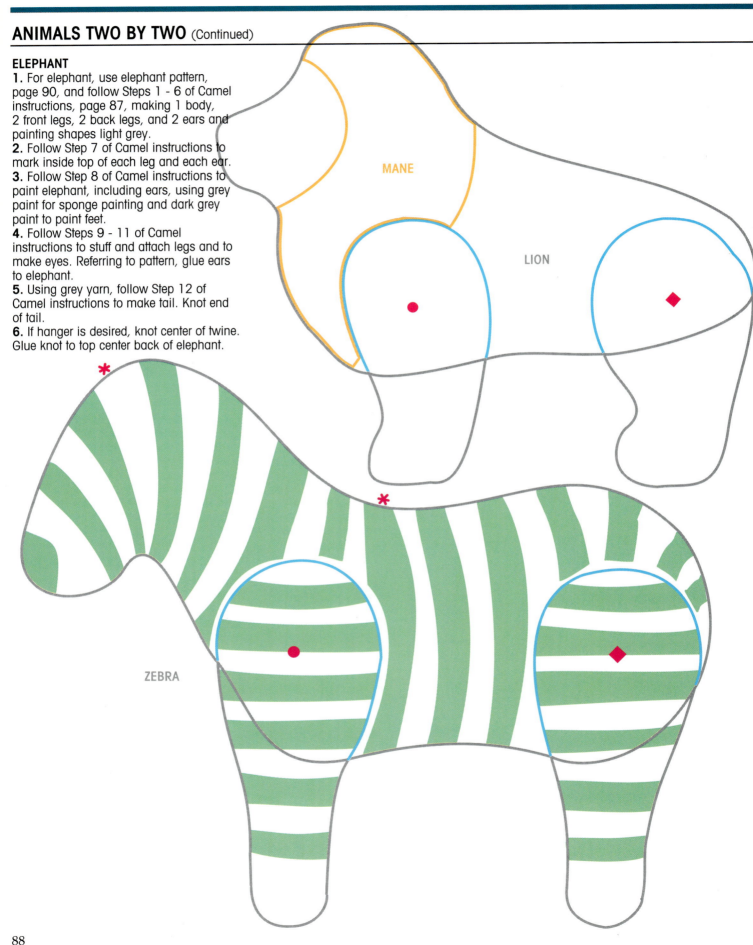

MANE

LION

ZEBRA

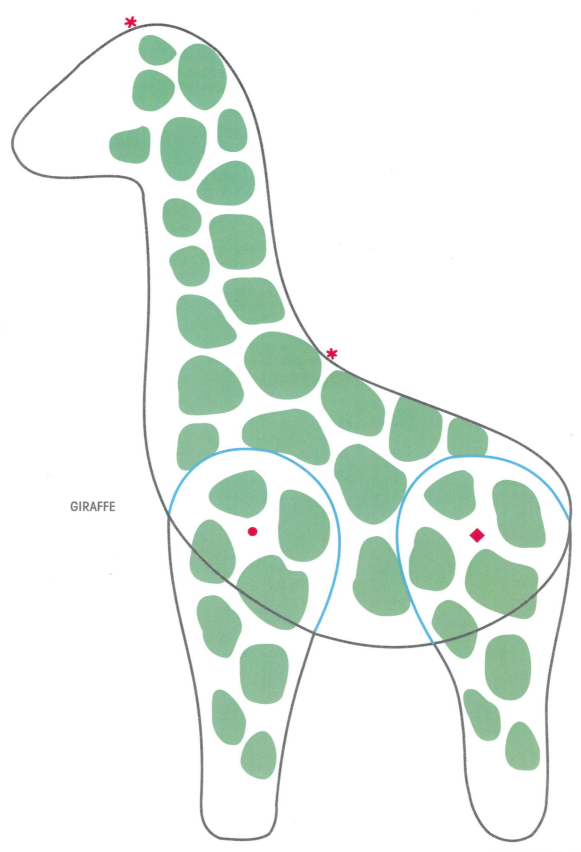

GIRAFFE

Patterns continued on page 90

NOAH'S ARK WALL HANGING (Shown on page 82)

For an approx. 35³/₄" x 47¹/₂" wall hanging, you will need fabrics for wall hanging front (see **Table**, page 91, for quantities), ¹/₂ yd of 44/45"w fabric for binding, one 42" x 54" piece each of fabric for backing (pieced as necessary) and low-loft polyester bonded batting, sewing and quilting thread to coordinate with fabrics, thread for appliqués (we used fine nylon thread), paper-backed fusible web, tear-away stabilizer, and tracing paper.

For ark panel appliqués, you will **also** need a 9" square of blue fabric for wave appliqués, a 5" x 10" piece of gold fabric for star appliqués, an 8" x 11" fabric piece for yo-yo s, thread to match yo-yo fabric, five ¹/₂" dia. black buttons for yo-yos, and a drawing compass.

For animal border appliqués, you will **also** need one 22" x 13" piece each of the following colors of fabric for animal appliqués: dark yellow for lions, rust for camels, light grey for elephants, very dark yellow for giraffes, and light beige for zebras; two 4¹/₂" lengths of 1" long brown fringe for giraffes' manes; two 3¹/₂" lengths of 1" long black fringe for zebras' manes; a 4" x 6" piece of light tan artificial fur for lions' manes; Design Master® glossy wood tone spray (optional; available at craft stores and florist shops); two 4" lengths each of light brown, rust, grey, and brown wool yarn and four 4" lengths of black wool yarn for tails; black wool yarn for eyes; black embroidery floss; twenty ³/₄" dia. black buttons; light rust, dark brown, grey, dark grey, and black acrylic paint; small round paintbrushes; small sponge pieces; stencil brushes; acetate for stencils for giraffe spots and zebra stripes; small sharp scissors; craft knife; cutting mat or thick layer of newspapers; graphite transfer paper; black permanent felt-tip pen with fine point; fabric glue; fabric marking pencil; removable tape (optional); paper towels; waxed paper; and pressing cloth.

For corner blocks, you will need a 6" x 21" piece of medium fabric for center squares; a 6" x 38" piece of light fabric for inner triangles; one 7" x 23" piece each of 2 dark fabrics for outer triangles; thread to match fabrics; and a rotary cutter, mat, and ruler (optional).

Note: Before beginning project, wash, dry, and press all fabrics. If using directional fabrics, lay out pieces for wall hanging as shown in **Diagram**, page 91, to make sure fabric direction is consistent. Unless otherwise indicated, match right sides and raw edges, pin fabric pieces together, and

use a ¹/₄" seam allowance for each sewing step. Press seam allowances toward darker fabric when possible.

MAKING ARK PANEL

1. For ark panel, refer to **Diagram** and **Table**, page 91, to cut pieces A - L from fabrics.

2. (**Note:** Refer to **Diagram** to assemble ark panel.) Sew two A's together. Sew one B to each A. Sew one D to each short edge of C. Sew D-C-D to A-A. Sew E to D-C-D. Sew one G to each short edge of F. Sew one H to each G. Sew G-F-G to E. Sew I's to J's. Sew one I-J to each side of pieced panel. Sew K to top of pieced panel. Sew L to bottom of pieced panel.

3. For wave and star appliqués, follow manufacturer's instructions to fuse web to wrong sides of fabrics. Trace wave pattern, this page, and star patterns, page 91, onto tracing paper; cut out.

4. Use patterns to cut 3 waves from wave fabric and 2 small stars and 1 large star from star fabric. Remove paper backing. Referring to photo, fuse waves and stars to ark panel.

5. Follow **Machine Appliqué**, page 158, to stitch over raw edges of waves and stars.

6. For yo-yo pattern, use compass to draw a 3" dia. circle on tracing paper; cut out.

7. (**Note:** Follow Step 7 to make 5 yo-yos.) For each yo-yo, use pattern to cut 1 circle from fabric. Use a double strand of thread to baste ¹/₈" from edge of fabric circle. Pull ends of thread to tightly gather circle; knot thread and trim ends. Fold raw edge to inside of circle.

8. With yo-yos flattened and gathers at center, space yo-yo s evenly across ark approx. 1" below top edge of E piece; pin in place. Sewing yo-yos to panel, sew one button to center of each yo-yo.

MAKING ANIMAL BORDERS

1. For animal borders, refer to **Diagram** and **Table**, page 91, to cut pieces M - U from fabrics.

2. (**Note:** Refer to **Diagram** to assemble animal borders.) For each sashing strip, sew 1 each of M, N, O, P, and Q pieces together. Repeat for a total of 6 sashing strips. For each side border, sew one R, one S, one T, and 2 sashing strips together. For top border, sew two U's and 1 sashing strip together; repeat for bottom border.

3. For animal appliqués, follow manufacturer's instructions to fuse web to wrong sides of fabrics. Trace grey and blue lines of each animal pattern, pages 87

through this page, onto tracing paper; cut out each pattern along outer lines.

4. Use fabric marking pencil to draw around camel pattern on right side of rust fabric piece; turn pattern over and draw around pattern again. Repeat to draw 2 elephants on grey fabric, 2 giraffes on very dark yellow fabric, 2 lions on dark yellow fabric, and 2 zebras on light beige fabric.

5. (**Note:** Cover work area with waxed paper. Refer to photo for remaining steps. Allow to dry after each paint step.) For camel appliqués, use a damp sponge piece to lightly sponge light rust paint over camel shapes. Use round paintbrush to paint dark brown hooves on legs. Repeat to sponge paint elephants with grey paint and paint dark grey feet on elephants.

6. Using giraffe spot pattern (shown in green), page 89, follow **Stenciling**, page 158, to stencil dark brown spots on giraffes. Using zebra stripe pattern (shown in green), page 88, repeat to stencil black stripes on zebras. Use round paintbrush to paint dark brown hooves on giraffes and black hooves on zebras.

7. Referring to patterns, pages 87 through this page, use transfer paper to transfer blue lines on patterns to each animal. Use black pen to draw over transferred lines.

8. Cut out animals and remove paper backing.

9. For mane on each giraffe, refer to pattern, page 89, and glue finished edge of 1 length of brown fringe to wrong side of appliqué between pink *'s. For mane on each zebra, refer to pattern, page 88, and repeat with black fringe.

10. To apply appliqués to borders, center camels on R pieces; use pressing cloth to fuse in place. Repeat to fuse elephants to S pieces, giraffes to T pieces, lions to top U pieces, and zebras to bottom U pieces. Using a medium width zigzag stitch with short stitch length, follow **Machine Appliqué**, page 158, to stitch over edges of appliqués.

MAKING CORNER BLOCKS

1. (**Note:** We recommend using a rotary cutter for Step 1.) For center squares, cut four 4¹/₂" squares. For inner triangles, cut eight 3³/₄" squares; cut each square in half diagonally to make 16 triangles. For outer triangles, cut four 4⁷/₈" squares from each fabric; cut each square in half diagonally to make a total of 16 triangles (8 from each fabric).

2. Follow Steps 2 and 3 of Noah's Star Quilt instructions, page 84, to make 4 blocks.

ELEPHANT

ASSEMBLING WALL HANGING FRONT

1. Sew side animal borders to sides of ark panel.
2. Sew 1 corner block to each end of top and bottom animal borders.
3. Sew top animal border to top of ark panel and side borders. Sew bottom animal border to bottom of ark panel and side borders.

FINISHING WALL HANGING

1. Place backing fabric wrong side up. Place batting on backing. Center wall hanging front right side up on batting. Pin layers together. Basting from center outward, baste layers together to each corner and to each side. With basting lines 3" to 4" apart, baste from top to bottom and from side to side. Baste 1/4" from each edge of wall hanging front.
2. Working from center of wall hanging outward and using quilting thread, use a medium straight stitch to machine quilt "in the ditch" (close to seamlines) along seams shown in blue in **Diagram** and around each animal.
3. Trim batting and backing 1/2" from edges of wall hanging front.

4. For binding, cut a 3"w x 4 3/4 yd fabric strip (pieced as necessary). Press 1 end of binding 1/2" to wrong side. Matching wrong sides, press strip in half lengthwise; unfold. Press long raw edges to center; refold binding.
5. To bind edges of wall hanging, unfold 1 long edge of binding. Beginning with pressed end of binding at least 3" away from a corner and matching right side of binding to wall hanging front, pin unfolded edge of binding along 1 edge of wall hanging. Using pressing line closest to raw edge as a guide, sew binding to quilt. Mitering binding at corners, continue pinning and sewing binding around wall hanging until ends of binding overlap 1/2"; trim excess binding. Fold binding over raw edges to back of quilt; hand stitch in place. Remove basting threads from wall hanging.
6. For lions' manes, trace mane pattern (shown in gold), page 88, onto tracing paper; cut out. Draw around pattern on back of fur; turn pattern over and draw around pattern again. Using small scissors and cutting through back of fur only, cut out manes. If desired, lightly spray fur with wood tone spray; allow to dry. Referring to pattern, glue manes to lions.
7. Use black floss to sew one 3/4" dia. button at top of each leg.
8. Using 1 strand of black yarn, work a French Knot, page 159, for each eye.
9. For each camel's tail, knot 1 end of 1 rust yarn length; trim short end of yarn close to knot. Glue knot to camel, allow to dry, and fray yarn. Repeat for each animal, using 1 grey yarn length for each elephant, 1 brown yarn length for each giraffe, 1 light brown yarn length for each lion, and 2 black yarn lengths for each zebra. Knot end of each elephant's and each lion's tail. Trim tails as desired.

TABLE

Fabric piece(s)	Size (w x h)	Number needed
A	8 3/8" triangle*	2
B	8 3/8" triangle*	2
C	11 1/2" x 4 1/2"	1
D	2 1/2" x 4 1/2"	2
E	15 1/2" x 7 1/4"	1
F	8" x 4 1/4"	1
G	4 5/8" triangle*	2
H	4 5/8" triangle*	2
I	2 3/8" x 15 1/2"	2
J	2 3/8" x 7 1/2"	2
K	19 1/4" x 5"	1
L	19 1/4" x 4 1/2"	1
M	1 1/4" x 2 1/2"	6
N	1 1/4" x 1 1/2"	6
O	1 1/4" x 3"	6
P	1 1/4" x 1 1/2"	6
Q	1 1/4" x 2"	6
R	8 1/2" x 10 1/2"	2
S	8 1/2" x 8 1/2"	2
T	8 1/2" x 11 1/2"	2
U	9 1/2" x 8 1/2"	4

* For triangles, cut a square the indicated size, then cut square in half diagonally.

DIAGRAM

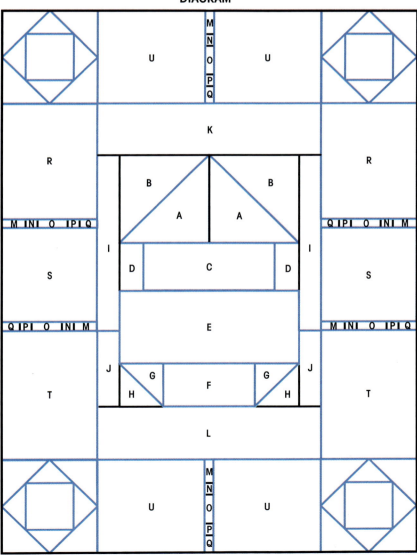

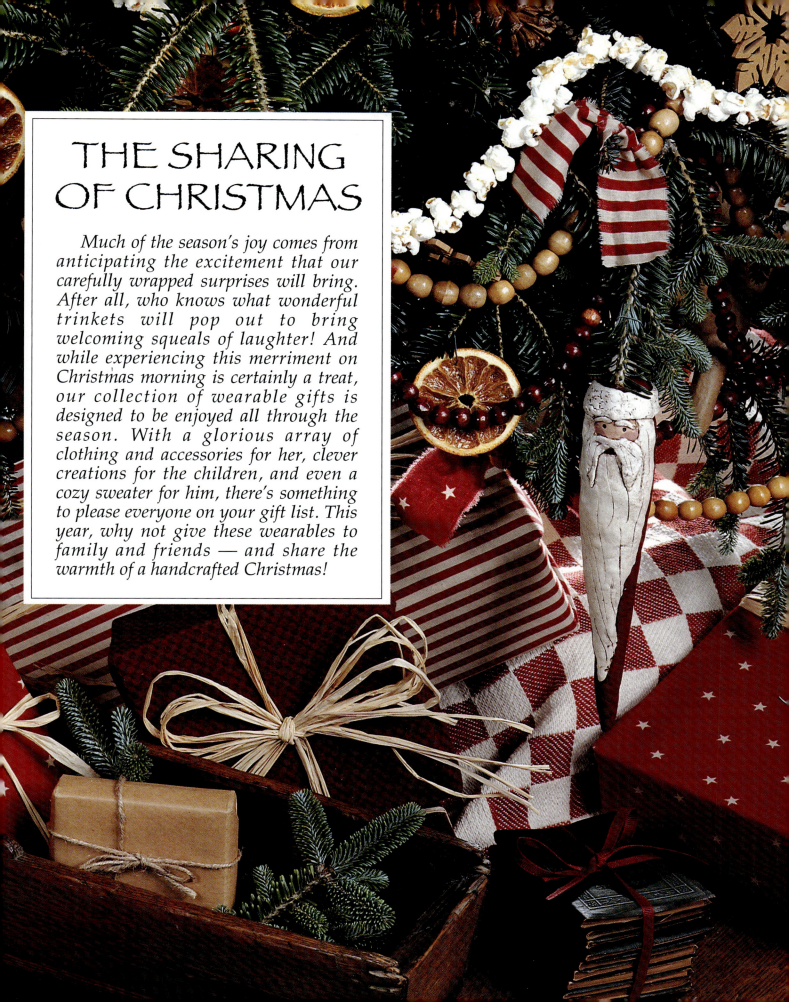

THE SHARING OF CHRISTMAS

Much of the season's joy comes from anticipating the excitement that our carefully wrapped surprises will bring. After all, who knows what wonderful trinkets will pop out to bring welcoming squeals of laughter! And while experiencing this merriment on Christmas morning is certainly a treat, our collection of wearable gifts is designed to be enjoyed all through the season. With a glorious array of clothing and accessories for her, clever creations for the children, and even a cozy sweater for him, there's something to please everyone on your gift list. This year, why not give these wearables to family and friends — and share the warmth of a handcrafted Christmas!

94

*W*hen the winter forecast calls for warm and comfortable clothing, give these stylish fashions! Buttons and bows bring added appeal to the charming **Feather Tree Sweater** (page 106). The embroidered tree is "displayed" in an appliquéd fabric flowerpot.

*B*earing a distinctly masculine design, the handsome **Men's Appliquéd Sweater** (page 111) is embellished with decorative blanket stitch embroidery on the appliqués and coordinating overcast stitches around the neckline.

A rustic scene from the North Woods is captured in cross stitch on the casual **Winter Forest Jumper** (page 107). This versatile winter warmer can be worn all through the season.

To Nattie—
Have Fun
coloring Your
own Shirt!

On our **"Merry Christmas" Cardigan** (page 104), Santa takes to the air in an unusual way to share his heartfelt holiday message. This cute cross-stitched design is a whimsical way to share Christmas cheer.

*L*ittle ones can jump right into the spirit of the season with this colorful collection of **Kids' Christmas Shoes** (page 106). Decorated with paints and holiday ribbons, they're wonderfully quick and easy to make.

*F*or a gift idea that's sure to paint a smile on the face of your favorite youngster, give a **Festive Reindeer Shirt Kit** (page 104) and watch the fun begin! The creative present contains everything a child will need to make an adorable Christmas sweatshirt — with just a little help from you, of course. The kits also make fun holiday party projects.

*D*azzle a special friend with this sparkling **"Ornament-al" Shirt** (page 107)! Embellished with metallic paints, sequin trims, jewel stones, and more, it's ideal for a Yuletide party or a night out on the town.

*T*hese **Beribboned Accessories** (page 109) will dress up a holiday wardrobe! An array of festive ribbons covers a plain purse and belt with a fashionable woven look. Decorated with ribbon, a multi-loop bow, and a gold button, the decorated hat will top off any outfit in style.

*B*looming with Christmas appeal, the **Poinsettia and Holly Jacket** (page 110) lends a classic touch to a Yuletide ensemble. The brilliant red petals are made from felt, and the stems and leaves are created with embroidery stitches.

*S*hare the warmth of a country celebration with these winter wearables! Offering a simple holiday greeting, the **Yo-Yo Wreath Sweatshirt** (page 111) is accented with buttons and a torn-fabric bow.

*B*orrowing a few techniques from patchwork quilting, you can turn a plain sweatshirt into this **Pieced Star Tunic** (page 108)! The pretty border is fashioned from coordinating homespun fabrics.

A sampling of favorite holiday motifs adorns the **Christmas Collage Sweatshirt** (page 102). To create this clever top, the front of an ordinary sweatshirt is replaced with a pieced fabric design. It'll spread country cheer wherever it's worn!

CHRISTMAS COLLAGE SWEATSHIRT (Shown on page 101)

You will need a sweatshirt with set-in sleeves and no side seams (shirt front should measure 26" to 29" from tops of shoulder seams to top of waist ribbing and 22" to 24" from side to side; we used a women's size medium shirt), fabrics for piecing shirt front (see **Table**, page 103), fabrics for appliqués, a 27" x 32" piece of muslin for shirt front backing, thread to match piecing fabrics and shirt, thread for appliqué stitching (we used fine clear nylon thread), black thread for Santa's eyes and details on bow, paper-backed fusible web, medium weight fusible interfacing, a ³/₈" dia. red shank button for Santa's nose, tracing paper, tear-away stabilizer or medium weight paper, disappearing ink fabric marking pen, yardstick, and seam ripper.

PIECING SHIRT FRONT

1. Wash, dry, and press shirt and fabrics.
2. Refer to **Table**, page 103, and cut fabrics for piecing shirt front.
3. Mark vertical center of muslin by using fabric marking pen and yardstick to draw a line from center of 1 short edge to center of remaining short edge.
4. (**Note:** Refer to **Diagram**, page 103, to piece shirt front. For all sewing, match right sides and raw edges and use a ¹/₄" seam allowance.) Sew A, B, C, and D together. With top edge of A 5" below 1 short edge (top edge) of muslin, center A-B-C-D right side up over drawn line on muslin; pin in place.
5. Sew E, F, and G together.
6. Place E-F-G right side down on A-B-C-D, matching left edge of E to right edge of A-B-C-D. Sewing through all layers along matched edges, sew pieces and muslin together. Turn E-F-G right side up and press.
7. Sew H and I together. Repeat Step 6 to sew top edge of H-I to bottom edges of D and E-F-G.
8. Sew J, K, and L together. Repeat Step 6 to sew right edge of J-K-L to left edges of A-B-C-D and H-I.
9. Repeat Step 6 to sew M, N, O, and P to previously sewn pieces and muslin, completing pieced front. Hand baste outer edges of M, N, O, and P to muslin.

APPLIQUÉING SHIRT FRONT

1. For Santa's mustache, tear two 1" x 3" pieces from fabric; topstitch close to edges of each piece to prevent fraying. Set aside.
2. For tree pattern, match dotted lines and align arrows and trace tree top and bottom patterns, this page, onto tracing paper. Trace remaining patterns, this page and page 103, onto tracing paper. Cut out patterns.
3. Follow manufacturer's instructions to fuse interfacing, then web, to wrong side of each appliqué fabric. Use patterns to cut 2 large stars and 1 of each remaining shape from fabrics. Remove paper backing.
4. (**Note:** Refer to photo for placement of appliqués.) Overlapping pieces slightly, arrange Santa pieces (except mustache) on piece B; fuse in place. Arrange and fuse stars to pieces H and J. Matching bottom edges, center and fuse tree trunk to piece L. Overlapping trunk ¹/₄", center and fuse tree to piece L. With bottom of letter "L" approx. ⁵/₈" from bottom of piece E and with letters approx. ¹/₂" apart, center and fuse letters to piece E. Fuse bow to letter "O".
5. Follow **Machine Appliqué**, page 158, to stitch over raw edges of appliqués.
6. For Santa's mustache, layer fabric pieces together. Use fingers to gather pieces at center. Place mustache on Santa and use a medium width zigzag stitch with a very short stitch length to stitch over gathered center. Sew button to Santa for nose.
7. Referring to patterns, use fabric marking pen to mark placement of eyes on Santa and to draw details on bow. Using black thread, use a medium width zigzag stitch with a very short stitch length to stitch eyes and a narrow width zigzag stitch with a very short stitch length to stitch details on bow.

ATTACHING SHIRT FRONT TO SHIRT

1. To mark cutting lines for removing front of shirt, use fabric marking pen and yardstick to draw a straight line on front of shirt from underarm seam to waist ribbing ¹/₄" from each side fold (**Fig. 1**).

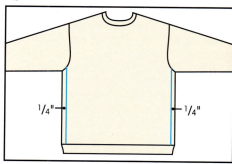

Fig. 1

2. On neck ribbing, use fabric marking pen to mark center front and back and positions of shoulder seams. On waist ribbing, mark center front and back.
3. Use seam ripper to remove neck and waist ribbings, take shoulder seams apart, and take each armhole seam apart at front of shirt from shoulder seam to drawn line at side of shirt. Cut away shirt front along drawn lines. Set ribbings and remainder of shirt aside.
4. Center shirt front right side up on pieced shirt front. Use fabric marking pen to draw around shirt front on pieced shirt front, drawing lines close to shirt front along neck edge and bottom edge, ¹/₄" from shirt front along each shoulder and armhole edge, and ¹/₂" from shirt front along each side edge (**Fig. 2**). Cut out pieced shirt front along drawn lines.

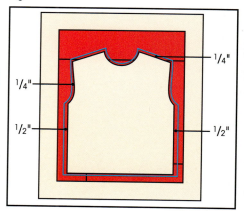

Fig. 2

5. (**Note:** When reassembling shirt, match right sides and raw edges; sew along previous seamlines unless otherwise indicated, easing pieces to fit as necessary.) Sew pieced shirt front to shirt back at shoulders. Using a ¹/₄" seam allowance, sew shirt front to shirt back at sides. Sew sleeves to shirt front. Turn shirt right side out and press.
6. Use fabric marking pen to mark center front and back on neck edge and bottom edge of shirt. Matching marks on ribbings to shoulder seams and marks on shirt, pin ribbings to shirt; sew in place.

TABLE

Fabric Piece	Size (width x length)
A	$5\frac{1}{2}$" x $3\frac{3}{4}$"
B	$5\frac{1}{2}$" x $10\frac{1}{2}$"
C	$5\frac{1}{2}$" x $1\frac{1}{4}$"
D	$5\frac{1}{2}$" x 1"
E	$3\frac{1}{2}$" x 15"
F	$1\frac{1}{2}$" x 15"
G	$2\frac{1}{2}$" x 15"
H	$11\frac{1}{2}$" x $6\frac{1}{4}$"
I	$11\frac{1}{2}$" x $1\frac{3}{4}$"
J	$6\frac{1}{2}$" x $6\frac{1}{4}$"
K	$6\frac{1}{2}$" x $1\frac{1}{2}$"
L	$6\frac{1}{2}$" x $15\frac{1}{4}$"
M	4" x 22"
N	21" x $4\frac{1}{2}$"
O	$4\frac{1}{2}$" x 26"
P	25" x $4\frac{1}{2}$"

DIAGRAM

SANTA HAT TRIM

SANTA FACE

SANTA HAT

SANTA BEARD

SANTA POM-POM

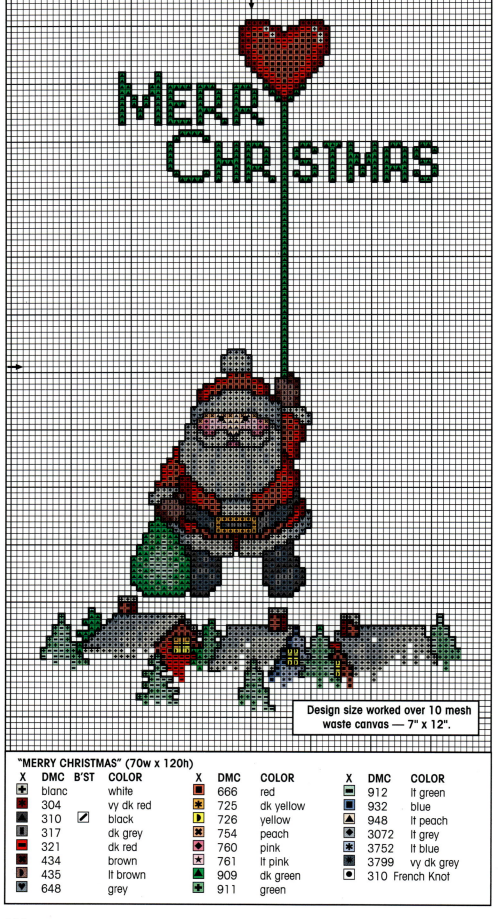

"MERRY CHRISTMAS" CARDIGAN
(Shown on page 97)

You will need a cardigan, one 11" x 16" piece each of 10 mesh waste canvas and lightweight non-fusible interfacing, embroidery floss (see color key), masking tape, thread, embroidery hoop (optional), tweezers, and a spray bottle filled with water.

Referring to photo for placement, follow Working on Waste Canvas, page 159, to stitch design on cardigan. Use 4 strands of floss for Cross Stitch, 2 for Backstitch, and 3 for French Knots.

FESTIVE REINDEER SHIRT KIT
(Shown on page 96)

You will need a children's polyester blend sweatshirt, black Sulky® Iron-on transfer pen, a piece of plain white paper, Crayola® Fabric Crayons (available at craft stores), two 12mm oval wiggle eyes, acrylic jewels, jewel glue, black permanent felt-tip pen with fine point, red and green felt-tip pens with fine points, a paper gift bag with handles, a small cellophane gift bag, a small piece of heavy white paper for tag, a hole punch, and curling ribbon.

ASSEMBLING KIT
1. Wash, dry, and press shirt. Use transfer pen to trace reindeer pattern, page 105, onto plain white paper. Place shirt, reindeer design, and glue in paper gift bag.
2. For tag, use black, red, and green pens to write message and to draw designs on heavy paper piece. Punch a small hole in 1 corner of tag.
3. Place crayons, wiggle eyes, acrylic jewels, and black permanent pen in cellophane bag. Tie several ribbon lengths together into a bow around top of bag. Thread another ribbon length through ribbon around bag; tie into a bow around handle of paper gift bag. Curl ribbon ends. Thread tag onto ribbon.
4. Give decorating instructions with kit.

DECORATING SHIRT
1. Use crayons to color reindeer design. Cutting as close to outline as possible, cut out design.
2. Follow crayon manufacturer's instructions to transfer colored design to shirt front.
3. If desired, use black permanent pen to draw over outlines and detail lines on design to darken.
4. Glue wiggle eyes and jewels to shirt; allow to dry.

Design size worked over 10 mesh waste canvas — 7" x 12".

"MERRY CHRISTMAS" (70w x 120h)

X	DMC	B'ST	COLOR	X	DMC	COLOR	X	DMC	COLOR
✚	blanc		white	■	666	red	▬	912	lt green
❈	304		vy dk red	✳	725	dk yellow	■	932	blue
▲	310	✎	black	▯	726	yellow	▲	948	lt peach
▮	317		dk grey	✖	754	peach	◆	3072	lt grey
▬	321		dk red	◉	760	pink	✳	3752	lt blue
✖	434		brown	✩	761	lt pink		3799	vy dk grey
▨	435		lt brown	▲	909	dk green	◉	310	French Knot
♥	648		grey	✚	911	green			

REINDEER

FEATHER TREE SWEATER (Shown on page 95)

For sweater with approx. 7¾" x 11¾" tree design, you will need a medium-gauge stockinette stitch cotton sweater (measuring across our medium-gauge sweater, there are 7 stitches to the inch); red, dark red, dark green, brown, and black embroidery floss; a 5" square of dark green fabric for pot; assorted buttons and washable charms; paper-backed fusible web; white vinegar; tracing paper; and fabric glue.

1. Unwrap floss skeins and soak for a few minutes in a mixture of 1 cup water and 1 tablespoon vinegar. Allow to dry.
2. (**Note:** Refer to photo for remaining steps.) Determine placement of design on sweater and mark placement for top of tree with a pin.
3. (**Note:** When stitching tree, refer to **Diagram** for length and placement of stitching lines; follow knit of sweater to keep stitches even. Use 12 strands of floss.) Use brown floss to work Running Stitch, page 159, for trunk. Use brown floss to work Running Stitch for branches. For needles on branches, use dark green floss and work long straight stitches.

4. For pot, trace pattern onto tracing paper; cut out. Follow manufacturer's instructions to fuse web to wrong side of fabric piece. Use pattern to cut pot from fabric. Fuse pot to sweater below tree.
5. Use 3 strands of black floss and Blanket Stitch, page 159, to stitch along edges of pot.
6. Use 6 strands of dark red floss to sew buttons to branches. Use 6 strands of red floss to sew charms to branches.
7. For each bow, thread needle with 9" of red floss (6 strands). Thread needle under 1 stitch of sweater; if desired, thread needle through loop of charm. Knot each end of floss; tie ends of floss into a bow. Use glue to secure knot of bow.

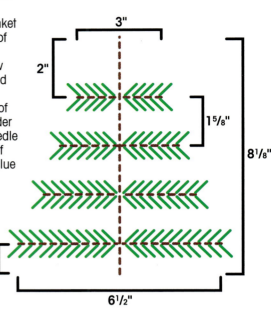

DIAGRAM

KIDS' CHRISTMAS SHOES (Shown on page 97)

MOON SANTA SHOES
You will need a pair of children's red lace-up canvas shoes; white, dark yellow, peach, pink, green, and black fabric paint; iridescent glitter dimensional fabric paint; small fabric paintbrushes; tracing paper; graphite transfer paper; ribbon to replace laces; and liquid fray preventative.

1. Remove laces from shoes.
2. Trace Santa pattern onto tracing paper. Use transfer paper to transfer Santa onto toe of each shoe, reversing pattern for 1 shoe.
3. (**Note:** Refer to photo for painting. Allow to dry between colors.) For each shoe, paint beard, hair, and hat trim white, hat green, face peach, and star dark yellow. Paint additional stars as desired on sides and back of shoe. Paint a large pink dot for cheek and a small black dot for eye. Follow paint manufacturer's instructions to heat-set designs if necessary.
4. Use paintbrush and glitter paint to paint over beards, hair, hat trims, hats, and stars.
5. Cut lengths of ribbon same length as laces. Re-lace shoes with ribbons. Trim ribbon ends and apply fray preventative to cut ends.

DOTTED SHOES
You will need a pair of children's white slip-on canvas shoes, red and green fabric paint, iridescent glitter dimensional fabric paint, fabric paintbrush, 1 yd of ribbon for bows, thread to match ribbon, liquid fray preventative, and fabric glue.

1. Use paintbrush and glitter paint to paint shoes; allow to dry. Use tip of paintbrush handle to paint red and green dots on toes of shoes; allow to dry.
2. Cut ribbon in half. Tie each length into a bow. Trim ribbon ends, apply fray preventative to cut ends, and allow to dry. Tack bows to shoes; glue streamers in place.

CANDY-STRIPED SHOES
You will need a pair of children's red lace-up canvas shoes, white fabric paint, liner paintbrush, red ribbon to replace laces, and liquid fray preventative.

1. Remove laces from shoes.
2. Paint diagonal white stripes approx. ⅛" apart on trim of shoes; allow to dry. Follow paint manufacturer's instructions to heat-set stripes if necessary.
3. For laces, follow Step 5 of Moon Santa Shoes instructions.

CANDY CANE SHOES
You will need a pair of children's green lace-up canvas shoes, white and red fabric paint, iridescent glitter dimensional fabric paint, small fabric paintbrushes, tracing paper, graphite transfer paper, ribbon to replace laces, and liquid fray preventative.

1. Remove laces from shoes.
2. Trace candy cane and heart pattern onto tracing paper. Use transfer paper to transfer design onto toe of each shoe.
3. (**Note:** Refer to photo for painting. Allow to dry between colors.) For each shoe, paint candy canes white and heart red. Paint red stripes on candy canes. Follow paint manufacturer's instructions to heat-set designs if necessary.
4. Use paintbrush and glitter paint to paint over candy canes and hearts.
5. For laces, follow Step 5 of Moon Santa Shoes instructions.

WINTER FOREST JUMPER
(Shown on page 94)

You will need a jumper with bib that measures at least 9" square, one 12" square each of 10 mesh waste canvas and lightweight non-fusible interfacing, embroidery floss (see color key), masking tape, thread, embroidery hoop (optional), tweezers, and a spray bottle filled with water.

Referring to photo for placement, follow Working on Waste Canvas, page 159, to stitch design on jumper. Use 5 strands of floss for Cross Stitch.

"ORNAMENT-AL" SHIRT (Shown on page 98)

You will need a white blouse with collar and cuffed sleeves, desired colors of fabric paint (we used red, green, and metallic gold), fabric paintbrushes, metallic gold appliqué thread, white thread, desired trims for ornaments (we used flat trims, fringes, rickrack, string sequins, half pearls, rhinestones, acrylic jewels, cord, beads, and a snowflake appliqué), black permanent felt-tip pen with fine point, fabric marking pencil, tracing paper, drawing compass, jewel glue (optional), and decorative buttons (optional).

1. (**Note:** Refer to photo for all steps.) Draw a 3" dia. and a 3½" dia. circle on tracing paper. Trace ornament patterns onto tracing paper. Cut out patterns.
2. Use fabric marking pencil to lightly draw around patterns on shirt as desired.

3. Paint ornaments desired colors; allow to dry.
4. Follow manufacturer's instructions to heat-set ornaments if necessary.
5. Use fabric marking pencil to draw an approx. ⅜" dia. loop for hanger at top of each ornament; use black pen to draw over each circle.
6. Use a ruler and fabric marking pencil to draw a line from top of each ornament hanger to shoulder seam of shirt. Using gold thread in top of sewing machine and white thread in bobbin, use a decorative stitch to machine stitch along drawn lines and ¼" from outer edges of collar and cuffs.
7. Sew or glue trims to ornaments as desired.
8. If desired, replace shirt buttons with decorative buttons.

WINTER FOREST (79w x 79h)			
X	**DMC**	**ANC.**	**COLOR**
★	ecru	387	ecru
▬	310	403	black
■	321	9046	red
✗	433	358	dk brown
▲	434	310	brown
◆	436	1045	lt brown
✕	561	212	dk green
♥	562	210	green
▬	3731	76	pink

Design size worked over 10 mesh waste canvas — 8" x 8".

PIECED STAR TUNIC (Shown on page 101)

You will need a sweatshirt (waist of sweatshirt just above ribbing must be large enough to fit around hips); light, medium, and dark fabrics for pieced blocks and borders (see **Diagram**, this page, and photo); thread to coordinate with fabrics; acetate for templates; permanent felt-tip pen with fine point; and a chalk pencil (optional).

1. Wash, dry, and press shirt and fabrics.
2. Cut ribbing from bottom of shirt.
3. To determine length of pieced band, measure around bottom edge of shirt; add 1/2". To determine number of pieced blocks needed, divide band measurement by 5 1/2 (approx. finished width of 1 block) and round up to the nearest whole number.
4. (**Note:** Patterns include a 1/4" seam allowance.) For templates, use permanent pen to trace patterns onto acetate. Label and cut out templates.
5. (**Note:** Follow Steps 5 - 11 and refer to **Diagram**, this page, and photo to assemble each star block. Refer to patterns for number of pieces to cut from each fabric.) For each piece, place template on wrong side of fabric, matching arrow on template to grain of fabric. Use a #2 or chalk pencil to lightly draw around template. Cut out pieces. Use a ruler and pencil to draw a seamline with an accurate 1/4" seam allowance on wrong side of each piece.
6. Arrange pieces to form 1 block.
7. (**Note:** For each sewing step, match right sides and raw edges and pin fabric pieces together. For Steps 7 - 9, sew along drawn seamlines, sewing from outer end of seamline toward inner end of seamline and stopping 2 - 3 stitches from center to allow center of star to lie flat; press all seam allowances in the same direction.) For 1 half of star, sew 1 light and 1 medium A piece together along 1 edge (**Fig. 1**). Sew a second light A piece to opposite side of medium A piece (**Fig. 2**).

Fig. 1 **Fig. 2**

8. For remaining half of star, repeat Step 7 with 2 medium A pieces and 1 light A piece.
9. Keeping points of pieces out of the way when stitching, sew halves of star together, stitching from left edge toward center, then from right edge toward center (**Fig. 3**).

Fig. 3

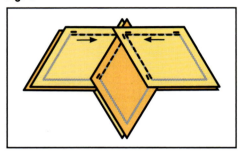

10. Sewing along drawn seamlines in the direction shown in **Fig. 4**, sew 1 dark A piece along 1 edge of star. Pivot dark A piece and sew adjacent edge of piece to adjacent edge of star (**Fig. 5**). Repeat to join remaining dark A pieces to star.

Fig. 4

Fig. 5

11. Sew 1 B piece to each side of star to complete block (see **Diagram**).
12. Referring to photo, sew blocks together to form a strip. Sew another B piece to each end of strip (**Fig. 6**).

Fig. 6

13. Trim ends of strip straight across so that length of strip equals band length measurement determined in Step 3.

DIAGRAM

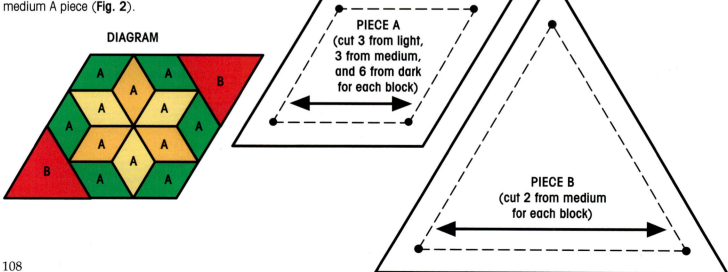

PIECE A
(cut 3 from light, 3 from medium, and 6 from dark for each block)

PIECE B
(cut 2 from medium for each block)

PIECED STAR TUNIC (Continued)

14. For borders, cut two 1¼"w strips, one 2"w strip, and one 6½"w strip of fabric same length as pieced strip.

15. (**Note:** For Steps 15 - 18, use a ¼" seam allowance.) Sew one 1¼"w strip to top and 1 to bottom of pieced strip. Sew 2"w strip to bottom of bottom 1¼"w strip.

16. Matching right sides and short edges, fold pieced strips in half. Sew short edges together to form a loop; press seam open. Repeat for 6½"w fabric strip.

17. Matching wrong sides and raw edges, press 6½"w loop in half. Aligning seams, sew raw edges of pressed loop to bottom of pieced loop.

18. With seam of pieced loop at 1 side fold of shirt, sew loop to bottom of shirt; press seam allowance toward loop.

BERIBBONED ACCESSORIES (Shown on page 98)

PURSE

For an approx. 8½" x 5¼" purse, you will need a 10" x 16" piece of fusible woven interfacing, a 12" x 18" piece of fabric for purse lining (we used black satin), eleven 16" lengths of ⅞"w ribbons, sixteen to twenty 10" lengths of ⅝"w to 1⅜"w ribbons (enough to cover length of interfacing), one 11" length of ⅝"w decorative woven ribbon for trim along bottom of flap, 3" of ⅛" dia. twisted cord, a ⅝" dia. shank button, a 3" long tassel, thread to match ribbons and lining fabric, pressing cloth, permanent felt-tip pen with fine point, spring-type clothespins, and fabric glue.

1. For ribbon backing, use permanent pen to make marks at 1" intervals along all edges on fusible side of interfacing. With long edges at top and bottom and fusible side up, place interfacing on ironing board; pin corners to ironing board.

2. (**Note:** Refer to photo for remaining steps. For Steps 2 and 3, place ribbons right side up on interfacing; use marks along edges of interfacing as a guide for keeping ribbons straight.) For lengthwise ribbons, center one 16" ribbon lengthwise on interfacing; pin ends to ironing board. Placing ribbons side by side, pin remaining 16" ribbons to ironing board over interfacing.

3. For crosswise ribbons, lay 10" ribbons side by side in desired order across lengthwise ribbons. One at a time, weave crosswise ribbons through lengthwise ribbons. Straighten ribbons, eliminating any gaps, and pin ends in place.

4. (**Note:** Use pressing cloth for each pressing step.) Follow manufacturer's instructions to fuse ribbons to interfacing. Trim edges of interfacing even with edges of woven ribbon.

5. Cut a piece from lining fabric same size as woven ribbon piece. Place woven ribbon piece and lining fabric piece right sides together. Using a ¼" seam allowance, sew pieces together along long edges and 1 short edge. Press remaining short edges of ribbon piece and lining ½" to wrong side. Clip corners, turn right side out, and press. Sew final closure by hand.

6. To form purse, press 1 short edge (bottom edge) of lined ribbon piece 4½" toward lining. Concealing edges of lining, hand stitch sides of purse together.

7. For ribbon trim on flap, press ends of 11" ribbon length ½" to wrong side; glue to secure. Matching 1 long edge of ribbon to bottom edge of flap, center and glue ribbon along bottom edge of flap; glue ends to inside of flap. Secure ribbon with clothespins until glue is dry.

8. For button closure, fold twisted cord in half. Wrap thread tightly around cord ⅜" from ends; knot and trim thread. Open flap and center loop along edge of flap with loop extending ⅞" beyond flap; securely hand-sew loop in place. Close flap; use a pin to mark placement of button. Sew button to purse.

9. Sew hanging loop of tassel inside top fold of purse lining.

BELT

You will need a 2"w belt, ¼"w to 1"w coordinating ribbons to decorate belt, 1¾"w matching grosgrain ribbon to line belt, a 3" long tassel, a ⅛" hole punch, hot glue gun, glue sticks, and liquid fray preventative.

1. (**Note:** Refer to photo for all steps.) For lengthwise ribbons, measure length of belt; add 3". Cut 2 lengths from coordinating ribbons the determined measurement. Leaving belt holes exposed, center ribbons lengthwise on right side of belt. At buckle end, fold 1½" of each ribbon through buckle to back of belt and glue in place.

2. For crosswise ribbons, cut desired number of 3½" lengths from coordinating ribbons. Leaving belt holes exposed, arrange ribbons on belt until desired spacing is achieved. Fold ¾" at top end of each crosswise ribbon to back of belt and glue in place.

3. Weave crosswise ribbons over and under top lengthwise ribbon, gluing top lengthwise ribbon to belt at points where crosswise ribbons overlap top ribbon. Repeat for bottom lengthwise ribbon.

4. Pulling ribbons taut, fold bottom end of each crosswise ribbon to back of belt and glue in place.

5. At pointed end of belt, fold ends of lengthwise ribbons to back of belt and glue in place, trimming ends to fit.

6. To cover loop of belt, measure around loop; add 1". Cut a length of coordinating ribbon the determined length. Overlapping ribbon ends at back of belt, wrap ribbon around loop and glue in place.

7. For belt lining, cut a length of 1¾"w ribbon 1" longer than belt. At 1 end of ribbon, press edges of ribbon to wrong side to match shape of pointed end of belt; glue to secure. Matching pointed end of ribbon to pointed end of belt, center and glue ribbon to back of belt, leaving 3" at buckle end unglued. At buckle end, trim ribbon even with end of belt. Press end of ribbon ½" to wrong side and glue in place.

8. Use hole punch to punch holes in ribbon lining to correspond with holes in belt. Apply fray preventative to holes in ribbon.

9. Cut hanging loop of tassel apart at top. Glue ends of loop inside bottom of loop of belt, trimming excess.

HAT

You will need a hat, ¼"w to 1½"w decorative ribbons, a large shank button, hot glue gun, glue sticks, and liquid fray preventative.

1. (**Note:** Refer to photo for all steps.) For band, measure around crown of hat; add 1". Cut wide ribbon the determined length. Overlapping ends at back, glue ribbon around crown of hat.

2. For band streamers, cut 2 lengths of wide ribbon desired length. Glue 1 end of each ribbon to back of hat over overlapped ends of ribbon on hat; trim remaining ends.

3. For bow loops, cut desired number of 21" ribbon lengths. With 1 ribbon end at top and 1 end at bottom of layers, fold 1 ribbon length into thirds; glue ribbon layers together at center to secure. Repeat with remaining 21" ribbon lengths. For bow center, cut a 5" length of wide ribbon. Place bow loops together and wrap 5" ribbon length around center; overlap ends at back and glue to secure. Glue bow to hat over tops of streamers.

4. Glue button to center of bow. Apply fray preventative to cut ends of ribbons.

POINSETTIA AND HOLLY JACKET (Shown on page 99)

You will need a dry-cleanable wool jacket to accommodate 5½" x 12½" design; red wool felt; dark yellow, red, green, dark green, and brown tapestry yarn; red embroidery floss; crewel needle; Sulky® Heat-Away™ Brush-Off Stabilizer (available at sewing supply stores); sewing thread; tracing paper; dry-cleanable paper-backed fusible web; and a permanent felt-tip pen with fine point.

1. Dry clean jacket, felt, yarn, and embroidery floss (to prevent dyes from fading onto jacket).
2. (**Note:** Refer to photo for Steps 2 - 9.) Leaving a 2½" space between stems for poinsettia, use pen to trace patterns for holly onto a 7" x 14" piece of stabilizer (**Fig. 1**). Pin pattern to jacket; baste in place.

3. (**Note:** Embroidery stitch diagrams are shown on page 159.) Follow stitch key and use 1 strand of yarn to work holly design over stabilizer.
4. Follow manufacturer's instructions to remove stabilizer.
5. Trace poinsettia petal patterns onto tracing paper; cut out.
6. Follow manufacturer's instructions to fuse web to 1 side (wrong side) of felt. Use patterns to cut indicated numbers of petals from felt; remove paper backing.
7. Referring to **Fig. 2**, arrange petals on jacket; fuse in place.

8. Using 2 strands of red embroidery floss, work Blanket Stitch along edges of petals.
9. Using 1 strand of dark yellow yarn, work French Knots in center of poinsettia.
10. Dry clean jacket when necessary.

Fig. 1

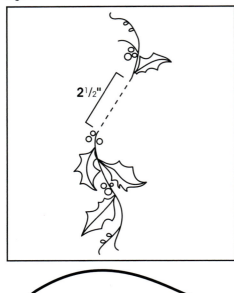

Fig. 2

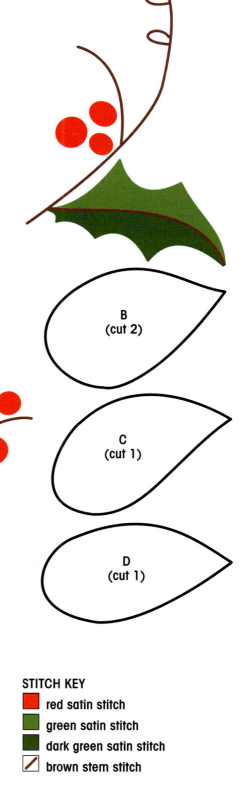

A
(cut 3,
1 in reverse)

B
(cut 2)

C
(cut 1)

D
(cut 1)

STITCH KEY
- 🟥 red satin stitch
- 🟩 green satin stitch
- 🟢 dark green satin stitch
- ╱ brown stem stitch

MEN'S APPLIQUÉD SWEATER (Shown on page 95)

You will need a sweater, fabric scraps for appliqués, lightweight fusible interfacing, paper-backed fusible web, coordinating embroidery floss, coordinating tapestry yarn (optional), and tracing paper.

1. Trace large tree, small tree, trunk, and bear patterns onto tracing paper; cut out.
2. Follow manufacturer's instructions to fuse interfacing, then web, to wrong sides of fabric scraps.
3. Use patterns to cut 2 large trees, 2 small trees, 2 trunks, and 1 bear from fabrics.
4. Remove paper backing and arrange appliqués on sweater front; fuse in place.
5. Use 4 strands of floss to work Blanket Stitch, page 159, over raw edges of appliqués. Use 12 strands of floss to work French Knot, page 159, for bear's eye.
6. If desired, use 2 strands of yarn to work Overcast Stitches, page 159, 1/2" apart along edge of sweater neck.

BEAR

TRUNK

SMALL TREE

LARGE TREE

YO-YO WREATH SWEATSHIRT (Shown on page 100)

For shirt with approx. 9 1/2" dia. wreath design, you will need a sweatshirt, a 10" square of fabric for wreath background, fabric scraps for yo-yos, a 2" x 20" torn fabric strip for bow, paper-backed fusible web, thread to coordinate with yo-yo fabrics, coordinating embroidery floss, assorted buttons, artist's tracing paper, dressmaker's tracing paper, safety pin, and a drawing compass.

1. (**Note:** Refer to photo for all steps.) Follow manufacturer's instructions to fuse web to wrong side of background fabric. Draw an 8" dia. circle on paper backing side of fabric; cut out circle. Remove paper backing and fuse circle to shirt.
2. Trace "Noel" pattern onto artist's tracing paper. Use dressmaker's tracing paper to transfer letters to center of circle on shirt. Use 6 strands of floss and Running Stitch, page 159, to stitch over letters. Remove any visible tracing marks.
3. For yo-yo patterns, draw a 3 1/2" dia. circle for large yo-yos, a 3" dia. circle for

medium yo-yos, and a 2 1/2" dia. circle for small yo-yos on artist's tracing paper; cut out.
4. (**Note:** Follow Step 4 to make enough yo-yos to cover edge of circle on shirt. We made 5 large, 6 medium, and 12 small yo-yos.) For each yo-yo, use pattern to cut a circle from fabric scrap. Use a double strand of thread to baste 1/8" from edge of fabric circle. Pull ends of thread to tightly gather circle; knot thread and trim ends. Fold raw edge to inside of circle. Flatten yo-yo with gathers at center (right side).
5. With yo-yos right side up and overlapping yo-yos slightly, arrange yo-yos along edge of fabric circle to form wreath; pin in place. Place a button over center of 1 yo-yo. Sew button and yo-yo to shirt at the same time. Repeat to sew remaining yo-yos to shirt.
6. Tie fabric strip into a bow. Use safety pin inside shirt to pin bow to shirt below wreath.

THE TASTES OF CHRISTMAS

As much as any beloved Christmas tradition, sumptuous holiday foods bring joy to our gatherings in a deliciously heartwarming way. We enjoy using a combination of old favorites and new recipes to create savory appetizers, glorious holiday meals, and delectable desserts — ensuring that the spirit of our family celebrations will endure with each coming generation. And when we share flavorful gifts from the kitchen, they're sure to be doubly appreciated when presented in creative handcrafted packaging. Whether you sample only a few of these delightful treats or prepare an entire buffet, we hope each dish will bring to mind the tastes of Christmas.

COZY LITTLE BUFFET

Home for the holidays — the words themselves awaken images of smiling faces, crackling fires, and holiday tables laden with hearty, heartwarming foods. During this festive season, generous portions of love, laughter, and Christmas cheer are served along with each delicious meal. To help you create a warm and cozy setting, this homestyle menu brings you a banquet of favorite holiday dishes.

A spicy stuffing makes moist Herb-Pecan Stuffed Turkey Breasts a succulent alternative to traditional holiday turkey. Kissed with a hint of orange, tart and tangy Cranberry-Port Sauce is the perfect condiment to serve with this entrée.

HERB-PECAN STU
TURKEY BREAS

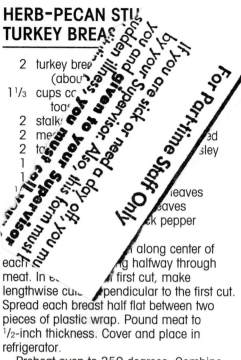

2   turkey bre
    (abou
1 1/3 cups cc
       too
2   stalk
2   me
2   to   sley
1
                            eaves
                            eaves
                            k pepper

along center of
each   ig halfway through
meat. In e.   first cut, make
lengthwise cu   pendicular to the first cut.
Spread each breast half flat between two
pieces of plastic wrap. Pound meat to
1/2-inch thickness. Cover and place in
refrigerator.

Preheat oven to 350 degrees. Combine
remaining ingredients in a food processor.
Process 15 to 20 seconds. Spread herb
mixture over each breast half. Beginning at
one long edge, roll each breast half jellyroll-
style; tie with twine. Place on a rack in a
roasting pan. Pour 1/2 inch of water into pan
(to add moisture and to help prevent
burning of meat drippings). Insert meat
thermometer into center of 1 breast
half. Loosely cover meat with foil. Roast
1 1/2 hours. Remove foil and twine. Continue
roasting 30 to 45 minutes or until
thermometer registers 180 degrees. Allow
meat to stand 15 minutes before slicing.
Serve warm with Cranberry-Port Sauce.
Yield: about 10 to 12 servings

CRANBERRY-PORT SAUCE

1   cup sugar
1/2 cup ruby port wine
1   package (12 ounces) fresh
    cranberries
1   tablespoon grated orange zest
4   tablespoons butter or margarine
1/4 cup chicken broth

In a medium saucepan over low heat, stir
sugar and wine until sugar dissolves; add
cranberries and orange zest. Increase heat
to medium-high and bring to a boil. Cook
about 10 minutes or until berries pop.
Reduce heat to medium-low. Adding one
tablespoon butter at a time, stir until well
blended. Stir in chicken broth. Serve warm
with Herb-Pecan Stuffed Turkey Breasts.
Yield: about 3 cups sauce

Puréed Tomato and Leek Bisque features the subtle flavor of fresh leeks
blended with tomatoes and fresh basil. Buttermilk and mashed sweet potatoes
add richness to tender Homestyle Sweet Potato Biscuits.

TOMATO AND LEEK BISQUE

1/4 cup olive oil
8   cups chopped leeks, white and pale
    green parts only (about 3 to
    4 leeks)
2   stalks celery, coarsely chopped
1   clove garlic, chopped
2   cans (14 1/2 ounces each) whole
    peeled tomatoes
1   can (14 1/2 ounces) chicken broth
3/4 cup dry white wine
1   tablespoon fresh lemon juice
1 1/2 tablespoons chopped fresh basil
    leaves **or** 2 teaspoons dried basil
    leaves
1/2 teaspoon salt
1/4 teaspoon ground white pepper
3/4 cup whipping cream

    Fresh or dried basil leaves to garnish

In a heavy Dutch oven, heat oil, leeks,
celery, and garlic over medium-high heat;
cook about 8 to 10 minutes or until leeks
are soft. Add tomatoes, chicken broth, wine,
and lemon juice. Bring mixture to a boil;
reduce heat to medium-low, cover, and
simmer 30 minutes. Remove from heat; add
1 1/2 tablespoons fresh basil, salt, and white
pepper. Purée soup mixture in a food
processor until smooth. Return soup to
Dutch oven over low heat. Stirring

occasionally, add cream and simmer about
10 minutes or until thickened. Garnish with
basil. Serve warm.
Yield: about 9 cups soup

HOMESTYLE SWEET POTATO
BISCUITS

2   cups all-purpose flour
2 1/2 teaspoons baking powder
1/2 teaspoon salt
1/4 cup butter or margarine, softened
1/4 cup vegetable shortening
1   cup cooked, mashed sweet potatoes
5   to 7 tablespoons buttermilk

Preheat oven to 450 degrees. In a large
bowl, combine flour, baking powder, and
salt. Using a pastry blender or 2 knives, cut
in butter and shortening until well blended.
Add sweet potatoes and enough buttermilk
to make a soft dough. Lightly knead dough
about 20 times. On a lightly floured surface,
roll out dough to 1/2-inch thickness. Use a
2-inch biscuit cutter to cut out biscuits.
Bake on an ungreased baking sheet 12 to
15 minutes or until biscuits are light golden
brown. Serve warm.
Yield: about 2 dozen biscuits

Delicate mushrooms are a tasty surprise in our Wild Rice Dressing (*left*). Orange zest and crystallized ginger awaken the flavor of Butternut Squash and Apple Purée (*right*), and Caramelized Onions have a buttery brown sugar glaze.

WILD RICE DRESSING

- 1   cup minced onions
- 1   cup finely chopped celery
- 1/2 cup olive oil
- 1/2 cup chopped green pepper
- 2   green onions, finely chopped
- 1   tablespoon chopped fresh parsley
- 1   clove garlic, minced
- 1   teaspoon dried basil leaves
- 1   teaspoon ground black pepper
- 1/2 teaspoon ground sage
- 1/2 teaspoon dried rosemary leaves
- 1/2 teaspoon dried thyme leaves
- 1   package (6.25 ounces) long grain and wild rice, cooked according to package directions
- 2   cups corn bread crumbs
- 1   can (14 1/2 ounces) chicken broth
- 1   cup sliced fresh mushrooms

Preheat oven to 350 degrees. In a heavy large skillet over medium heat, cook minced onions and celery in olive oil until vegetables are almost tender. Add green pepper, green onions, parsley, and garlic to skillet; continue cooking 2 minutes, stirring frequently. Remove from heat; stir in basil, black pepper, sage, rosemary, and thyme until well blended. In a large bowl, combine onion mixture and remaining ingredients; spoon into a greased 8 x 11 1/2-inch baking dish. Bake 35 to 40 minutes or until lightly browned.
Yield: about 8 to 10 servings

BUTTERNUT SQUASH AND APPLE PURÉE

- 1   butternut squash (about 2 1/2 pounds), peeled, seeded, and cut into 1/2-inch cubes
- 1   tart baking apple, peeled, cored, and coarsely chopped
- 2   tablespoons butter or margarine
- 1   tablespoon honey
- 1   teaspoon grated orange zest
- 1   teaspoon finely chopped crystallized ginger
- 1/8 teaspoon ground nutmeg

In a heavy large saucepan, cover squash and apple with water. Cover and cook over medium-high heat 15 to 20 minutes or until tender; drain. Reduce heat to medium-low; add remaining ingredients to squash mixture. Stirring constantly, cook squash mixture until smooth or about 10 minutes. Serve warm.
Yield: about 8 servings

CARAMELIZED ONIONS

- 2 pounds pearl onions, peeled
- 1/4 cup butter or margarine
- 2 tablespoons firmly packed brown sugar
- 1 tablespoon grated orange zest
- 1/8 teaspoon salt
- 1/8 teaspoon paprika

In a large saucepan, cover onions with water. Cover and cook over medium-high heat 10 to 12 minutes or until onions are almost tender; drain. In a heavy large skillet, combine onions and butter. Stirring frequently, cook over medium-high heat about 30 minutes or until golden brown. In a small bowl, combine remaining ingredients. Add brown sugar mixture to onions. Stirring constantly, cook until onions are evenly coated and browned. Remove from heat. Serve warm.

Yield: about 6 servings

PARMESAN SPINACH AND ARTICHOKES

- 1/2 cup chopped green onions
- 1/2 cup chopped celery
- 1/2 cup butter or margarine
- 2 packages (10 ounces each) frozen chopped spinach, cooked and drained
- 2 cups sour cream
- 1 can (14 ounces) artichoke hearts, drained and chopped
- 1/2 teaspoon hot pepper sauce
- 1/2 teaspoon salt
- 1/4 teaspoon ground black pepper
- 8 ounces bacon, cooked, crumbled, and divided
- 1/2 cup freshly grated Parmesan cheese

Preheat oven to 350 degrees. In a small saucepan over medium heat, cook onions and celery in butter until vegetables are tender. In a greased 2-quart baking dish, combine onion mixture, spinach, sour cream, artichoke hearts, hot pepper sauce, salt, and pepper. Reserving 2 tablespoons bacon for garnish, stir remaining bacon into spinach mixture. Sprinkle cheese over top of casserole. Bake 30 to 40 minutes or until edges are lightly browned. Garnish with reserved bacon.

Yield: about 8 to 10 servings

Topped with crisp bacon pieces and freshly grated cheese, creamy Parmesan Spinach and Artichokes will be a family favorite.

HERBED ZUCCHINI BUNDLES

1 pound unpeeled zucchini, cut into 3-inch-long by ⅛-inch-thick julienne strips
2 medium sweet red peppers, sliced into ten ¼-inch rings
2 tablespoons butter or margarine
1 teaspoon dried marjoram leaves
¼ teaspoon dried oregano leaves

Divide zucchini strips into 10 equal bundles and place a pepper ring around each bundle. Place in a microwave-safe baking dish and cover with plastic wrap. Make 2 slits in top of plastic wrap. Microwave on medium-high power (90%) 3½ to 4 minutes, turning dish halfway through cooking time. Remove dish from microwave. Place butter, marjoram, and oregano in a small microwave-safe bowl. Microwave on high power (100%) 20 to 30 seconds or until butter is melted; pour over zucchini. Serve warm.
Yield: 10 servings

Festive Herbed Zucchini Bundles are quick and easy to prepare in the microwave.

Remind guests to save room for Deep-Dish Berry Pie. The old-fashioned treat has a treasure of cherries, blueberries, and raspberries hidden beneath a flaky sugar-coated crust.

DEEP-DISH BERRY PIE

CRUST
2¼ cups all-purpose flour
½ teaspoon salt
½ cup vegetable shortening, chilled
¼ cup butter or margarine, chilled
¼ cup ice water

FILLING
2 cans (16 ounces each) tart red pitted cherries, drained
1 package (12 ounces) frozen whole blueberries
1 package (12 ounces) frozen whole red raspberries
1½ cups plus 2 tablespoons sugar, divided
2 tablespoons fresh lemon juice
¼ teaspoon ground cinnamon
⅓ cup cornstarch
⅓ cup cold water
2 tablespoons butter or margarine, chilled
1 egg white, beaten

For crust, combine flour and salt in a medium bowl. Using a pastry blender or 2 knives, cut in shortening and butter until mixture resembles coarse meal. Sprinkle with water; mix until a soft dough forms. Shape dough into a ball; divide dough in half. Cover each half with plastic wrap and chill while preparing filling.

For filling, combine cherries, blueberries, raspberries, 1½ cups sugar, lemon juice, and cinnamon in a large saucepan over medium-high heat; stir until well blended. In a small bowl, combine cornstarch and water. Stirring constantly as fruit mixture begins to boil, add cornstarch mixture. Stir until mixture thickens. Remove from heat; place pan in cool water in sink. Allow filling to cool while rolling out dough. Use a rolling pin to roll out half of dough between pieces of plastic wrap to ⅛-inch thickness. Transfer to a 9-inch deep-dish pie plate. Leaving ½ inch of dough over edge, use a sharp knife to trim dough. Cover crust and chill in refrigerator while filling cools to room temperature.

Preheat oven to 375 degrees. Roll out remaining dough for top crust. Spoon filling into bottom pie crust. Cut butter into small pieces and place over filling. Place top crust over filling; crimp edges of crust and make several slits in top. Brush with egg white and sprinkle remaining 2 tablespoons sugar over crust. Bake on a baking sheet 50 to 60 minutes or until crust is golden brown. (If edge of crust browns too quickly, cover edge with aluminum foil.) Serve warm.
Yield: about 10 servings

PUMPKIN CHEESECAKE WITH GINGER CREAM TOPPING

CRUST
¾ cup graham cracker crumbs
½ cup finely chopped pecans
¼ cup firmly packed brown sugar
¼ cup granulated sugar
4 tablespoons butter or margarine, melted

FILLING
1 can (16 ounces) pumpkin
3 eggs
½ cup firmly packed brown sugar
1 teaspoon vanilla extract
1½ teaspoons ground cinnamon
½ teaspoon ground ginger
½ teaspoon ground nutmeg
¼ teaspoon salt
3 packages (8 ounces each) cream cheese, softened
½ cup granulated sugar
1 tablespoon all-purpose flour

TOPPING
1 cup whipping cream
1 cup sour cream
2 tablespoons sugar
3 tablespoons dark rum
½ teaspoon vanilla extract
¼ cup minced crystallized ginger

16 pecan halves to garnish

For crust, combine cracker crumbs, pecans, and sugars in a medium bowl until well blended; stir in melted butter. Press mixture into bottom and halfway up sides of a greased 9-inch springform pan; chill 1 hour.

Preheat oven to 350 degrees. For filling, beat pumpkin, eggs, brown sugar, vanilla, spices, and salt in a medium bowl. In a large bowl, beat cream cheese and granulated sugar until well blended. Beat flour and pumpkin mixture into cream cheese mixture until smooth. Pour filling into crust; bake 50 to 55 minutes or until center is set. Cool completely in pan.

For topping, chill a medium bowl and beaters from an electric mixer in freezer. In chilled bowl, whip cream, sour cream, and sugar until stiff peaks form. Fold in rum, vanilla, and ginger. Spread topping over cheesecake. Cover and refrigerate overnight.

To serve, remove sides of pan and garnish top with pecan halves.
Yield: 16 servings

A luscious after-dinner treat, Pumpkin Cheesecake with Ginger Cream Topping has an irresistible whipped topping spiked with dark rum.

A GLORIOUS GATHERING

Amid the gaiety and excitement of the Christmas season, we delight in opening our homes to friends and family. Merriment and laughter abound at these glorious gatherings, and scrumptious tidbits are generously served with each cup of holiday cheer. The tempting assortment of foods on the following pages will help you create memorable appetizers for the people you love.

Pepper and Olive Crostini feature a marinated mixture of roasted red and green peppers, stuffed green olives, and tangy capers on slices of crispy French bread. Cherry Tomatoes Stuffed with Basil Cheese are delicious little bites, and spirited Cherry-Mocha Warmer is laced with crème de cacao and cherry brandy.

PEPPER AND OLIVE CROSTINI

- 2 large green peppers
- 2 large sweet red peppers
- 1 jar (5 ounces) stuffed green olives, drained and sliced
- 2 tablespoons minced red onion
- 1 tablespoon drained capers
- 6 tablespoons olive oil, divided
- 1 tablespoon balsamic vinegar
- 4 tablespoons butter
- 1 clove garlic, minced
- 2 loaves 2½-inch diameter French bread, sliced into ½-inch slices

To roast peppers, cut in half lengthwise and remove seeds and membranes. Place skin side up on an ungreased baking sheet; flatten with hand. Broil about 3 inches from heat about 15 to 20 minutes or until peppers are blackened and charred. Immediately seal peppers in a plastic bag and allow to steam 10 to 15 minutes. Remove charred skin. Cut peppers into thin 2½-inch-long strips. Combine peppers, olives, onion, capers, 2 tablespoons olive oil, and vinegar in a medium bowl.

Preheat oven to 300 degrees. In a small saucepan over medium-low heat, combine remaining 4 tablespoons olive oil, butter, and garlic; heat about 7 minutes. Brush butter mixture on both sides of French bread slices and place on an ungreased baking sheet. Bake 10 to 12 minutes or until light golden and crisp. Spread pepper mixture over warm bread slices and serve immediately.

Yield: about 44 appetizers

CHERRY-MOCHA WARMER

- 2 cups very hot strongly brewed coffee **or** 2 cups boiling water and 2 tablespoons instant coffee granules
- 4 ounces semisweet baking chocolate, chopped
- ⅔ cup granulated sugar
- ⅛ teaspoon salt
- 4 cups half and half
- 2 cups milk
- ¾ cup crème de cacao
- ¾ cup cherry brandy
- 1 cup whipping cream
- 4 tablespoons sifted confectioners sugar

Maraschino cherries with stems to garnish

Chill a small bowl and beaters from an electric mixer in freezer. In a double boiler over hot water, combine coffee, chocolate, granulated sugar, and salt. Whisk until

Awaken the table with this colorful dish! Our Festive Shrimp Appetizer is tossed in a zesty blend of olive oil, rice vinegar, and red and green peppercorns.

chocolate is melted and smooth. In a medium saucepan, scald half and half and milk; whisk into chocolate mixture. Add crème de cacao and brandy. Keep chocolate mixture warm.

In chilled bowl, whip cream until soft peaks form. Gradually add confectioners sugar and beat until stiff peaks form. Serve warm beverage with a dollop of whipped cream and a maraschino cherry.

Yield: about fourteen 6-ounce servings

CHERRY TOMATOES STUFFED WITH BASIL CHEESE

- 20 cherry tomatoes
- ½ cup part-skim ricotta cheese
- 2 tablespoons freshly grated Parmesan cheese
- 1 tablespoon chopped fresh basil **or** ½ teaspoon dried basil leaves
- 1 small clove garlic, minced
- ⅛ teaspoon crushed red pepper flakes
- ⅛ teaspoon salt
- ⅛ teaspoon ground black pepper

Cut a small slice off bottom of each tomato. Cut around stem of each tomato and use a small melon baller to scoop out pulp; invert in a colander to drain.

In a food processor, combine remaining ingredients; process until well blended. Place cheese mixture in a pastry bag fitted with a large star tip; pipe cheese into each tomato. Serve chilled.

Yield: 20 tomatoes

FESTIVE SHRIMP APPETIZER

- 2 pounds medium shrimp, cooked, peeled, and deveined
- 1 medium white onion, cut into bite-size pieces
- 1 large sweet red pepper, cut into bite-size pieces
- 1 large green pepper, cut into bite-size pieces
- 1 jar (5 ounces) stuffed green olives, drained
- ½ cup olive oil
- ¼ cup white rice vinegar
- ¾ teaspoon red peppercorns
- ½ teaspoon green peppercorns

In a large bowl, combine all ingredients; lightly toss until well blended. Cover and refrigerate overnight to allow flavors to blend. Serve chilled.

Yield: about 7 cups shrimp

MUSHROOMS IN CREAM CHEESE PASTRY

2½ cups all-purpose flour
½ teaspoon salt
2 packages (8 ounces each) cream
    cheese, softened
¾ cup butter or margarine, softened
12 ounces fresh mushrooms,
    quartered
½ cup freshly grated Parmesan
    cheese
2 tablespoons dry white wine
2 tablespoons chopped fresh parsley
2 tablespoons chopped pimiento
1 clove garlic, minced
1 teaspoon dried marjoram leaves
¼ teaspoon salt
⅛ teaspoon ground white pepper
⅛ teaspoon dry mustard
1 egg, beaten

In a medium bowl, combine flour and salt. Using a pastry blender or 2 knives, cut in cream cheese and butter until mixture resembles coarse meal. Lightly knead dough. Divide dough in half and wrap in plastic wrap; chill 1 hour.

In a food processor, process next 10 ingredients until coarsely chopped. Allow mushroom mixture to stand 15 minutes; drain in a colander.

Preheat oven to 400 degrees. On a lightly floured surface, use a floured rolling pin to roll out half of dough to ⅛-inch thickness. Use a 3-inch-diameter fluted-edge cookie cutter to cut out dough. For each dough circle, place a scant teaspoon of mushroom filling on half of dough circle; brush edge with beaten egg. Fold dough over filling. Use a floured fork to crimp edges of dough together and to prick top of pastry. Repeat with remaining dough and filling. Place on an ungreased baking sheet. Bake 15 to 20 minutes or until lightly browned. Serve warm.

Unbaked pastries may be placed on a baking sheet and frozen. Store frozen pastries in an airtight container. Bake frozen pastries 20 to 25 minutes in a preheated 400-degree oven.
Yield: about 5 dozen pastries

CHEESY PEPPER RICE SQUARES

4 cups cooked white rice
1½ cups (6 ounces) shredded
    Monterey Jack cheese, divided
1½ cups (6 ounces) shredded
    Cheddar cheese, divided
1 cup sour cream

Mushrooms in Cream Cheese Pastry *(top)* offer a filling of fresh mushrooms and Parmesan cheese nestled in a rich crust. Made with red peppers and green chilies, Cheesy Pepper Rice Squares are smothered with two kinds of cheese.

2 cans (4 ounces each) whole
    green chilies, drained
1 jar (7 ounces) roasted red
    peppers, drained

Preheat oven to 325 degrees. In a medium bowl, combine rice, 1 cup Monterey Jack cheese, 1 cup Cheddar cheese, and sour cream until well blended. Firmly press half of rice mixture into bottom of a greased 7 x 11-inch baking pan. Cut green chilies open; place over rice mixture. Press remaining rice mixture over green chilies. Place roasted red peppers over rice mixture. Bake uncovered 25 to 30 minutes; sprinkle remaining cheeses over red peppers. Bake 5 minutes longer or until cheese melts. Place pan on a wire rack and allow to cool 15 minutes. Cut into 2-inch squares. Serve warm.
Yield: about 15 servings

PIZZA BITES

DOUGH

- 1 package dry yeast
- 1 cup warm water
- 1 teaspoon sugar
- 2 tablespoons vegetable oil
- 1 teaspoon salt
- 2½ cups all-purpose flour, divided
  Vegetable cooking spray

TOPPINGS

- 5 plum tomatoes, thinly sliced and divided
- 1 sweet yellow pepper, thinly sliced
- 1 to 2 ounces feta cheese, crumbled
- 1 to 2 cloves garlic, minced
- 1 teaspoon dried basil leaves
- 4 tablespoons olive oil, divided
- 2 ounces Canadian bacon, cut into bite-size pieces
- 1 sweet red pepper, thinly sliced
- 1 green pepper, thinly sliced
- 1 small onion, thinly sliced and separated into rings
- 1 can (2¼ ounces) sliced black olives, drained
- 2 tablespoons finely chopped fresh cilantro **or** 2 teaspoons dried cilantro
- ½ teaspoon ground cumin
- 1 cup (4 ounces) shredded mozzarella cheese

For dough, dissolve yeast in warm water in a medium bowl. Add sugar, oil, salt, and 2 cups flour; stir until a soft dough forms. Turn onto a lightly floured surface; using remaining ½ cup flour, knead 5 minutes or until dough becomes smooth and elastic. Place in a medium bowl sprayed with cooking spray, turning once to coat top of dough. Cover and let rise in a warm place (80 to 85 degrees) 1 hour or until doubled in size.

Preheat oven to 400 degrees. Using half of dough, shape into eight 1½-inch balls. Use a floured rolling pin to roll out each ball into a 5-inch circle. Transfer dough circles to an ungreased baking sheet. Place half of tomato slices on dough circles. Layer yellow pepper, feta cheese, garlic, and basil over tomato slices; drizzle 2 tablespoons olive oil evenly over toppings. Repeat procedure with remaining dough, layering with remaining tomato slices, Canadian bacon, red and green peppers, onion rings, black olives, cilantro, cumin, and mozzarella cheese. Drizzle with remaining 2 tablespoons olive oil. Bake 20 to 25 minutes. Cut each pizza into 4 wedges; serve warm.

Yield: about 5 dozen pizza bites

Delectable Pizza Bites are zippy delights! Topped with lots of fresh veggies and Canadian bacon or feta cheese, these flavorful snacks add Italian flair to the buffet.

SPICY ROASTED PEANUTS

2 tablespoons vegetable oil
4 cloves garlic, minced
1 tablespoon crushed red pepper flakes
2 cans (16 ounces each) salted peanuts
2 teaspoons paprika
1 teaspoon chili powder

Preheat oven to 350 degrees. In a heavy large skillet, cook oil, garlic, and red pepper flakes over medium heat about 1 minute. Remove from heat. Add peanuts and stir until well blended. Pour peanut mixture onto a baking sheet. Stirring occasionally, bake about 20 minutes or until lightly browned. Sprinkle paprika and chili powder over peanuts and stir. Allow peanuts to cool completely.
Yield: about 6 cups peanuts

HUMMUS DIP

2 cans (15 ounces each) chick-peas, drained
½ cup olive oil
3 tablespoons fresh lemon juice
2 cloves garlic, coarsely chopped
1 tablespoon tahini (ground sesame seeds)
1 tablespoon coarsely chopped onion
1 tablespoon minced fresh parsley
¼ teaspoon salt
¼ teaspoon ground black pepper
⅛ teaspoon curry powder

Sliced black olives, fresh parsley, and red onion wedges to garnish
Pita bread triangles to serve

In a food processor, combine all ingredients; process until smooth. Spoon hummus into serving dish. Garnish with black olives, parsley, and red onion wedges. Serve at room temperature with pita bread triangles.
Yield: about 3 cups dip

Spicy Roasted Peanuts are coated with garlic, red pepper flakes, chili powder, and paprika. Chick-peas are used to make Hummus Dip, a creamy Middle Eastern substitute for bean dip that's delicious served with pita triangles.

Toasted almonds are a pleasant surprise in Creamy Chicken-Mushroom Dip. Robust Mustard Rolls are the perfect accompaniment for Herbed Beef Brisket. Sure to satisfy hearty appetites, the tender meat is stuffed with sliced garlic and sprinkled with fennel seeds that impart an aromatic flavor.

HERBED BEEF BRISKET

  4 pound beef brisket
 12 to 15 cloves garlic, thinly
       sliced
  3 tablespoons fennel seed
  1 tablespoon all-purpose flour
  1 cup hot water
  1 teaspoon beef bouillon granules
  2 tablespoons Worcestershire sauce
  1 teaspoon dried marjoram leaves
  1 teaspoon dried thyme leaves
  1 teaspoon ground oregano
  1 teaspoon ground black pepper

     Mustard Rolls and desired
       condiments to serve

Preheat oven to 325 degrees. Trim excess fat from brisket. Make 1/2-inch-deep cuts in meat across the grain. Insert garlic slices into cuts. Sprinkle fennel seed over top of brisket. Place flour in a large (14 x 20-inch) oven cooking bag; shake to coat bag. Place brisket into bag. Pour water into a small bowl; dissolve bouillon in water. Add remaining ingredients to bouillon mixture; pour into cooking bag. Seal and puncture cooking bag according to package directions. Bake 2 1/4 hours to 2 1/2 hours or until tender. Allow meat to stand in bag 10 to 15 minutes. Remove meat from bag; thinly slice across the grain. Serve warm on Mustard Rolls with desired condiments.
Yield: 30 to 40 appetizers

MUSTARD ROLLS

  2 packages dry yeast
 1/4 cup warm water
  1 tablespoon sugar
  1 cup milk
 2/3 cup prepared mustard
  2 tablespoons butter or margarine
  4 cups all-purpose flour
     Vegetable cooking spray
  1 egg yolk
  1 tablespoon water

In a small bowl, combine yeast, 1/4 cup warm water, and sugar; stir until well blended. In a small saucepan, heat milk, mustard, and butter over medium-high heat until butter melts. In a large bowl, combine yeast mixture, milk mixture, and flour. Stir until a soft dough forms. Turn onto a lightly floured surface and knead about 8 minutes or until dough becomes smooth and elastic. Place in a large bowl sprayed with cooking spray, turning once to coat top of dough. Cover and let rise in a warm place (80 to 85 degrees) 1 hour or until doubled in size. Turn dough onto a lightly floured surface and punch down. Shape dough into 1 1/2-inch balls and place 2 inches apart on a greased baking sheet. Lightly spray tops of rolls with cooking spray, cover, and let rise in a warm place 1 hour or until doubled in size.

Preheat oven to 400 degrees. In a small bowl, whisk egg yolk with 1 tablespoon water; brush over tops of rolls. Bake 12 to 15 minutes or until golden brown. Serve warm with Herbed Beef Brisket.
Yield: about 3 1/2 dozen rolls

CREAMY CHICKEN-MUSHROOM DIP

  1 can (10 3/4 ounces) golden
       mushroom soup, undiluted
  1 package (8 ounces) cream cheese,
       softened
  1 can (5 ounces) chunk white
       chicken, drained
 1/2 cup sliced fresh mushrooms
 1/2 cup slivered almonds, toasted
  2 tablespoons white wine
  1 small clove garlic, minced
 1/8 teaspoon ground white pepper

     Chips or crackers to serve

In a heavy medium saucepan, combine soup and cream cheese. Stir over medium heat until smooth. Add remaining ingredients; stir until well blended and heated through. Serve warm with chips or crackers.
Yield: about 2 1/2 cups dip

Miniature Bacon-Cheese New Potatoes are savory twice-baked treats. A sassy alternative to ordinary dips, Tomatillo Salsa is an unusual Mexican snack. Thin and crispy, Spicy Corn Wafers are perfect for nibbling or dipping.

BACON-CHEESE NEW POTATOES

- 1½ pounds small unpeeled new potatoes
- 2 tablespoons olive oil
- 1 cup (2 ounces) finely shredded Gruyère cheese
- ½ cup sour cream
- ½ cup minced green onions (about 3 large onions)
- 1 package (3 ounces) cream cheese, softened
- 2 tablespoons minced fresh basil **or** 1 teaspoon dried basil leaves
- 1 clove garlic, minced
- ¼ teaspoon salt
- ¼ teaspoon ground black pepper
- 8 ounces bacon, cooked and finely chopped

Preheat oven to 400 degrees. Rub potatoes with olive oil and place on an ungreased baking sheet; bake 1 hour or until tender. Allow potatoes to cool enough to handle. Cut potatoes in half. Cut a small slice off bottom of each potato half. Using a small melon baller, scoop out a small portion of potato pulp, leaving at least a ¼-inch shell; reserve potato pulp.

In a medium bowl, combine potato pulp and next 8 ingredients with an electric mixer; stir in bacon. Spoon potato mixture into each potato shell; place on a greased baking sheet. Broil 5 to 7 minutes or until lightly browned. Serve warm.
Yield: about 26 potato halves

SPICY CORN WAFERS

- 1½ cups white cornmeal
- 1 teaspoon garlic powder
- ¾ teaspoon salt
- ½ teaspoon ground red pepper
- 2¼ cups boiling water
- 4 tablespoons butter or margarine, melted

Preheat oven to 425 degrees. In a medium bowl, combine cornmeal, garlic powder, salt, and red pepper. Stirring constantly, pour boiling water over dry ingredients and mix well; stir in butter. For each wafer, drop 1 tablespoon batter onto an ungreased nonstick baking sheet. Using back of spoon, spread batter to form a 3-inch circle; add hot water to thin batter if necessary. Repeat with remaining batter. Bake 18 to 20 minutes or until edges are golden brown. Serve warm.
Yield: about 3 dozen wafers

TOMATILLO SALSA

- 1 small onion, quartered
- ¼ cup water
- ¼ teaspoon salt
- 1¼ pounds fresh tomatillos, husked (about 12 tomatillos)
- ½ cup coarsely chopped green pepper
- 2 jalapeño peppers, seeded
- 2 tablespoons chopped fresh cilantro
- 1 tablespoon fresh lime juice
- 1 clove garlic, coarsely chopped

  Tortilla chips to serve

In a medium saucepan over medium heat, combine onion, water, and salt; cover and cook about 5 minutes or until onion is soft. Add whole tomatillos, green pepper, and jalapeño peppers to saucepan. Reduce heat, cover, and cook 15 minutes or until tomatillos are tender; drain. Place tomatillo mixture and remaining ingredients in food processor; process mixture until coarsely chopped. Pour into a serving dish; cover and allow to stand 1 hour for flavors to blend. Serve at room temperature with tortilla chips.
Yield: about 3 cups salsa

MINIATURE CRAB CAKES WITH TARTAR SAUCE

TARTAR SAUCE
- 2 cups mayonnaise
- 2/3 cup finely chopped dill pickle
- 4 tablespoons fresh lemon juice
- 4 tablespoons finely minced scallions (use white and a small portion of green tops)
- 2 tablespoons drained capers, chopped
- 1/2 teaspoon creamed horseradish
- 1/2 teaspoon hot pepper sauce

CRAB CAKES
- 3 cans (6 ounces each) crabmeat, drained
- 1/2 cup finely chopped green pepper
- 1/2 cup finely chopped sweet red pepper
- 3 tablespoons minced onion
- 1/3 cup freshly prepared tartar sauce
- 2 teaspoons minced fresh parsley
- 1 egg, beaten
- 1/2 cup finely crushed butter-type crackers (about 12 crackers)
- 1/4 teaspoon salt
- 1/8 teaspoon ground black pepper
- 3/4 cup corn flake crumbs

For tartar sauce, combine all ingredients in a small bowl; stir until well blended. Reserve 1/3 cup for crab cakes; refrigerate remaining sauce until ready to serve.

Preheat oven to 350 degrees. For crab cakes, combine crabmeat, green and red peppers, onion, tartar sauce, parsley, egg, cracker crumbs, salt, and black pepper in a medium bowl. Carefully blend ingredients, just until mixed. Use 1 tablespoon of crab mixture to form each patty. Roll in corn flake crumbs until well coated. Place on an ungreased baking sheet. Bake 20 to 25 minutes or until golden brown. Serve warm with tartar sauce.

Crab cakes may be prepared 1 day in advance and refrigerated until ready to bake.

Yield: about 40 crab cakes and about 2 1/3 cups tartar sauce

Miniature Crab Cakes are breaded with a crunchy corn flake coating and baked. The fresh Tartar Sauce gets its tangy flavor from dill pickles, scallions, capers, and creamed horseradish.

BUSY ELVES' BRUNCH

This Christmas, why not get the season rolling with a fun-filled gift-wrapping party! With all of Santa's elves busily (and somewhat secretly) preparing for the big day, half the fun will be keeping the lucky recipients from discovering their presents. The rest of the merriment is served up with our hearty brunch menu, which features delicious delights to make the gathering even more special. Your holiday hostess duties will be all wrapped up with this collection!

Italian Sausage Frittata is a filling breakfast casserole that layers fresh vegetables, spicy Italian sausage, and eggs.

ITALIAN SAUSAGE FRITTATA

- 1 small onion, thinly sliced
- 1 medium potato, peeled and thinly sliced
- 1 pound Italian sausage, cooked and crumbled
- 3 ounces fresh mushrooms, sliced
- 1 small zucchini, thinly sliced
- 1 small sweet red pepper, sliced into rings
- 12 eggs, beaten
- 1/3 cup freshly grated Parmesan cheese

Preheat oven to 350 degrees. In a greased 12-inch ovenproof skillet, layer onion, potato, crumbled sausage, mushrooms, zucchini, and red pepper. Pour eggs over vegetables; sprinkle cheese over eggs. Bake 40 to 45 minutes or until eggs are almost set. Place skillet under broiler; broil about 3 minutes or until edges are lightly browned. Cut into wedges and serve immediately.

Yield: 8 to 10 servings

CHOCOLATE WAFFLES WITH CINNAMON-MARSHMALLOW TOPPING

WAFFLES
- 1/2 cup butter or margarine, softened
- 1 cup sugar
- 1/2 cup milk
- 2 eggs
- 1 teaspoon vanilla extract
- 1 1/2 cups cake flour
- 2 teaspoons baking powder
- 1/4 teaspoon salt
- 2 ounces semisweet baking chocolate, melted

TOPPING
- 1 jar (7 ounces) marshmallow creme
- 2 tablespoons light corn syrup
- 1/2 teaspoon clear vanilla extract (used in cake decorating)
- 1/4 teaspoon ground cinnamon

    Shaved semisweet baking chocolate to garnish

For waffles, preheat waffle iron. In a large bowl, cream butter and sugar until fluffy. Add milk, eggs, and vanilla; beat until smooth. In a small bowl, combine cake flour, baking powder, and salt. Add dry ingredients and melted chocolate to creamed mixture and blend; do not overmix. For each waffle, pour about 1/2 cup batter into waffle iron. Bake 5 to 7 minutes or according to manufacturer's instructions.

They'll think you're a sweetheart for serving Chocolate Waffles, a delicious alternative to typical morning fare. Presented with a drizzling of creamy Cinnamon-Marshmallow Topping, they're a unique and elegant dessert, too!

For topping, heat marshmallow creme and corn syrup over medium-low heat in a medium saucepan until marshmallow creme melts. Stir in vanilla and cinnamon.

Serve waffles hot with warm topping. Garnish with shaved chocolate.

Yield: about six 7-inch waffles

A confetti of color, Rice and Barley Pilaf is flavored with bacon and chicken broth. Coated with coarse ground pepper and a tangy honey-mustard sauce, spicy Peppered Ham is tender and juicy.

PEPPERED HAM

    4   pound boneless fully cooked ham
    1/4 cup honey
    2   tablespoons prepared mustard
    1   clove garlic, minced
    3   tablespoons coarse ground black
        pepper
    1/8 teaspoon ground cloves

Preheat oven to 325 degrees. Place ham on a rack in a shallow roasting pan. In a small bowl, combine remaining ingredients. Brush honey mixture over ham. Loosely cover ham with aluminum foil. Bake 1¾ hours to 2¼ hours or until heated through. Serve warm.
Yield: about 14 servings

RICE AND BARLEY PILAF

    6   slices bacon
    1   medium onion, chopped
    1/2 cup chopped celery
    2   cans (16 ounces each) chicken broth
    1   cup uncooked brown rice
    1   cup uncooked barley
    1   package (10 ounces) frozen green
        peas
    2   medium carrots, shredded
    1/4 cup cooking sherry
    3/4 teaspoon turmeric
    1/2 teaspoon ground black pepper
    1   bay leaf

In a large skillet over medium-high heat, cook bacon until crisp. Reserving drippings, remove bacon from pan; set bacon aside. In same skillet, add onion and celery to bacon drippings; cook until barely tender, stirring frequently. Remove onion mixture from pan and set aside. In same skillet, combine chicken broth, rice, and barley. Cover and cook over medium-low heat 45 minutes or until most of liquid is absorbed. Stir in onion mixture, peas, carrots, sherry, turmeric, pepper, and bay leaf. Reduce heat to low; simmer 10 minutes or until peas are crisp-tender. Remove bay leaf. Crumble bacon on top of pilaf; serve warm.
Yield: 15 to 18 servings

LIGHT YEAST BISCUITS

      1 package dry yeast
      2 tablespoons warm water
      2 tablespoons sugar, divided
 2¹/₂ cups all-purpose flour
   ¹/₂ teaspoon baking powder
   ¹/₂ teaspoon baking soda
   ¹/₂ teaspoon salt
   ¹/₂ cup butter or margarine, softened
      1 cup warm buttermilk
         Vegetable cooking spray

In a small bowl, dissolve yeast in warm water; stir in 1 tablespoon sugar. In a large bowl, combine remaining 1 tablespoon sugar, flour, baking powder, baking soda, and salt. Using a pastry blender or two knives, cut butter into dry ingredients until mixture resembles coarse cornmeal. Add buttermilk and yeast mixture to dry ingredients; stir until a soft dough forms. Turn onto a lightly floured surface and knead 4 minutes or until dough becomes smooth and elastic. Place in a large bowl sprayed with cooking spray, turning once to coat top of dough. Cover and let rise in a warm place (80 to 85 degrees) 1 to 1¹/₂ hours or until doubled in size. Turn dough onto a lightly floured surface and punch down. Roll out dough to ¹/₂-inch thickness; use a 2-inch-diameter biscuit cutter to cut out biscuits. Place biscuits 1 inch apart on an ungreased baking sheet. Spray tops with cooking spray, cover, and let rise in a warm place 30 to 45 minutes or until doubled in size. Preheat oven to 400 degrees. Bake 12 to 15 minutes or until golden brown. Serve warm.
Yield: about 2 dozen biscuits

HOT MAPLE CREAM

      2 cups milk
      2 cups half and half
      1 teaspoon vanilla extract
   ¹/₂ cup maple syrup
   ¹/₈ teaspoon ground nutmeg

         Freshly grated nutmeg to garnish

Combine milk, half and half, vanilla, maple syrup, and ¹/₈ teaspoon nutmeg in a heavy medium saucepan over medium-low heat. Stirring occasionally, heat mixture thoroughly without boiling. Garnish with grated nutmeg. Serve warm.
Yield: about six 6-ounce servings

For tasty help-yourself tidbits, set out a basket of buttery Light Yeast Biscuits along with jelly, jam, or sliced meats. A dash of nutmeg adds spice to Hot Maple Cream, a flavorful winter warmer.

Baked Spiced Fruit is a warm, flavorful compote of spiced apples, peaches, pineapple, and cherries cooked in a cinnamony brown sugar sauce. Your guests can take a Christmas coffee break with hearty Banana-Raisin Bran Muffins.

BAKED SPICED FRUIT

1   can (29 ounces) peach halves
     in heavy syrup, drained
1   can (20 ounces) pineapple slices
     in fruit juice, drained, reserving
     ³/₄ cup of juice
1   jar (about 14 ounces) spiced apple
     rings, drained
¹/₂ cup drained maraschino cherries
³/₄ cup firmly packed brown sugar
¹/₃ cup butter or margarine
1   teaspoon ground cinnamon

¹/₄ teaspoon ground cloves
¹/₄ teaspoon curry powder
4   teaspoons cornstarch
4   teaspoons water

Preheat oven to 350 degrees. Arrange fruit in a 9 x 13-inch baking dish. In a small saucepan over medium heat, combine reserved pineapple juice, brown sugar, butter, cinnamon, cloves, and curry powder. Stirring pineapple juice mixture frequently, cook 7 to 8 minutes. In a small bowl, combine cornstarch and water. Stirring constantly, add cornstarch mixture and continue to cook about 2 minutes or until mixture thickens. Pour sauce over fruit. Bake 25 to 30 minutes. Serve warm.
Yield: about 14 servings

BANANA-RAISIN BRAN MUFFINS

1 cup all-purpose flour
³/₄ cup whole-wheat flour
¹/₃ cup sugar
2 teaspoons baking powder
¹/₂ teaspoon baking soda
¹/₂ teaspoon salt
2 eggs
¹/₂ cup buttermilk
¹/₂ cup vegetable oil
2 medium bananas, mashed
2 cups raisin bran flakes

Preheat oven to 350 degrees. In a medium bowl, combine flours, sugar, baking powder, baking soda, and salt. In a small bowl, whisk eggs, buttermilk, oil, and bananas. Add buttermilk mixture and raisin bran flakes to dry ingredients; stir until ingredients are moistened. Fill paper-lined muffin tins two-thirds full. Bake 25 to 30 minutes or until golden brown.
Yield: about 18 muffins

APPLE-PEAR SKILLET CAKE

1 cup firmly packed brown sugar
6 tablespoons butter or margarine, cut into pieces
1 medium unpeeled baking apple, cored and sliced
1 medium unpeeled pear, cored and sliced
1¹/₃ cups all-purpose flour
1 cup granulated sugar
2 teaspoons ground cinnamon
1¹/₄ teaspoons baking soda
¹/₂ teaspoon salt
2 eggs
¹/₂ cup sour cream
2 tablespoons vegetable oil
1 teaspoon vanilla extract

Preheat oven to 350 degrees. Place brown sugar and butter in a 10¹/₂-inch cast-iron or ovenproof skillet. Place skillet in oven about 5 minutes or until butter melts. Remove skillet from oven and whisk brown sugar mixture until well blended. Arrange fruit slices over brown sugar mixture. In a medium bowl, combine flour, granulated sugar, cinnamon, baking soda, and salt. In a small bowl, whisk eggs, sour cream, oil, and vanilla; beat into flour mixture. Pour batter over fruit; bake 30 to 35 minutes or until a toothpick inserted in center of cake comes out clean. Remove from oven and place on a wire rack to cool 10 minutes. Run knife around edge of cake; invert onto a serving plate. Serve warm.
Yield: about 12 servings

Fresh fruit and a buttery brown sugar topping make Apple-Pear Skillet Cake a sumptuous upside-down treat. It's best when prepared in a cast-iron skillet.

HEAVENLY CONFECTIONS

Sweetening the mood of an already joyous celebration, heavenly desserts are the grand finale to a delicious holiday feast. Moist cakes, creamy pies, and buttery candies invite us to linger and visit over coffee or tea. And for those who usually resist the sweet temptation of the dessert tray, we've included several sinless delights, too! This year, entice all your darling angels with these delectable confections.

Deliciously light in fat and calories, Mexican Chocolate Angel Food Cake is a divine completion for Christmas dinner. Its lacy decoration is created by sprinkling cinnamon and confectioners sugar over a paper doily.

MEXICAN CHOCOLATE ANGEL FOOD CAKE

1³/₄ cups sifted confectioners sugar,
    divided
1 cup sifted all-purpose flour
¹/₄ cup sifted cocoa
2¹/₄ teaspoons ground cinnamon, divided
1¹/₂ cups egg whites (10 to 12 large
    eggs)
1¹/₂ teaspoons cream of tartar
1 teaspoon vanilla extract
1 cup granulated sugar

    Sugared grapes to garnish

Preheat oven to 350 degrees. In a medium bowl, sift 1¹/₂ cups confectioners sugar, flour, cocoa, and 2 teaspoons cinnamon 3 times.

In a large bowl, beat egg whites, cream of tartar, and vanilla with an electric mixer until soft peaks form. Gradually add granulated sugar, 2 tablespoons at a time, and beat until stiff peaks form.

Sift about one-fourth of confectioners sugar mixture over egg white mixture; fold in gently by hand. Continue to sift and fold in confectioners sugar mixture in small batches. Lightly spoon batter into an ungreased 10-inch tube pan and place on lower rack of oven. Bake 40 to 45 minutes or until top springs back when lightly touched. Remove from oven and invert pan onto neck of a bottle; cool completely. Remove cake from pan, placing bottom side up on a serving plate.

To decorate, combine remaining ¹/₄ cup confectioners sugar and ¹/₄ teaspoon cinnamon in a small bowl. Place a 10-inch round paper doily on top of cake and lightly sift confectioners sugar mixture over doily. Carefully remove doily. Garnish with sugared grapes.
Yield: about 12 servings

OLD-FASHIONED MINTS

¹/₄ cup butter or margarine
3³/₄ cups sifted confectioners sugar,
    divided
¹/₃ cup light corn syrup
¹/₂ teaspoon peppermint extract
¹/₂ teaspoon vanilla extract
    Red paste food coloring

In a heavy medium saucepan over medium heat, melt butter. Add 2 cups confectioners sugar and corn syrup; stir until well blended. Stirring constantly, cook about 4 minutes or until mixture comes to a boil. Remove from heat and add remaining 1³/₄ cups confectioners sugar; stir about

Serve creamy Old-fashioned Mints as delectable after-dinner treats. The soft, buttery pinwheels taste just like the ones Grandmother used to make.

3 minutes or until mixture thickens. Stir in extracts. Pour mixture onto a smooth, damp surface; use a spatula to knead mixture until cool enough to handle with lightly greased hands. Continue kneading until very smooth and creamy. Divide mixture in half, wrapping one half in plastic wrap. Tint remaining half red. Using a rolling pin, quickly roll red mixture into a 5 x 18-inch rectangle on plastic wrap. Cover with another piece of plastic wrap while preparing second layer. Repeat to roll out white mint mixture; place over red layer. Beginning at 1 long edge, roll layers tightly together. Using a serrated knife and a sawing motion, carefully cut roll into ³/₈-inch slices. Store in an airtight container in a cool place.
Yield: about 4 dozen mints

There's only one word for this luscious frozen confection — *Mmmm*! A sinfully rich combination of flavors, Jamocha Toffee Mud Pie features a chocolate cookie crumb crust filled with coffee-flavored ice cream and chunks of buttery chocolate-almond toffee. A chocolaty topping laced with coffee liqueur crowns this heavenly confection. You'll want to make an extra batch of the crunchy toffee for snacking, too. It's an unforgettable treat in its own right!

JAMOCHA TOFFEE MUD PIE

TOFFEE
- 1/2 cup plus 1 teaspoon butter or margarine, divided
- 1/2 cup sugar
- 1 tablespoon water
- 1/2 tablespoon light corn syrup
- 1/4 teaspoon almond extract
- 1/4 teaspoon vanilla extract
- 1 1/4 cups (about 10 ounces) sliced almonds, toasted
- 1/2 cup semisweet chocolate chips

CRUST
- 1 1/2 cups chocolate sandwich cookie crumbs (about 18 cookies)
- 3 tablespoons butter or margarine, melted

FILLING
- 1 quart coffee-flavored ice cream, softened

TOPPING
- 1 package (6 ounces) semisweet chocolate chips
- 1 can (5 ounces) evaporated milk
- 1/2 cup sugar
- 2 tablespoons coffee-flavored liqueur
- 1 tablespoon butter or margarine

For toffee, use 1 teaspoon butter to coat sides of a heavy large saucepan. Combine remaining 1/2 cup butter, sugar, water, and corn syrup in saucepan. Stirring constantly, cook over medium-low heat until sugar dissolves. Using a pastry brush dipped in hot water, wash down any sugar crystals on sides of pan. Attach a candy thermometer to pan, making sure thermometer does not touch bottom of pan. Increase heat to medium and bring to a boil. Cook, without stirring, until syrup reaches soft-crack stage (approximately 270 to 290 degrees). Test about 1/2 teaspoon syrup in ice water. Syrup will form hard threads in ice water but will soften when removed from the water. Remove from heat and stir in extracts and almonds. Pour onto a baking sheet lined with greased aluminum foil. Sprinkle chocolate chips over hot toffee. As chocolate melts, spread over toffee. Chill until firm; break into small pieces.

Preheat oven to 350 degrees. For crust, combine cookie crumbs and melted butter in a small bowl. Press crumbs into bottom of a 9-inch springform pan. Bake 10 minutes. Remove from oven; place pan on a wire rack to cool completely.

For filling, reserve a few toffee pieces for garnish and combine remaining toffee pieces and ice cream in a large bowl. Wrap aluminum foil under and around outside of springform pan. Spoon ice cream mixture over crust. Cover with plastic wrap; freeze until firm.

For topping, combine chocolate chips, evaporated milk, and sugar in a heavy medium saucepan over medium heat. Stirring constantly, bring to a boil. Remove from heat; add liqueur and butter, stirring until butter melts. Remove pie from springform pan. Drizzle about 1/2 cup topping over pie. Garnish pie with reserved toffee pieces. Serve remaining topping warm with individual servings.
Yield: 10 to 12 servings

ULTIMATE CHOCOLATE PUDDING

    3 ounces semisweet baking chocolate,
          coarsely chopped
    3 ounces unsweetened baking
          chocolate, coarsely chopped
    4 tablespoons butter or margarine
    3 cups milk
1 1/4 cups sugar, divided
    2 eggs
    4 egg yolks
  1/2 cup cocoa
    2 teaspoons cornstarch
    2 cups whipping cream, divided
    1 teaspoon vanilla extract
    1 tablespoon finely chopped bittersweet
          baking chocolate and fresh mint
          leaves to garnish

In a double boiler over simmering water, melt chocolates and butter, stirring until well blended. Remove from heat and allow to cool. In a heavy large saucepan over medium heat, whisk milk, 1 cup sugar, eggs, and egg yolks. Attach a candy thermometer to pan, making sure thermometer does not touch bottom of pan. Stirring constantly, cook until mixture reaches 180 degrees on candy thermometer or begins to thicken. Strain custard through a fine mesh strainer into a large bowl. In a heavy small saucepan, sift cocoa and cornstarch into 1 cup whipping cream. Stirring constantly, bring mixture to a boil; cook until slightly thickened. Add chocolate mixture, cornstarch mixture, and vanilla to custard; stir until well blended. Pour into individual serving dishes; cover and chill.

To serve, chill a small bowl and beaters from an electric mixer in freezer. In chilled bowl, beat remaining 1 cup whipping cream and remaining 1/4 cup sugar until stiff peaks form. Spoon mixture into a pastry bag fitted with a large star tip. Pipe whipped cream mixture onto pudding. Garnish with chopped bittersweet chocolate and mint leaves.
Yield: 8 to 10 servings

PENUCHE

    2 cups firmly packed brown sugar
  2/3 cup half and half
1 1/2 tablespoons light corn syrup
  1/8 teaspoon salt
    2 tablespoons butter or margarine,
          softened
    1 teaspoon vanilla extract
    1 cup chopped pecans

Four kinds of chocolate are used to create our creamy Ultimate Chocolate Pudding. Packed with tasty pecans, Penuche is a delightful brown sugar fudge.

Butter sides of a heavy large saucepan. Combine brown sugar, half and half, corn syrup, and salt in pan. Stirring constantly, cook over medium-low heat until sugar dissolves. Using a pastry brush dipped in hot water, wash down any sugar crystals on sides of pan. Attach a candy thermometer to pan, making sure thermometer does not touch bottom of pan. Increase heat to medium and bring to a boil. Cook, without stirring, until syrup reaches soft-ball stage (approximately 234 to 240 degrees). Test about

1/2 teaspoon syrup in ice water. Syrup will easily form a ball in ice water but will flatten when held in your hand. Place pan in cold water in sink. Cool, without stirring, to approximately 110 degrees. Add butter and vanilla. Using an electric mixer, beat fudge until thickened and no longer glossy. Stir in pecans. Line a 7 x 11-inch baking pan with aluminum foil, extending foil over ends of pan; butter foil. Pour mixture into pan. Cool completely. Remove fudge by lifting foil from pan. Cut into 1-inch squares.
Yield: about 5 dozen pieces fudge

WHITE CHOCOLATE PROFITEROLES

CREAM PUFF PASTRY
- 1 cup plus 1 teaspoon water, divided
- 1/2 cup butter or margarine
- 1 cup all-purpose flour
- 5 large eggs, divided
- 1/8 teaspoon salt

FILLING
- 1 3/4 cups whipping cream, divided
- 1/3 cup sugar
- 4 ounces white chocolate, coarsely chopped
- 1/8 teaspoon salt

TOPPING
- 3 ounces white chocolate
  Red and green paste food coloring

Preheat oven to 400 degrees. For cream puff pastry, bring 1 cup water and butter to a boil in a heavy large saucepan over high heat. Remove from heat. Add flour all at once; stir with a wooden spoon until mixture forms a ball. Place flour mixture in a medium bowl. Add 4 eggs, one at a time, beating well with an electric mixer after each addition. Spoon batter into a pastry bag fitted with a large round tip (1/2-inch opening). Placing 2 inches apart on a greased and floured baking sheet, pipe 1 1/2-inch-diameter x 1-inch-high puffs. In a small bowl, whisk remaining egg, remaining 1 teaspoon water, and salt until well blended. Brush egg wash over tops of puffs, gently rounding out tops. Bake puffs 10 minutes in upper one-third of oven. Reduce heat to 350 degrees; bake 25 to 30 minutes longer or until puffs are firm to the touch and golden. Transfer puffs to a wire rack and cool completely.

For filling, chill a medium bowl and beaters from an electric mixer in freezer. Combine 1/4 cup whipping cream and sugar in a double boiler. Stirring frequently, cook over simmering water until sugar dissolves. Stirring constantly, add white chocolate and salt; continue to cook until chocolate melts. Remove from heat; allow mixture to cool. In chilled bowl, beat remaining 1 1/2 cups whipping cream until stiff peaks form; gradually add chocolate mixture while continuing to beat. Chill until ready to fill puffs.

For topping, melt white chocolate in top of a double boiler over simmering water. Divide melted chocolate into 2 small bowls; tint red and green. Spoon chocolate into separate pastry bags fitted with small round tips. To serve, slice puffs in half horizontally with a sharp serrated knife;

Airy White Chocolate Profiteroles (*top*) feature a fluffy white chocolate filling piped into individual cream puff pastries. Topped with a rich cream cheese icing and toasted coconut, Coconut-Orange Squares are moist and chewy.

place 1 1/2 tablespoons of filling between halves. Drizzle each color of chocolate over puffs.
Yield: about 2 dozen puffs

COCONUT-ORANGE SQUARES

CAKE
- 3/4 cup butter or margarine, softened
- 3/4 cup sugar
- 1 can (16 ounces) sliced carrots, drained and mashed
- 1 egg
- 1 1/2 teaspoons grated orange zest
- 1/2 teaspoon vanilla extract
- 1/4 teaspoon orange extract
- 2 cups all-purpose flour
- 2 teaspoons baking powder
- 3/4 teaspoon salt
- 3/4 cup sweetened shredded coconut

ICING
- 1 package (8 ounces) cream cheese, softened
- 1/4 cup butter or margarine, softened
- 2 teaspoons milk
- 1/2 teaspoon grated orange zest
- 1/2 teaspoon orange extract
- 1/4 teaspoon vanilla extract
- 3 1/2 cups sifted confectioners sugar
- 1/2 cup toasted sweetened shredded coconut to garnish

Preheat oven to 350 degrees. For cake, cream butter and sugar in a large bowl until fluffy. Add carrots, egg, orange zest, and extracts; beat until smooth. In a medium bowl, combine flour, baking powder, and salt. Add dry ingredients to creamed mixture; stir until well blended. Stir in coconut. Pour batter into a lightly greased 9 x 13-inch pan. Bake 20 to 25 minutes or until a toothpick inserted in center comes out clean. Place pan on a wire rack to cool completely.

For icing, beat cream cheese, butter, milk, orange zest, and extracts in a medium bowl until smooth. Stir in confectioners sugar until smooth. Spread icing over cooled cake. Garnish with toasted coconut. Cut into 2-inch squares.
Yield: about 24 squares

ORANGE TART

CRUST

- 1 tablespoon light corn syrup
- 1 tablespoon water
- 1½ cups graham cracker crumbs
- 1 tablespoon butter or margarine, chilled
- 1 tablespoon canola oil
- ¼ teaspoon ground cinnamon

FILLING

- 1 envelope unflavored gelatin
- ½ cup orange juice
- 1 package (8 ounces) Neufchâtel cheese
- 1 container (8 ounces) nonfat vanilla-flavored yogurt
- 1 teaspoon grated orange zest
- 1 packet (.035 ounces) sugar substitute (equivalent to 2 teaspoons sugar)
- ½ teaspoon clear vanilla extract (used in cake decorating)
- 3 cans (11 ounces each) mandarin oranges, well drained
- 3 tablespoons orange marmalade

Preheat oven to 375 degrees. For crust, combine corn syrup and water in a small bowl until well blended. In a food processor, combine cracker crumbs, butter, oil, and cinnamon. Add corn syrup mixture to processor. Process until ingredients are well blended. Press cracker crumb mixture into bottom and up sides of a greased 8 x 11-inch tart pan with removable bottom. Bake 7 to 9 minutes or until lightly browned and firm. Place pan on a wire rack to cool completely.

For filling, sprinkle gelatin over orange juice in a small saucepan; allow to stand 5 minutes. Heat gelatin mixture over medium heat and stir until gelatin dissolves; remove from heat and allow to cool. In a food processor, combine Neufchâtel cheese, yogurt, orange zest, sugar substitute, vanilla, and gelatin mixture; process until well blended and smooth. Pour cheese mixture into crust. Cover and chill 1 hour or until filling is set.

To serve, remove sides of tart pan. Place orange segments on filling. Melt marmalade in a small saucepan over medium heat; brush segments with melted marmalade. Serve immediately.
Yield: about 12 servings

No one will believe that this refreshing Orange Tart is a low-calorie, low-fat dessert — but it is! Flavorful mandarin oranges cover the creamy filling that's prepared with Neufchâtel cheese, nonfat yogurt, and sugar substitute.

ORANGE-NUT POUND CAKE

CAKE

- 1¼ cups butter or margarine, softened
- 1½ cups firmly packed brown sugar
- 6 eggs, separated
- 1 cup canned pumpkin
- ½ cup buttermilk
- 3 cups all-purpose flour
- 1 teaspoon ground cinnamon
- ½ teaspoon ground cardamom
- ½ teaspoon salt
- ½ teaspoon baking powder
- ½ teaspoon baking soda
- 1 cup finely chopped walnuts
- 1 tablespoon grated orange zest
- 1 tablespoon orange-flavored liqueur
- 1 teaspoon vanilla extract
- ½ cup granulated sugar

SYRUP

- ¼ cup firmly packed brown sugar
- ¼ cup butter or margarine
- 2 tablespoons water
- ¼ cup orange-flavored liqueur

Preheat oven to 325 degrees. For cake, cream butter and brown sugar in a large bowl until fluffy. Reserving egg whites, add egg yolks, one at a time, beating well after each addition. Add pumpkin and buttermilk; stir until well blended. In a medium bowl, sift flour, cinnamon, cardamom, salt, baking powder, and baking soda. Add dry ingredients to creamed mixture; stir until well blended. Stir in walnuts, orange zest, liqueur, and vanilla; stir until well blended. Beat reserved egg whites until frothy; gradually add granulated sugar and beat until stiff peaks form. Fold beaten egg whites into cake batter. Pour batter into a greased and lightly floured 10-inch fluted tube pan. Bake 1 hour to 1¼ hours or until a toothpick inserted in center of cake comes out clean. Cool in pan 15 minutes; invert onto a serving plate.

For syrup, combine brown sugar, butter, and water in a small saucepan over medium-high heat. Stirring frequently, bring mixture to a slow boil; boil about 2 minutes or until sugar dissolves. Remove from heat; add liqueur. While cake is still warm, use a wooden skewer to poke holes about 1 inch apart in cake; slowly spoon syrup over cake. Cool cake completely and cover. Allow cake to absorb syrup overnight.
Yield: about 16 servings

Covered with a caramelized topping, custard-like Amaretto-Apricot Flan (*top*) is a delicious alternative to traditional pumpkin or sweet potato pie. Moist Orange-Nut Pound Cake is saturated with an orange liqueur syrup.

AMARETTO-APRICOT FLAN

- ¾ cup plus 2 tablespoons sugar, divided
- 2 tablespoons water
- 1 can (17 ounces) apricot halves, drained
- 1 can (14 ounces) sweetened condensed milk
- 5 eggs
- ½ cup apricot nectar
- 5 tablespoons amaretto
- 1 tablespoon grated orange zest
- ¼ teaspoon salt
- ¼ teaspoon ground nutmeg

Canned apricot halves and toasted slivered almonds to garnish

Preheat oven to 150 degrees. Place a 9-inch round cake pan in oven to preheat. In a heavy medium skillet, combine ¾ cup sugar and water. Over medium-high heat, swirl skillet to dissolve sugar while allowing mixture to come to a rolling boil; do not stir. Using a pastry brush dipped in hot water, wash down any sugar crystals on sides of skillet. Continue to cook about 15 minutes or until syrup is a deep golden brown. Pour syrup into heated cake pan. Rotate pan to spread syrup evenly over bottom and halfway up sides; set aside.

Increase oven temperature to 350 degrees. In a food processor, combine apricots, condensed milk, eggs, apricot nectar, amaretto, orange zest, salt, nutmeg, and remaining 2 tablespoons sugar. Pulse process until apricots are finely chopped; pour apricot mixture into pan over syrup. Place cake pan in a larger baking pan and fill baking pan with hot water to come halfway up sides of cake pan. Bake 1¼ hours to 1½ hours or until a knife inserted in center comes out clean. Remove from oven; cool slightly. Cover and chill 8 hours or overnight.

To serve, place cake pan in a pan of very hot water about 5 minutes. Run a knife around edge of pan to loosen flan. Invert onto a serving plate. Garnish with apricots and toasted almonds.
Yield: 8 to 10 servings

LEMON-FILLED PUMPKIN ROLL

CAKE

- 1 cup pasteurized egg substitute (equivalent to 4 eggs)
- ³/₄ cup granulated sugar
- ²/₃ cup canned pumpkin
- ¹/₄ cup nonfat buttermilk
- 2 tablespoons vegetable oil
- ³/₄ cup all-purpose flour
- 2¹/₂ teaspoons ground cinnamon
- 1¹/₄ teaspoons baking powder
- ¹/₂ teaspoon salt
- ¹/₂ teaspoon ground nutmeg
- ¹/₄ teaspoon ground ginger
- 1 tablespoon confectioners sugar

FILLING

- 1 package (0.3 ounces) sugar-free lemon-flavored gelatin
- ¹/₂ cup boiling water
- 1 can (5 ounces) evaporated skimmed milk, chilled overnight
- 1 container (8 ounces) nonfat lemon-flavored yogurt

  Lemon slices to garnish

Preheat oven to 375 degrees. For cake, beat egg substitute in a large bowl at high speed of an electric mixer until foamy; gradually add granulated sugar. While mixing at low speed, add pumpkin, buttermilk, and oil. In a small bowl, combine next 6 ingredients. Add flour mixture to egg mixture; beat until well blended. Spread batter evenly in a greased 10 x 15-inch jellyroll pan. Bake 12 to 15 minutes or until cake springs back when lightly touched. Sift confectioners sugar onto a smooth dish towel; immediately turn cake out onto towel. Beginning at 1 short edge, roll up warm cake in towel. Cool completely on a wire rack; wrap in plastic wrap and chill while preparing filling.

For filling, chill a small bowl and beaters from electric mixer in freezer. Add gelatin to boiling water in a small bowl; stir until gelatin dissolves. Cool gelatin mixture by placing bowl over ice. In chilled bowl from freezer, beat evaporated milk until stiff peaks form. Continue beating and quickly add gelatin mixture; fold in yogurt.

To assemble, carefully unroll cake, removing towel. Reserving about ¹/₂ cup filling for garnish, spread remaining lemon filling evenly over cake. Reroll cake. Spoon reserved filling into a pastry bag fitted with a small star tip. Garnish roll with lemon slices; pipe remaining filling onto lemon slices.

Yield: 8 to 10 servings

Lighten up your holiday menu with luscious Lemon-Filled Pumpkin Roll! The low-calorie treat features a fluffy filling wrapped in a spicy low-fat chiffon cake.

CHOCOLATE-MINT TORTE

CAKE
- ½ cup butter or margarine, softened
- 1¾ cups sugar
- 2 eggs
- 1 teaspoon vanilla extract
- 2 cups all-purpose flour
- 1 teaspoon baking powder
- 1 teaspoon baking soda
- ¼ teaspoon salt
- ¾ cup buttermilk
- ½ cup coffee-flavored liqueur
- 4 ounces unsweetened baking chocolate, melted

FILLING
- 8 ounces semisweet baking chocolate, finely chopped
- 1 cup whipping cream
- 2 tablespoons crème de menthe
- 4 egg whites
- ⅛ teaspoon salt
- ¼ teaspoon cream of tartar

- 15 individually wrapped chocolate wafer mints to garnish

Preheat oven to 350 degrees. For cake, cream butter and sugar in a large bowl until fluffy. Add eggs and vanilla; stir until smooth. In a medium bowl, sift flour, baking powder, baking soda, and salt. Alternately add buttermilk, liqueur, and dry ingredients to creamed mixture; beat until well blended. Stir in melted chocolate. Line bottoms of 3 ungreased 9-inch round cake pans with waxed paper. Divide batter evenly in pans. Bake 20 to 25 minutes or until a toothpick inserted in center of cake comes out clean. Cool in pans 10 minutes; remove from pans and cool completely on a wire rack.

For filling, chill a small bowl and beaters from an electric mixer in freezer. Stirring constantly, melt chocolate in a heavy medium saucepan over low heat. Remove from heat and cool to room temperature. In chilled bowl, beat whipping cream and crème de menthe until stiff peaks form; refrigerate. In a large bowl, beat egg whites and salt with an electric mixer until frothy. Add cream of tartar; beat until stiff peaks form. Gently fold chocolate and whipped cream mixture into egg white mixture. Refrigerate until ready to use.

To assemble cake, place one cake layer on a cake plate; spread one-third of filling on cake layer. Repeat with remaining layers. To garnish, use a vegetable peeler to shave chocolate curls from mints; place on top of cake. Cover and store in refrigerator.
Yield: about 12 servings

A chocolate fancier's delight, elegant Chocolate-Mint Torte layers melt-in-your-mouth buttermilk chocolate cake with a crème de menthe filling. Curls of mint-chocolate candy top off this exquisite offering.

WHITE CHRISTMAS CAKES

CAKE

- 1 cup granulated sugar
- 6 eggs
- 1 cup all-purpose flour
- $^1/_2$ cup butter or margarine, melted, at room temperature
- 2 teaspoons almond extract

ICING

- $4^1/_2$ cups granulated sugar
- $2^1/_4$ cups hot water
- $^1/_4$ teaspoon cream of tartar
- 1 teaspoon clear vanilla extract (used in cake decorating)
- $4^1/_2$ cups sifted confectioners sugar

ROYAL ICING

- $2^1/_4$ cups sifted confectioners sugar
- $1^1/_2$ tablespoons meringue powder
- 2 to 3 tablespoons warm water
- $^1/_2$ teaspoon almond extract

Preheat oven to 350 degrees. For cake, whisk granulated sugar and eggs in a double boiler over simmering water. Stirring occasionally, cook 5 to 10 minutes or until sugar dissolves. Pour mixture into a large bowl and beat with an electric mixer 10 to 12 minutes or until volume is tripled and mixture is cooled. Using low speed of electric mixer and adding $^1/_3$ cup flour at a time, sift and stir flour into egg mixture. Gently fold in melted butter and almond extract. Line a greased 9 x 13-inch baking pan with a sheet of waxed paper that extends over each end of pan. Spread batter in pan. Bake 18 to 20 minutes or until a toothpick inserted in center of cake comes out clean. Cool cake in pan 5 minutes. Remove cake by lifing waxed paper from pan; transfer to a wire rack. Invert onto a second wire rack and remove paper. Cool completely.

For icing, place granulated sugar, water, and cream of tartar in a medium saucepan. Stirring constantly, cook mixture over medium-high heat until sugar dissolves. Stirring frequently, bring mixture to a boil. Reduce heat to medium. Using a pastry brush dipped in hot water, wash down any sugar crystals on sides of pan. Attach a candy thermometer to pan, making sure thermometer does not touch bottom of pan. Allow mixture to boil about 15 minutes or until thermometer reaches 226 degrees, stirring only if icing begins to stick. Remove from heat and allow to cool at room temperature without stirring about 1 hour or until thermometer reaches 110 degrees. Add vanilla; stir in confectioners sugar until icing is a good consistency to spoon over

Kissed with almond flavor, dainty White Christmas Cakes are sumptuous tidbits that few can resist. Indulge your sweet tooth with Strawberry-Banana Frozen Yogurt. Wonderfully low in fat and calories, it's a frosty treat!

cakes. If necessary, beat icing with an electric mixer to remove any lumps.

Cut cake into 2-inch squares. Place wire rack containing cakes over a jellyroll pan. Spoon icing over cakes. Allow icing to harden.

For royal icing, beat confectioners sugar, meringue powder, water, and almond extract in a medium bowl 7 to 10 minutes or until stiff. Spoon icing into a pastry bag fitted with a small round tip. Pipe desired decorations onto tops of cakes.
Yield: 20 cakes

STRAWBERRY-BANANA FROZEN YOGURT

- $^1/_2$ cup sugar
- 1 envelope unflavored gelatin
- 1 cup cold skim milk
- $2^1/_2$ cups nonfat strawberry-banana-flavored yogurt
- 1 cup puréed frozen unsweetened strawberries
- 1 banana, puréed

  Frozen or fresh strawberry slices and fresh mint leaves to garnish

In a medium saucepan, combine sugar and gelatin; add milk and allow to stand 1 minute. Stirring constantly, cook over low heat 5 minutes or until gelatin dissolves. Allow mixture to cool. Add yogurt, strawberries, and banana; stir until well blended. Freeze in an ice cream freezer according to manufacturer's instructions (or freeze overnight in an airtight container; remove from freezer, beat 5 minutes, and refreeze). To serve, garnish with strawberry slices and mint leaves.
Yield: about $1^1/_4$ quarts yogurt

THE CHRISTMAS COOKIE JAR

A delicious holiday tradition, freshly baked cookies tickle our noses with their sweet, spicy aromas. Whether crunchy, crispy, chewy, or gooey, these little tastes of Christmas invite us to slow down and remember the goodness of an old-fashioned celebration. For an added touch of nostalgia, we displayed our treats in a collection of heirloom cookie jars. This Yuletide, may your Christmas cookie jar overflow with taste-tempting treats and warm, wonderful holiday memories.

GINGERBREAD HOUSE COOKIES

COOKIES
- 1/2 cup butter or margarine, softened
- 1/2 cup firmly packed brown sugar
- 1/2 cup molasses
- 1 egg
- 2 1/2 cups all-purpose flour
- 2 teaspoons ground ginger
- 1 teaspoon ground cinnamon
- 1 teaspoon baking soda
- 1/2 teaspoon ground nutmeg
- 1/4 teaspoon ground cloves
- 1/4 teaspoon salt

ROYAL ICING
- 2 2/3 cups sifted confectioners sugar
- 4 tablespoons warm water
- 2 tablespoons meringue powder
- 1/2 teaspoon lemon extract

  Candies, mints, and gumdrops to decorate

Preheat oven to 350 degrees. For cookies, cream butter and brown sugar in a large bowl until fluffy. Add molasses and egg; beat until smooth. In a medium bowl, combine remaining ingredients; add to creamed mixture and stir until a soft dough forms. On a lightly floured surface, use a floured rolling pin to roll out dough to 1/4-inch thickness. Use a floured 5 x 7 1/2-inch gingerbread house-shaped cookie cutter to cut out cookies. Transfer to a greased baking sheet. Bake 10 to 12 minutes or until edges are firm. Transfer to a wire rack with waxed paper underneath to cool completely.

For royal icing, beat confectioners sugar, water, meringue powder, and lemon extract in a medium bowl with an electric mixer 7 to 10 minutes or until stiff. Spoon icing into a pastry bag fitted with a medium round tip. Pipe icing on cookies. Use candies, mints, and gumdrops to decorate cookies as desired. Allow icing to harden. Store in an airtight container.

Yield: 6 cookies

(Opposite) The heartwarming taste of home-baked gingerbread is always a holiday favorite. This year, share the goodness with the whole family as you gather to decorate these Gingerbread House Cookies.

Lacy patterns of royal icing create the look of delicate crochet atop tangy Lemon Snowflake Cookies.

LEMON SNOWFLAKE COOKIES

COOKIES
- 1/2 cup butter or margarine, softened
- 1 cup sugar
- 1 egg
- 2 tablespoons milk
- 1 teaspoon grated lemon zest
- 1/2 teaspoon lemon extract
- 2 cups all-purpose flour
- 1/2 teaspoon baking soda
- 1/2 teaspoon cream of tartar
- 1/4 teaspoon salt

ROYAL ICING
- 1 3/4 cups sifted confectioners sugar
- 2 tablespoons warm water
- 1 tablespoon meringue powder
- 1/8 teaspoon lemon extract

For cookies, cream butter and sugar in a large bowl until fluffy. Add egg, milk, lemon zest, and lemon extract; beat until smooth. In a small bowl, combine remaining ingredients; add to creamed mixture and stir until a soft dough forms. Wrap in plastic wrap and chill 2 hours or until dough is firm.

Preheat oven to 375 degrees. On a lightly floured surface, use a floured rolling pin to roll out dough to 1/8-inch thickness. Use a 3-inch-diameter fluted-edge cookie cutter to cut out cookies. Transfer to a lightly greased baking sheet. Bake 8 to 10 minutes or until bottoms of cookies are lightly browned. Transfer to a wire rack to cool completely.

For royal icing, beat confectioners sugar, water, meringue powder, and lemon extract in a medium bowl with an electric mixer 7 to 10 minutes or until stiff. Spoon icing into a pastry bag fitted with a small round tip. Pipe snowflake design on each cookie. Allow icing to harden. Store in an airtight container.

Yield: about 2 1/2 dozen cookies

Chunky Chocolate-Caramel Chewies *(lower right)* are a gooey, nutty delight. A dusting of powdered sugar adds sweetness to light Butter-Nut Cookies. Striped with vanilla candy coating, Chocolate Squares have a hint of almond flavor.

CHOCOLATE SQUARES

- 1/2 cup butter or margarine, softened
- 1 cup sugar
- 1/3 cup (about 4 ounces) almond paste
- 2 eggs
- 1 teaspoon vanilla extract
- 1 teaspoon chocolate extract
- 1 3/4 cups all-purpose flour
- 3/4 cup cocoa
- 1 teaspoon baking powder
- 1/4 teaspoon salt
- 4 ounces vanilla-flavored candy coating

In a medium bowl, cream butter and sugar until fluffy. Add almond paste, eggs, and extracts. Beat 2 minutes at high speed of an electric mixer. In a small bowl, combine flour, cocoa, baking powder, and salt. Add dry ingredients to creamed mixture; stir until a soft dough forms. Shape dough into 2 balls. Wrap in plastic wrap and chill 1 hour.

Preheat oven to 350 degrees. On a lightly floured surface, use a floured rolling pin to roll out each half of dough to 1/4-inch thickness. Using a sharp knife, cut dough into 2-inch squares. Transfer to a greased baking sheet. Bake 10 to 12 minutes or until firm. Transfer to a wire rack to cool completely.

In a small saucepan, melt candy coating over low heat, stirring constantly. Spoon candy coating into a pastry bag fitted with a medium round tip. Pipe stripes on cookies. Allow coating to harden. Store in an airtight container.
Yield: about 4 dozen cookies

BUTTER-NUT COOKIES

- 1 cup butter or margarine, softened
- 1 1/2 cups sifted confectioners sugar, divided
- 1 teaspoon vanilla-butter-nut flavoring
- 2 cups all-purpose flour
- 1/4 teaspoon salt
- 3/4 cup coarsely ground pecans, toasted

Preheat oven to 375 degrees. In a large bowl, cream butter, 3/4 cup confectioners sugar, and vanilla-butter-nut flavoring until fluffy. In a small bowl, combine flour and salt. Add dry ingredients and pecans to creamed mixture; stir until well blended. Shape dough into 1-inch balls; place on an ungreased baking sheet. Bake 12 to 14 minutes or until firm to touch and bottoms are lightly browned. When cool

enough to handle, roll in remaining 3/4 cup confectioners sugar. Transfer cookies to waxed paper; allow to cool completely. Roll in confectioners sugar again. Store in an airtight container.
Yield: about 5 1/2 dozen cookies

CHOCOLATE-CARAMEL CHEWIES

- 3/4 cup butter or margarine, softened
- 1/2 cup firmly packed brown sugar
- 2 eggs
- 1 teaspoon vanilla extract
- 1 1/2 cups all-purpose flour
- 1/4 teaspoon baking soda
- 1/4 teaspoon salt
- 1 1/2 cups chopped pecans
- 1 cup milk chocolate chips
- 22 caramel candies, quartered

Preheat oven to 350 degrees. In a medium bowl, cream butter and brown sugar until fluffy. Add eggs and vanilla; stir until smooth. In a small bowl, combine flour, baking soda, and salt. Add dry ingredients to creamed mixture; stir until a soft dough forms. Stir in pecans, chocolate chips, and caramel pieces. Drop tablespoonfuls of dough 2 inches apart onto a greased baking sheet. Bake 8 to

10 minutes or until edges are lightly browned. Allow cookies to cool slightly on pan; transfer to a wire rack to cool completely. Store in an airtight container.
Yield: about 4 dozen cookies

CHRISTMAS ORNAMENT COOKIES

COOKIES

- ³/₄ cup butter or margarine, softened
- ¹/₂ cup granulated sugar
- 1 egg
- 1 teaspoon vanilla extract
- 1³/₄ cups all-purpose flour
- 3 tablespoons cornstarch
- ¹/₂ teaspoon baking powder
- ¹/₈ teaspoon salt
- 2 tablespoons confectioners sugar

FILLING

- 2 tablespoons butter or margarine, softened
- 2 tablespoons vegetable shortening
- ³/₄ cup sifted confectioners sugar
- 2 teaspoons milk
- ³/₄ teaspoon peppermint extract
  Red and green powdered food coloring

Preheat oven to 350 degrees. For cookies, cream butter and granulated sugar in a medium bowl until fluffy. Add egg and vanilla; beat until smooth. In a small bowl, combine flour, cornstarch, baking powder, and salt. Add dry ingredients to creamed mixture; stir until a soft dough forms. On a lightly floured surface, use a floured rolling pin to roll out dough to ¹/₈-inch thickness. Use a 3-inch-diameter fluted-edge cookie cutter to cut out cookies. Transfer to a greased baking sheet. Use a 2-inch star-shaped cookie cutter to cut out centers of half of cookies on baking sheet. Bake 10 to 12 minutes or until edges are lightly browned. Transfer to a wire rack with waxed paper underneath to cool completely. Sift confectioners sugar over warm star cutout cookies.

For filling, cream butter, shortening, and confectioners sugar in a medium bowl until well blended. Stir in milk and peppermint extract. Divide filling into 2 small bowls. Using ¹/₂ teaspoon of each food coloring, tint filling red and green. Spread a thin layer of filling on top of each whole cookie and place a star cutout cookie on top. Allow filling to harden. Store in an airtight container.
Yield: about 20 cookies

Santa won't be able to resist these yummy treats! As pretty as holiday jewels, Christmas Ornament Cookies *(right)* get four stars for their buttery taste and creamy peppermint filling. Chewy Chocolate-Raspberry Squares are capped with a delightful hazelnut meringue-like topping.

CHOCOLATE-RASPBERRY SQUARES

- 1 cup butter or margarine, softened
- 1¹/₂ cups sugar, divided
- 4 eggs, separated and divided
- 2¹/₂ cups all-purpose flour
- 1 jar (12 ounces) raspberry jelly
- 1 cup semisweet chocolate mini chips
- ¹/₄ teaspoon salt
- 2 cups coarsely ground hazelnuts

Preheat oven to 350 degrees. In a medium bowl, cream butter and ¹/₂ cup sugar until fluffy. Reserve egg whites in a small bowl. Add 2 egg yolks to butter mixture; beat until smooth. Set aside remaining egg yolks for another use. Stir in flour until well blended. Press dough into bottom of a greased 10 x 15-inch jellyroll pan. Bake 15 to 20 minutes or until lightly browned. Spread jelly over hot crust; sprinkle chocolate chips over jelly. Beat 4 reserved egg whites until foamy. Gradually add remaining 1 cup sugar and salt; beat until stiff peaks form. Fold in hazelnuts. Gently spread egg white mixture over chocolate layer. Bake 20 to 25 minutes or until lightly browned on top. Cool completely in pan. Cut into 2-inch squares. Store in an airtight container.
Yield: about 3 dozen squares

CHEWY PECAN SQUARES

CRUST
- 1 package (18.25 ounces) yellow cake mix
- 1 egg
- 1/3 cup vegetable oil

FILLING
- 1 cup sugar
- 4 eggs
- 1/2 teaspoon salt
- 1 cup dark corn syrup
- 1/4 cup butter or margarine, melted
- 1 teaspoon vanilla extract
- 2 cups chopped pecans

Preheat oven to 350 degrees. For crust, combine cake mix, egg, and oil in a medium bowl. Press mixture into bottom of a greased 9 x 13-inch baking pan. Bake 20 minutes.

For filling, beat sugar, eggs, and salt in a large bowl until well blended. Beat in corn syrup, melted butter, and vanilla. Stir in pecans. Pour over hot crust. Bake at 350 degrees 30 to 35 minutes or until brown around edges and center is set. Cool completely. Cut into 1 1/2-inch squares. Store in an airtight container.

Yield: about 3 dozen squares

PECAN-CINNAMON COOKIES

- 1/2 cup vegetable shortening
- 1/4 cup butter or margarine, softened
- 1 cup firmly packed brown sugar
- 1/4 cup light corn syrup
- 1 egg
- 1 tablespoon vanilla extract
- 2 cups all-purpose flour
- 2 teaspoons ground cinnamon
- 1 teaspoon baking soda
- 1/2 teaspoon salt
- 1 1/2 cups chopped pecans, toasted

Preheat oven to 350 degrees. In a medium bowl, cream shortening, butter, and brown sugar until fluffy. Add corn syrup, egg, and vanilla; beat until smooth. In a small bowl, combine flour, cinnamon, baking soda, and salt. Add dry ingredients to creamed mixture; stir until a soft dough forms. Stir in pecans. Drop tablespoonfuls of dough 2 inches apart onto a greased baking sheet. Bake 8 to 10 minutes or until bottoms are lightly browned. Allow cookies to cool on pan 5 minutes; transfer to a wire rack to cool completely. Store in an airtight container.

Yield: about 4 dozen cookies

Pecan-Cinnamon Cookies (*top left*) are bursting with nuts. A delicious variation on a Southern favorite, Chewy Pecan Squares (*right*) taste like miniature pecan pies! Coffee-flavored Mocha Crunch Cookies are loaded with chocolate mini chips.

MOCHA CRUNCH COOKIES

- 1/2 cup butter or margarine, softened
- 1/4 cup vegetable shortening
- 1/2 cup plus 2 tablespoons granulated sugar, divided
- 1/2 cup firmly packed brown sugar
- 1 egg yolk
- 1 1/2 teaspoons vanilla extract
- 1 3/4 cups all-purpose flour
- 1 tablespoon instant coffee granules
- 1/4 teaspoon baking powder
- 1/4 teaspoon baking soda
- 1/4 teaspoon salt
- 1/2 cup semisweet chocolate mini chips

Preheat oven to 375 degrees. In a large bowl, cream butter, shortening, 1/2 cup granulated sugar, and brown sugar until fluffy. Add egg yolk and vanilla; beat until smooth. In a small bowl, combine flour, instant coffee, baking powder, baking soda, and salt. Add dry ingredients to creamed mixture; stir until a soft dough forms. Stir in chocolate chips. Shape dough into 1-inch balls; place 2 inches apart on an ungreased baking sheet. Flatten cookies with bottom of a glass dipped in remaining 2 tablespoons granulated sugar. Bake 10 to 12 minutes or until edges are lightly browned. Allow cookies to cool on pan 2 minutes; transfer cookies to a wire rack to cool completely. Store in an airtight container.

Yield: about 4 dozen cookies

CHOCOLATE-ORANGE LOGS

COOKIES
1 cup butter or margarine, softened
1 cup sugar
1 egg
1 teaspoon grated orange zest
2¼ cups all-purpose flour
1 teaspoon baking powder

ICING
½ cup semisweet chocolate chips
1 teaspoon vegetable shortening
¼ teaspoon orange extract
¾ cup finely chopped pecans

For cookies, cream butter and sugar in a large bowl until fluffy. Add egg and orange zest; beat until smooth. In a medium bowl, combine flour and baking powder. Add dry ingredients to creamed mixture; stir until a soft dough forms.

Spoon mixture into a pastry bag fitted with a large star tip (we used tip #6B). Pipe 2½-inch strips of dough 2 inches apart onto an ungreased baking sheet. Chill cookies 30 minutes. Preheat oven to 375 degrees. Bake about 8 minutes or until golden and firm. Allow cookies to cool on pan 2 minutes; transfer to a wire rack to cool completely.

For icing, place chocolate chips and shortening in a small microwave-safe bowl; microwave on medium power (50%) 3 minutes or until chips are soft. Stir chips until smooth; stir in orange extract. Dip one end of each cookie in chocolate mixture and then in pecans. Place on waxed paper; allow chocolate to harden. Store in an airtight container.
Yield: about 5 dozen cookies

SPRINGERLE

Make cookies at least 2 weeks in advance to allow flavor to develop.

4 eggs
2 cups sugar
1 teaspoon grated lemon zest
1 teaspoon anise extract **or**
    2 teaspoons anise seed, crushed
3¾ cups all-purpose flour
1 teaspoon baking powder

In a large bowl, beat eggs at high speed of an electric mixer 1 minute. Gradually add sugar, beating at high speed 10 minutes. Add lemon zest and anise extract. In a medium bowl, combine flour and baking powder. Stir in dry ingredients (dough will be stiff). Shape dough into 2 balls. Wrap in plastic wrap and chill 1 hour.

The raised designs on the Springerle (*top*) are created using a springerle rolling pin or cookie molds. A traditional German sweet, the licorice-flavored treats are best when dunked in coffee or cocoa. Chocolate-Orange Logs (*left*) are melt-in-your-mouth wonderful. Baked-on Christmas trees, made by piping on chocolate batter, adorn yummy White Chocolate Cookies.

Work with 1 ball of dough at a time. On a lightly floured surface, use a floured rolling pin to roll out dough into a ¼-inch-thick rectangle the width of a springerle rolling pin. Pressing firmly, roll designs into dough using springerle rolling pin (or press dough into individual cookie molds). If using rolling pin, cut out cookies along design lines (a pizza cutter works well). Place cookies on a lightly greased baking sheet; allow to stand uncovered at room temperature overnight.

Preheat oven to 350 degrees. Place baking sheet in oven; immediately reduce heat to 300 degrees. Bake 15 to 20 minutes or until bottoms are lightly browned. Transfer cookies to a wire rack to cool completely. Store in an airtight container.
Yield: about 7½ dozen cookies

WHITE CHOCOLATE COOKIES

¾ cup butter or margarine, softened and divided
¼ cup vegetable shortening
½ cup granulated sugar
½ cup firmly packed brown sugar
1 egg yolk
½ teaspoon vanilla extract
1⅓ cups plus 6 tablespoons all-purpose flour, divided
½ teaspoon baking powder
⅛ teaspoon salt
½ cup coarsely chopped walnuts
2 ounces white chocolate, coarsely chopped
1 tablespoon chocolate-flavored syrup

In a large bowl, beat ½ cup butter and shortening until well blended; add sugars and beat until fluffy. Add egg yolk and vanilla; beat until smooth. In a small bowl, combine 1⅓ cups flour, baking powder, and salt. In a food processor, process walnuts and chocolate until finely ground. Add dry ingredients and walnut mixture to creamed mixture; stir until a soft dough forms. Wrap in plastic wrap and chill 1 to 2 hours.

Preheat oven to 350 degrees. Shape chilled dough into ¾-inch balls; place 2 inches apart on an ungreased baking sheet. Flatten cookies with bottom of a glass dipped in 2 tablespoons flour. In a small bowl, mix remaining ¼ cup butter, remaining 4 tablespoons flour, and syrup; stir until well blended. Spoon chocolate mixture into a pastry bag fitted with a small round tip. Pipe tree design onto each cookie. Bake 8 to 10 minutes or until edges are lightly browned. Transfer to a wire rack to cool completely. Store in an airtight container.
Yield: about 6 dozen cookies

PEPPERMINT SNOWBALLS

1¼ cups crushed peppermint candies (about 45 round candies)
1⅓ cups sugar, divided
½ cup butter or margarine, softened
¼ cup vegetable shortening
2 eggs
1 teaspoon peppermint extract
¾ teaspoon vanilla extract
2½ cups all-purpose flour
¼ teaspoon salt

Preheat oven to 350 degrees. In a food processor, finely grind peppermint candies and ⅓ cup sugar to a powdery consistency; transfer to a small bowl. In a large bowl, cream butter, shortening, and remaining 1 cup sugar until fluffy. Add eggs and extracts; beat until smooth. In a medium bowl, combine flour and salt. Add dry ingredients to creamed mixture; stir until a soft dough forms. Shape dough into 1-inch balls. Roll balls in candy mixture. For best results, place 6 cookies at a time on an ungreased baking sheet. Bake 8 minutes; immediately roll hot cookies in candy mixture. Transfer to a wire rack to cool completely. Repeat with remaining dough. Store in an airtight container.
Yield: about 5½ dozen cookies

CHINESE NEW YEAR COOKIES

½ cup butter or margarine, softened
1 cup sugar
2 eggs
½ teaspoon vanilla extract
2¼ cups all-purpose flour
2 teaspoons baking powder
1 teaspoon Chinese five spice powder
1 teaspoon finely chopped crystallized ginger
¼ teaspoon salt

Preheat oven to 375 degrees. In a large bowl, cream butter and sugar until fluffy. Add eggs and vanilla; beat until smooth. In a medium bowl, combine remaining ingredients. Add dry ingredients to creamed mixture; stir until a soft dough forms. On a lightly floured surface, use a floured rolling pin to roll out dough to ⅛-inch thickness. Use a 3-inch-wide dog-shaped cookie cutter to cut out cookies. Transfer to an ungreased baking sheet. Bake 8 to 10 minutes or until edges are lightly browned. Transfer to a wire rack to cool completely. Store in an airtight container.
Yield: about 4 dozen cookies

Celebrate 1994, the Year of the Dog, with crispy Chinese New Year Cookies (*top*). A taste-tempting treat, they're made with Chinese five spice powder and crystallized ginger. Cool Peppermint Snowballs (*right*) are flavored with peppermint extract and rolled in a mixture of crushed peppermints and sugar. Soft and chewy, Chocolate Mint-Topped Cookies pair almond-flavored cookies with a chocolate-mint icing.

CHOCOLATE MINT-TOPPED COOKIES

¾ cup butter or margarine, softened
¾ cup sugar
1 egg
4 teaspoons milk
1 teaspoon vanilla extract
½ teaspoon almond extract
2 cups all-purpose flour
1½ teaspoons baking powder
¼ teaspoon salt
1 package (12 ounces) individually wrapped layered chocolate mints

Green candied cherry halves to decorate

In a large bowl, cream butter and sugar until fluffy. Add egg, milk, and extracts; beat until smooth. In a small bowl, combine flour, baking powder, and salt. Add dry ingredients to creamed mixture; stir until a soft dough forms. Shape dough into a ball. Wrap in plastic wrap and chill 1 hour.

Preheat oven to 375 degrees. On a lightly floured surface, use a floured rolling pin to roll out dough to ⅛-inch thickness. Use a 2¼-inch-diameter fluted-edge cookie cutter to cut out cookies. Transfer to a greased baking sheet. Bake 7 to 9 minutes or until bottoms are lightly browned. Remove from oven and immediately place 1 mint on top of each hot cookie; allow to soften. Spread softened mint evenly over each cookie. Decorate each cookie with a cherry half. Transfer to a wire rack to cool completely. Store in an airtight container.
Yield: about 4 dozen cookies

ORANGE-MOLASSES CRISPIES

  1/3 cup butter or margarine, softened
  1/2 cup vegetable shortening
  3/4 cup sugar
  1/4 cup molasses
    2 tablespoons orange liqueur
    2 teaspoons grated orange zest
  1/2 teaspoon vanilla extract
 1 1/2 cups all-purpose flour
    1 teaspoon baking soda
    1 cup finely chopped walnuts

Preheat oven to 350 degrees. In a large bowl, cream butter, shortening, and sugar until fluffy. Stir in molasses, orange liqueur, orange zest, and vanilla until well blended. In a small bowl, combine flour and baking soda. Add dry ingredients to creamed mixture; stir until a soft dough forms. Stir in walnuts. Drop teaspoonfuls of dough 1 inch apart onto a greased baking sheet. Bake 8 to 10 minutes or until cookies are golden brown. Allow cookies to cool on pan 3 minutes; transfer to a wire rack to cool completely. Store in an airtight container.
Yield: about 5 dozen cookies

CHRISTMAS TREE COOKIES

    1 cup butter or margarine, softened
    1 cup sugar
    2 eggs
    1 teaspoon vanilla extract
 3 1/3 cups all-purpose flour
    1 teaspoon baking powder
  1/2 teaspoon salt
    1 cup finely crushed hard red
        candies (about 20 candies)

In a large bowl, cream butter and sugar until fluffy. Add eggs and vanilla; beat until smooth. In a medium bowl, combine flour, baking powder, and salt. Add dry ingredients to creamed mixture; stir until a soft dough forms. Wrap in plastic wrap and chill 1 hour.

Preheat oven to 350 degrees. On a lightly floured surface, use a floured rolling pin to roll out dough to 1/8-inch thickness. Use a 4 1/2-inch tree-shaped cookie cutter to cut out cookies. Transfer cookies to a lightly greased aluminum foil-lined baking sheet. Use a heart-shaped aspic cutter to cut out heart from center of each cookie. Bake 8 to 10 minutes or until cookies are firm. Cool completely on pan; leave cookies on foil to decorate.

In a small saucepan, melt candies over medium heat; reduce heat to low. Spoon melted candies into each heart cutout. Allow

Cake-like Russian Rock Cookies (*left*) are studded with dates, maraschino cherries, and pecans. Perfect with coffee or tea, Orange-Molasses Crispies (*right*) will be a hit with those who enjoy brickly cookies. Deliver sweet holiday wishes with Christmas Tree Cookies. Their heart-shaped centers are filled with melted hard candies.

candies to harden. Carefully remove cookies from foil. Store in an airtight container.
Yield: about 5 1/2 dozen cookies

RUSSIAN ROCK COOKIES

    1 cup butter or margarine, softened
    1 cup granulated sugar
  1/2 cup firmly packed brown sugar
  1/2 cup light corn syrup
  1/2 cup buttermilk
    3 eggs, beaten
    1 teaspoon vanilla extract
 3 1/4 cups all-purpose flour, divided
    1 package (8 ounces) chopped dates
    1 tablespoon ground cinnamon
    1 teaspoon ground cloves
    1 teaspoon ground nutmeg
  1/2 teaspoon baking soda
  1/4 teaspoon salt
    1 jar (10 ounces) maraschino
        cherries, drained and chopped
    2 cups chopped pecans

Preheat oven to 350 degrees. In a large bowl, cream butter and sugars until fluffy. Add corn syrup, buttermilk, eggs, and vanilla; beat until smooth. In a small bowl, combine 1/4 cup flour and dates; stir until dates are coated with flour. In a medium bowl, combine remaining 3 cups flour, cinnamon, cloves, nutmeg, baking soda, and salt. Add dry ingredients to creamed mixture; stir until a soft dough forms. Stir in dates, cherries, and pecans. Drop teaspoonfuls of dough 1 inch apart onto a greased baking sheet. Bake 12 to 15 minutes or until edges are lightly browned. Transfer to a wire rack to cool completely. Store in an airtight container.
Yield: about 8 dozen cookies

Gifts from the Kitchen

Spread the festive Christmas spirit among friends and neighbors with luscious homemade gifts prepared in your holiday kitchen! The lucky recipients will enjoy the tasty treats and admire the creative packaging custom-made with your loving hands. Simple to create, our delicious recipes and easy crafts will leave you ample time to enjoy the Yuletide season.

Entice the chocolate lovers on your list with sumptuous Brandied Fruit Balls. The spirited candies are created by coating a mixture of dried fruit, walnuts, and brandy with semisweet chocolate. Gold foil candy cups and a handsome gift tag add opulence to your gift boxes.

BRANDIED FRUIT BALLS

- 1 pound dried fruit (we used a mixture of cherries, peaches, dates, prunes, cranberries, and apricots)
- 1 cup chopped walnuts
- 4 tablespoons brandy
- $\frac{1}{2}$ cup sifted confectioners sugar
- $4\frac{1}{2}$ ounces semisweet chocolate chips
- 7 ounces chocolate-flavored candy coating

In a food processor, combine dried fruit, walnuts, and brandy; process until finely chopped. Chill in an airtight container 1 hour. Press brandied fruit into 1-inch balls; roll lightly in confectioners sugar and place on a baking sheet.

In a heavy medium saucepan over low heat, melt chocolate chips and candy coating. Remove chocolate from heat. Placing each fruit ball on a fork and holding over saucepan, spoon chocolate over balls. Transfer to a baking sheet covered with waxed paper. Place in refrigerator; allow chocolate to harden. Store in an airtight container in refrigerator.

Yield: about 4 dozen fruit balls

For poinsettia tag, press a 4" length of $1\frac{1}{2}$"w ribbon in half lengthwise. Follow manufacturer's instructions to fuse $\frac{3}{4}$"w paper-backed fusible web tape along 1 short edge of a $3\frac{3}{4}$" x 5" piece of heavy ivory paper; do not remove paper backing. Turn paper over and fuse another length of web tape along same edge. Remove paper backing from both lengths. Insert edge of paper into fold of ribbon and fuse ribbon in place. Trim ends of ribbon even with edges of paper. Hot glue a silk poinsettia with leaves to tag. Use a green pen to write greeting on tag.

CHERRY-NUT CAKES

- 12 ounces dried cherries (available at gourmet food stores)
- $1\frac{1}{2}$ cups orange-flavored liqueur
- 6 tablespoons finely chopped crystallized ginger
- 1 cup butter or margarine, softened
- $\frac{3}{4}$ cup firmly packed brown sugar
- 6 eggs
- 1 tablespoon vanilla extract
- $1\frac{1}{2}$ cups all-purpose flour
- 1 teaspoon ground cinnamon
- $\frac{1}{2}$ teaspoon ground nutmeg
- $\frac{1}{4}$ teaspoon ground cloves

- 2 cups chopped unsalted pecans
- 2 cups chopped unsalted walnuts
- 2 cups chopped unsalted cashews

In a small bowl, combine cherries, liqueur, and ginger. Cover and let stand at room temperature 8 hours or overnight.

Preheat oven to 350 degrees. In a large bowl, cream butter and brown sugar until fluffy. Beat in eggs and vanilla. In a small bowl, combine flour, cinnamon, nutmeg, and cloves. Add flour mixture to creamed mixture; stir until smooth. Stir in cherry mixture and nuts. Spoon batter into greased and floured $2\frac{1}{2}$ x $4\frac{1}{2}$-inch loaf pans. Bake 35 to 40 minutes or until a toothpick inserted in center of cake comes out clean. Cool in pans 10 minutes; remove from pans and cool completely on a wire rack. Store in an airtight container.

Yield: about $1\frac{1}{2}$ dozen cakes

For cherry tag, glue a $2\frac{1}{4}$" x $3\frac{5}{8}$" piece of ivory paper to a $2\frac{3}{8}$" x $3\frac{3}{4}$" piece of green paper. Use a ruler and a red pen to draw a border on ivory paper $\frac{1}{4}$" from edges. Use black and red pens to write greeting on tag. Use a large needle to make a hole in 1 corner of tag. Loop 8" of $\frac{1}{16}$" dia. red cord around stem of cherry jingle bell ornament. Thread cord through hole in tag and knot cord at back.

A batch of our spicy Cherry-Nut Cakes makes plenty of individually wrapped goodies to share with coworkers or other groups. To pass them out in style, finish a decorated basket with a hand-lettered tag trimmed with colorful cherry jingle bells. Your colleagues will clamor for more of these sweet cakes!

A delicious new twist on the traditional holiday decoration, our Cherry-Almond Christmas Wreath blends colorful candied cherries and crunchy almonds in a rich yeast bread. A buttery almond-flavored filling and a drizzling of sweet icing add richness to this pretty present. For a wonderful treat, deliver the fresh-baked wreath covered with cellophane and trimmed with a seasonal bow!

CHERRY-ALMOND CHRISTMAS WREATH

BREAD
1	package dry yeast
1/4	cup warm water
1/2	cup butter or margarine, softened
1/4	cup warm milk
2	tablespoons sugar
1	teaspoon ground cardamom
1/2	teaspoon salt
3	to 3 1/2 cups all-purpose flour, divided
2	eggs
	Vegetable cooking spray

FILLING
1/2	cup sugar
1/2	cup almond paste
1/3	cup butter or margarine, softened
1	teaspoon almond extract
3/4	cup red and green candied cherries, divided
1/2	cup sliced almonds, toasted

ICING
1	cup sifted confectioners sugar
2	tablespoons milk
1/4	teaspoon almond extract

In a large bowl, dissolve yeast in warm water; stir in butter, milk, sugar, cardamom, salt, and 1 cup flour. Stir in eggs and enough remaining flour to form a soft dough. Turn onto a lightly floured surface and knead 5 minutes or until dough becomes smooth and elastic. Place in a large bowl sprayed with cooking spray, turning once to coat top of dough. Cover and let rise in a warm place (80 to 85 degrees) 1 hour or until doubled in size.

For filling, combine sugar, almond paste, butter, and almond extract in a small bowl until well blended. Set aside.

Turn dough onto a lightly floured surface and punch down. Use a floured rolling pin to roll out dough to a 9 x 30-inch rectangle. Spread filling over dough to within 1/2 inch of edges; sprinkle with 1/2 cup cherries and almonds. Beginning with 1 long edge, roll dough jellyroll-style; pinch seam to seal. Cut dough in half lengthwise; turn cut sides up. Wrap dough halves around each other with cut sides up. Place dough on a greased baking sheet; shape into a wreath and pinch ends together to seal. Place remaining 1/4 cup cherries on top of wreath. Spray with cooking spray. Cover loosely with plastic wrap and let rise in a warm place about 30 minutes or until doubled in size.

Preheat oven to 350 degrees. Bake 30 to 40 minutes or until lightly browned. Transfer to a wire rack to cool completely.

For icing, combine all ingredients in a small bowl; stir until smooth. Drizzle icing over bread. Allow icing to harden; wrap in cellophane.

Yield: about 20 servings

Your friends will relish the sweet, zesty flavor of Roasted Red Pepper Jelly! A versatile condiment, it makes a savory accompaniment to a meat dish, and it's perfect for perking up an appetizer such as cream cheese and crackers. For a country presentation, top the lids with homespun fabric and nestle the jars in little baskets adorned with torn-fabric bows and handmade gift tags.

ROASTED RED PEPPER JELLY

- 6 large sweet red peppers
- 6 cups sugar
- 1 cup white wine vinegar
- 2 pouches (3 ounces each) liquid fruit pectin

Follow manufacturer's instructions to prepare canning jars, lids, and bands.

To roast peppers, cut in half lengthwise and remove seeds and membranes. Place skin side up on an ungreased baking sheet; flatten with hand. Broil about 3 inches from heat about 15 to 20 minutes or until peppers are blackened and charred. Immediately seal peppers in a plastic bag and allow to steam 10 to 15 minutes. Remove charred skin. In a food processor, process peppers until finely chopped. In a heavy large saucepan, combine peppers, sugar, and vinegar until well blended. Stirring constantly over high heat, bring pepper mixture to a rolling boil. Stir in liquid pectin. Stirring constantly, bring to a rolling boil again and boil 1 minute. Remove from heat; skim off foam. Fill sterilized jars to within 1/4 inch of tops. Wipe jar rims and threads. Quickly cover with lids and screw bands on tightly. Using water-bath method as directed by the USDA, process jars 5 minutes. When jars have cooled, check seals. Lids should be curved down or remain so when pressed. Refrigerate all unsealed jars.
Yield: about 3 1/2 pints

JELLY BASKETS

For each basket, you will need a basket to hold jar, fabric for bow, fabric scraps for tag, paper-backed fusible web, brown craft paper, heavy paper for tag backing, 20" of jute twine, tracing paper, pinking shears, a 1/8" hole punch, and black felt-tip pen with fine point.
For jar lid insert, you will need fabric, polyester bonded batting, lightweight cardboard, and craft glue.

1. For bow, measure around top of basket; add 18". Tear a 1"w strip of fabric the determined measurement. Tie fabric strip into a bow around top of basket.
2. For tag, follow manufacturer's instructions to fuse web to wrong sides of brown paper and fabric scraps. Remove paper backing from brown paper. Fuse brown paper to heavy paper. Use pinking shears to cut an approx. 2 3/4" x 3 1/2" piece from paper.
3. Trace house, roof, and tree patterns onto tracing paper; cut out. Use patterns to cut shapes from fabric scraps. Remove paper backing from shapes. Arrange shapes on tag; fuse in place.
4. Use black pen to draw window and door on house, dashed lines around house to resemble stitching, and trunks for trees; use pen to write "MERRY CHRISTMAS" on tag.
5. Punch holes approx. 1/2" apart 1/4" from edges of tag. Beginning at top left corner, thread twine through holes. Tie tag to fabric strip on basket.
6. For jar lid insert, use flat part of a jar lid (same size as jar lid used in storing food) as a pattern to cut 1 circle each from fabric, batting, and cardboard. Matching edges, glue batting to cardboard. Glue edges of fabric to batting.
7. (**Note:** If jar has been sealed in canning, be careful not to break seal of lid. If seal of lid is broken, jar must be refrigerated.) Remove band from filled jar; place jar lid insert in band and screw in place over lid.

Your neighbors will sing "Let it snow!" when you treat them to a chill-chasing coffee break featuring crunchy Cinnamon-Walnut Biscotti! Presented in a basket lined with a snowy cross-stitched bread cloth, the nutty goodies are especially delicious when dunked in hot coffee, cocoa, or tea.

CINNAMON-WALNUT BISCOTTI

- 2 cups all-purpose flour
- 1 cup plus 2 tablespoons sugar, divided
- $1/2$ teaspoon baking soda
- $1/2$ teaspoon baking powder
- $1/4$ teaspoon salt
- 3 eggs, divided
- 1 egg yolk
- 1 teaspoon vanilla extract
- 1 tablespoon grated orange zest
- $1 1/2$ cups walnuts, coarsely chopped and toasted
- $1/4$ teaspoon ground cinnamon
- 1 teaspoon water

Preheat oven to 300 degrees. Using an electric mixer with a dough hook attachment, combine flour, 1 cup sugar, baking soda, baking powder, and salt in a large bowl until well blended. In a small bowl, whisk 2 eggs, 1 egg yolk, vanilla, and orange zest. Add egg mixture to flour mixture; continue beating until a soft dough forms. Turn onto a lightly floured surface. Add walnuts and knead 3 minutes or until walnuts are evenly distributed. Divide dough in half. On a greased and floured baking sheet, shape each piece of dough into a $2 1/2$ x 10-inch loaf, flouring hands as necessary. Allow 3 inches between loaves on baking sheet. In a small bowl, combine remaining 2 tablespoons sugar and cinnamon. In another small bowl, beat remaining egg and water. Brush loaves with egg mixture; sprinkle with sugar and cinnamon mixture. Bake 45 to 50 minutes or until loaves are lightly browned; cool 10 minutes on baking sheet. Cut loaves diagonally into $1/2$-inch slices. Lay cut cookies flat on a baking sheet. Bake 15 minutes, turn cookies over, and bake 15 minutes longer. Transfer cookies to a wire rack to cool completely. Store in an airtight container.
Yield: about $2 1/2$ dozen cookies

LET IT SNOW! (47w x 47h)

X	DMC	B'ST	ANC.	COLOR
	322	✎	978	blue
★	3325		129	lt blue
●	322	French Knot		blue

Grey area indicates beginning of fringe.

Work design on 1 corner of a White Charles Craft Soft Touch™ Bread Cover (14 ct), placing design 4 fabric threads from fringe. Use 3 strands of floss for Cross Stitch and 2 for Backstitch and French Knot.

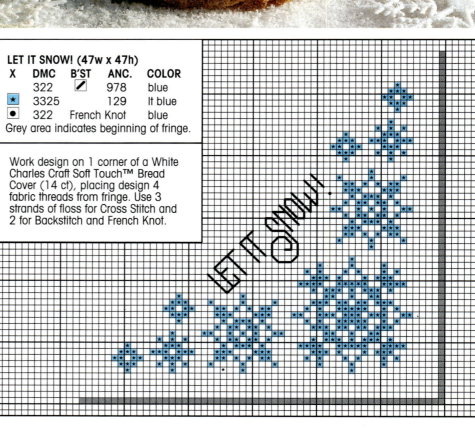

A zesty treat delivered in a personalized gift bag is the perfect token of gratitude during the holiday season. Accented with clever trimmings and filled with jars of colorful Sweet Christmas Pickles, these unique bags are thoughtful ways to remember your dependable postman, a favorite teacher, or other special people on your list. You'll want to bag up extra jars of pickles and keep them on hand for last-minute gift-giving, too!

SWEET CHRISTMAS PICKLES

2	cups pickling lime
2	gallons cold water
7$^1/_2$	pounds cucumbers, peeled
5	pounds sugar (10 cups)
2	quarts white vinegar (5% acidity)
2	tablespoons pickling spice
	Red and green food coloring

Follow manufacturer's instructions to prepare canning jars, lids, and bands.

In a large non-metal bowl, mix pickling lime with water; stir until well blended. Slice cucumbers in half lengthwise; scoop out seeds. Cut into $^1/_2$-inch slices; place in pickling lime mixture. Cover and allow to stand 24 hours. Using a colander, drain and thoroughly rinse cucumber slices with cold water. Return slices to large bowl and cover with cold water; soak 3 hours. Drain again and return to bowl. In another large bowl, combine sugar and vinegar. Place 1 tablespoon pickling spice in each of 2 small cheesecloth squares and tie with string; place in bowl with cucumbers. Pour vinegar mixture over cucumbers; cover and allow to stand 12 hours. Divide cucumber mixture in half, placing each half in a separate large Dutch oven with a spice bag; tint red and green. Boil slowly 50 to 60 minutes or until cucumbers begin to look translucent. Fill sterilized jars to within $^1/_2$ inch of tops. Wipe jar rims and threads. Quickly cover with lids and screw bands on tightly. Using water-bath method as directed by the USDA, process jars 15 minutes. When jars have cooled, check seals. Lids should be curved down or remain so when pressed. Refrigerate all unsealed jars.
Yield: about 7 pints pickles

PERSONALIZED GIFT BAGS

For each bag, you will need a gift bag with handles, paper-backed fusible web, florist wire, craft glue, hot glue gun, and glue sticks.
For "Season's Greetings" bag, you will **also** need fabric, $^5/_8$"w ribbon for bow, heavy white paper and $^3/_8$"w ribbon for tag, a 1" dia. jingle bell, and a black felt-tip pen with fine point.
For Teacher's bag, you will **also** need black construction paper, $^5/_8$"w "ruler" ribbon, a white colored pencil, $^7/_8$"w ribbon for bow, and a small artificial apple with leaves.
For Postman's bag, you will **also** need wrapping paper with stamp motif, a 3" x 4$^1/_4$" piece of heavy white paper for tag, a canceled postage stamp, a black felt-tip pen with fine point, and 1"w and $^1/_2$"w ribbons for bow.

"SEASON'S GREETINGS" BAG
1. Follow manufacturer's instructions to fuse web to wrong side of fabric.
2. Measure length and width of front of bag; cut a piece of fabric the determined measurements. Remove paper backing and fuse fabric to front of bag.
3. Form a multi-loop bow from $^5/_8$"w ribbon; wrap bow with wire at center to secure. Hot glue ribbon around center of bow, covering wire. Hot glue jingle bell to bow. Wire bow to handle of bag.

4. For tag, cut desired size piece of paper. Use craft glue to glue $^3/_8$"w ribbon lengths along top and bottom edges of paper piece. Use pen to write greeting on tag. Hot glue tag to bag.

TEACHER'S BAG
1. Follow Steps 1 and 2 of "Season's Greetings" Bag instructions to fuse black paper to bag.
2. Use craft glue to glue "ruler" ribbon along edges on front of bag, trimming ribbon to fit.
3. Use white pencil to write greeting on black paper.
4. Form a multi-loop bow from $^7/_8$"w ribbon; wrap bow with wire at center to secure. Hot glue apple and leaves to bow. Wire bow to handle of bag.

POSTMAN'S BAG
1. Follow Steps 1 and 2 of "Season's Greetings" Bag instructions to fuse wrapping paper to bag.
2. Form a multi-loop bow from 1"w ribbon; wrap bow with wire at center to secure. Hot glue $^1/_2$"w ribbon around center of bow, covering wire. Wire bow to handle of bag.
3. For tag, use craft glue to glue stamp to upper right corner of paper piece. Use pen and a ruler to draw a line 2$^1/_2$" from left edge of paper piece. Write greeting and address on tag. Hot glue tag to bag.

157

TRACING PATTERNS

When one-half of pattern (indicated by dashed line on pattern) is shown, fold tracing paper in half and place fold along dashed line of pattern. Trace pattern half, including all placement symbols and markings; turn folded paper over and draw over all markings. Unfold pattern and lay flat. Cut out pattern.

When entire pattern is shown, place tracing paper over pattern and trace pattern, including all placement symbols and markings. Cut out pattern.

SEWING SHAPES

1. Center pattern on wrong side of 1 fabric piece and use fabric marking pencil or pen to draw around pattern. **DO NOT CUT OUT SHAPE.**
2. Place fabric pieces right sides together. Leaving an opening for turning, carefully sew pieces together **directly on pencil line**.
3. Leaving a $1/4$" seam allowance, cut out shape. Clip seam allowance at curves and corners. Turn shape right side out.

STENCILING

1. For stencil, cut a piece of acetate 1" larger on all sides than entire pattern. Center acetate over pattern and use permanent felt-tip pen with fine point to trace pattern. Place acetate piece on cutting mat and use craft knife to cut out stencil, making sure edges are smooth.
2. (**Note:** If desired, use removable tape to mask any cutout areas on stencil next to area being painted.) Hold or tape stencil in place. Use a clean, dry stencil brush for each color of paint. Dip brush in paint and remove excess on a paper towel. Brush should be almost dry to produce good results. Beginning at edge of cutout area, apply paint in a stamping motion. If desired, shade design by stamping additional paint around edge of cutout area. Carefully remove stencil and allow paint to dry. To reverse design, carefully clean stencil and turn stencil over.

MACHINE APPLIQUÉ

Note: Follow individual project instructions to prepare appliqués and attach them to background fabric. Unless otherwise indicated in project instructions, set sewing machine for a medium width zigzag stitch

($1/16$"w to $1/8$"w) with a very short stitch length (18 to 24 stitches per inch). When using fine nylon thread for appliquéing, use regular thread in bobbin. Test stitching on project fabric and adjust upper tension as necessary.

1. Cut a piece of tear-away stabilizer or medium weight paper slightly larger than design. Place on wrong side of background fabric under design; baste in place.
2. Beginning on a straight edge if possible, position fabric under presser foot so that most of stitching will be on appliqué piece. Hold upper thread toward you and sew over it for 2 - 3 stitches to prevent thread from raveling. Do not backstitch at end of stitching; all thread ends will be pulled to wrong side of background fabric and secured when stitching is complete. Following Steps 3 and 4 for stitching corners and curves, stitch over all exposed raw edges of appliqués and along detail lines as indicated in project instructions.
3. For **outside corners**, stitch $1/16$" to $1/8$" past corner, stopping with needle in background fabric on side of stitching line farthest from appliqué. Raise presser foot and pivot project; lower presser foot and stitch adjacent side. For **inside corners**, stitch $1/16$" to $1/8$" past corner, stopping with needle in appliqué fabric on side of stitching line farthest from background fabric. Raise presser foot and pivot project; lower presser foot and stitch adjacent side.
4. For **slight curves**, turn project as needed while stitching. For **extreme outside curves**, stop with needle in background fabric. Raise presser foot and pivot project; lower presser foot and continue stitching, pivoting as often as necessary. For **extreme inside curves**, stop with needle in appliqué fabric. Raise presser foot and pivot project; lower presser foot and continue stitching, pivoting as often as necessary.
5. When stitching is complete, remove basting thread and stabilizer from background fabric. Pull loose threads to wrong side of fabric; knot and trim ends.

CROSS STITCH

COUNTED CROSS STITCH (X)
Work 1 Cross Stitch to correspond to each colored square in the chart. For horizontal rows, work stitches in 2 journeys (**Fig. 1**). For vertical rows, complete each stitch as

shown in **Fig. 2**. When working over 2 fabric threads, work Cross Stitch as shown in **Fig. 3**. When the chart shows a Backstitch crossing a colored square (**Fig. 4**), a Cross Stitch (**Fig. 1, 2, or 3**) should be worked first; then the Backstitch (**Fig. 8 or 9, page 159**) should be worked on top of the Cross Stitch.

Fig. 1
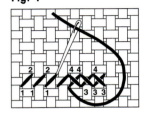

Fig. 2
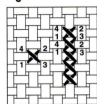

Fig. 3

Fig. 4

QUARTER STITCH ($1/4$X)
Quarter Stitches are denoted by triangular shapes of color in chart and color key. Come up at 1 (**Fig. 5**); then split fabric thread to go down at 2. **Fig. 6** shows the Quarter Stitch when working over two fabric threads.

Fig. 5
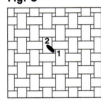

Fig. 6
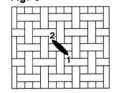

HALF CROSS STITCH ($1/2$X)
This stitch is 1 journey of the Cross Stitch and is worked from lower left to upper right. **Fig. 7** shows the Half Cross Stitch when working over 2 fabric threads.

Fig. 7
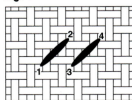

BACKSTITCH (B'ST)

For outline detail, Backstitch (shown in chart and color key by black or colored straight lines) should be worked after the design has been completed (**Fig. 8**). When working over 2 fabric threads, work Backstitch as shown in **Fig. 9**.

Fig. 8

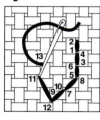

Fig. 9

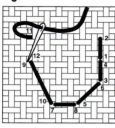

WORKING OVER TWO FABRIC THREADS

(**Note:** Using a hoop is optional.) Roll excess fabric from left to right until stitching area is in proper position. Use the sewing method, keeping stitching hand on right side of fabric and taking needle down and up with 1 stroke. To add support to stitches, place first Cross Stitch on fabric with stitch 1-2 beginning and ending where a vertical fabric thread crosses over a horizontal fabric thread (**Fig. 10**).

Fig. 10

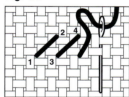

WORKING ON WASTE CANVAS

1. Cover edges of canvas with masking tape.
2. Find desired stitching area on garment and mark center of area with a pin. Match center of canvas to pin. Use blue threads in canvas to place canvas straight on garment; pin canvas to garment. Pin interfacing to wrong side of garment under canvas. Basting through all layers, baste around edges of canvas, from corner to corner, and from side to side.
3. (**Note:** Using a hoop is recommended when working on a large garment. We recommend a hoop that is large enough to encircle entire design.) Using a sharp needle, work design, stitching from large holes to large holes.
4. Remove basting threads and trim canvas to within $3/4$" of design. Dampen canvas until it becomes limp. Use tweezers to pull out canvas threads one at a time. Trim interfacing close to design.

EMBROIDERY

RUNNING STITCH

Make a series of straight stitches with stitch length equal to the space between stitches (**Fig. 1**).

Fig. 1

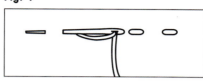

STEM STITCH

Referring to **Fig. 2**, bring needle up at 1; keeping thread below stitching line, go down at 2 and come up at 3. Go down at 4 and come up at 5.

Fig. 2

SATIN STITCH

Referring to **Fig. 3**, bring needle up at odd numbers and go down at even numbers with stitches touching but not overlapping.

Fig. 3

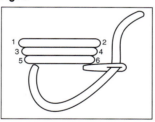

BLANKET STITCH

Referring to **Fig. 4**, bring needle up at 1. Go down at 2 and come up at 3, keeping thread below point of needle. Keeping stitches even, continue going down at even numbers and coming up at odd numbers (**Fig. 5**).

Fig. 4

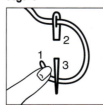

Fig. 5

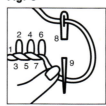

OVERCAST STITCH

Referring to **Fig. 6**, bring needle up at 1; take thread around edge of fabric and bring needle up at 2. Continue stitching along edge of fabric.

Fig. 6

FRENCH KNOT

Bring needle up at 1. Wrap floss once around needle and insert needle at 2, holding end of floss with non-stitching fingers (**Fig. 7**). Tighten knot; then pull needle through fabric, holding floss until it must be released. For a larger knot, use more strands; wrap only once.

Fig. 7

QUILTING

Thread quilting needle with an 18" to 20" length of quilting thread; knot 1 end. Insert needle into quilt top and batting approx. $1/2$" from location of first quilting stitch. Bring needle up where you wish to begin quilting; when knot catches on quilt top, give thread a short quick pull to pop knot through fabric into batting (**Fig. 1**). To quilt, use small Running Stitches (**Fig. 2**). At the end of a length of thread, knot thread close to quilt top and take needle down through all layers of fabric and batting; when knot catches on quilt top, pop knot through fabric into batting. Clip thread close to backing fabric.

Fig. 1

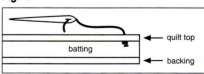

Fig. 2

CREDITS

We want to extend a warm *thank you* to the generous people who allowed us to photograph our projects in their homes.

- *Snowmen's Frolic:* Frank and Carol Clawson
- *Angels of Gold:* Dick and Susan Wildung
- *Visions of Santa:* Becky Owen
- *Enchanting Elegance:* Jerry and Linda Wardlaw
- *A Festival of Trees:* Dr. Reed and Becky Thompson, Frank and Carol Clawson, and Jan and Sandy Scruggs
- *Nostalgic Toyland:* Dick and Susan Wildung
- *Bountiful Glory:* Spencer and Patricia Elrod
- *Noah and Friends:* John and Anne Childs

We also thank Shirley Held and Nancy Gunn Porter for allowing us to photograph portions of *The Sharing of Christmas* and *Gifts From the Kitchen* in their homes.

To Magna IV Color Imaging of Little Rock, Arkansas, we say thank you for the superb color reproduction and excellent pre-press preparation.

We want to especially thank photographers Ken West, Larry Pennington, Mark Mathews, and Karen Shirey of Peerless Photography, Little Rock, Arkansas; and Jerry R. Davis of Jerry Davis Photography, Little Rock, Arkansas, for their time, patience, and excellent work.

We offer a very special *thank you* to Dr. and Mrs. Michael Grounds for the use of their antique cookie jars shown on pages 144-151.

To the talented people who helped in the creation of the following projects in this book, we extend a special word of thanks.

- *Crocheted Snowflake Ornaments*, page 48: Theresa Dyke Bickley
- *Madonna and Child*, page 77: Needlework adaptation by Carol Emmer
- *"Merry Christmas" Cardigan*, page 104: Vicky Howard (Needlework adaptation by Jane Chandler)
- *Winter Forest Jumper*, page 107: Polly Carbonari
- *"Let It Snow!" Bread Cover*, page 156: Deborah Lambein

We extend a sincere *thank you* to all the people who assisted in making and testing the projects in this book: Carrie Clifford, Lynette M. Cook, Joyce Graves, Risa Johnson, Barbara Middleton, Sherri Mode, Colleen Moline, Dee Ann Younger, and the members of the First Assembly of God Church Women's Ministry, Searcy, Arkansas: Frances Blackburn, Louella English, Wanda Fite, Nan Goode, Bonnie Gowan, Juanita Hodges, Ida Johnson, Ruby Johnson, Richedeen Lewis, and Velrie Louks.